T0207396

Communications in Computer and Information Science   1860

Rationale

The CCIS series is devoted to the publication of proceedings of computer science conferences. Its aim is to efficiently disseminate original research results in informatics in printed and electronic form. While the focus is on publication of peer-reviewed full papers presenting mature work, inclusion of reviewed short papers reporting on work in progress is welcome, too. Besides globally relevant meetings with internationally representative program committees guaranteeing a strict peer-reviewing and paper selection process, conferences run by societies or of high regional or national relevance are also considered for publication.

Topics

The topical scope of CCIS spans the entire spectrum of informatics ranging from foundational topics in the theory of computing to information and communications science and technology and a broad variety of interdisciplinary application fields.

Information for Volume Editors and Authors

Publication in CCIS is free of charge. No royalties are paid, however, we offer registered conference participants temporary free access to the online version of the conference proceedings on SpringerLink (http://link.springer.com) by means of an http referrer from the conference website and/or a number of complimentary printed copies, as specified in the official acceptance email of the event.

CCIS proceedings can be published in time for distribution at conferences or as post-proceedings, and delivered in the form of printed books and/or electronically as USBs and/or e-content licenses for accessing proceedings at SpringerLink. Furthermore, CCIS proceedings are included in the CCIS electronic book series hosted in the SpringerLink digital library at http://link.springer.com/bookseries/7899. Conferences publishing in CCIS are allowed to use Online Conference Service (OCS) for managing the whole proceedings lifecycle (from submission and reviewing to preparing for publication) free of charge.

Publication process

The language of publication is exclusively English. Authors publishing in CCIS have to sign the Springer CCIS copyright transfer form, however, they are free to use their material published in CCIS for substantially changed, more elaborate subsequent publications elsewhere. For the preparation of the camera-ready papers/files, authors have to strictly adhere to the Springer CCIS Authors' Instructions and are strongly encouraged to use the CCIS LaTeX style files or templates.

Abstracting/Indexing

CCIS is abstracted/indexed in DBLP, Google Scholar, EI-Compendex, Mathematical Reviews, SCImago, Scopus. CCIS volumes are also submitted for the inclusion in ISI Proceedings.

How to start

To start the evaluation of your proposal for inclusion in the CCIS series, please send an e-mail to ccis@springer.com.

Alfredo Cuzzocrea · Oleg Gusikhin ·
Slimane Hammoudi · Christoph Quix
Editors

Data Management Technologies and Applications

10th International Conference, DATA 2021
Virtual Event, July 6–8, 2021
and 11th International Conference, DATA 2022
Lisbon, Portugal, July 11–13, 2022
Revised Selected Papers

 Springer

Editors
Alfredo Cuzzocrea
University of Calabria
Rende, Italy

Oleg Gusikhin
Ford Motor Company
Commerce Township, MI, USA

Slimane Hammoudi
Siège du Groupe ESEO
Angers, France

Christoph Quix
Hochschule Niederrhein
Krefeld, Nordrhein-Westfalen, Germany

ISSN 1865-0929 ISSN 1865-0937 (electronic)
Communications in Computer and Information Science
ISBN 978-3-031-37889-8 ISBN 978-3-031-37890-4 (eBook)
https://doi.org/10.1007/978-3-031-37890-4

This Springer imprint is published by the registered company Springer Nature Switzerland AG
The registered company address is: Gewerbestrasse 11, 6330 Cham, Switzerland

Preface

The present book includes extended and revised versions of a set of selected papers from the 10th and 11th International Conferences on Data Science, Technology and Applications (DATA 2021 and DATA 2022). DATA 2021 was held as an online event due to the Covid-19 pandemic, from 6–8 July 2021, and DATA 2022 was held in Lisbon, Portugal, from 11–13 July 2022.

DATA 2021 received 64 paper submissions from 27 countries, of which 5% were included in this book, and DATA 2022 received 84 paper submissions from 36 countries, of which 10% were also included in this book. The papers were selected by the event chairs and their selection is based on a number of criteria that include the classifications and comments provided by the program committee members, the session chairs' assessment and also the program chairs' global view of all papers included in the technical program. The authors of selected papers were then invited to submit a revised and extended version of their papers having at least 30% innovative material.

The purpose of the International Conference on Data Science, Technology and Applications (DATA) is to bring together researchers, engineers and practitioners interested on databases, big data, data mining, data management, data security and other aspects of information systems and technology involving advanced applications of data.

The papers selected to be included in this book contribute to the understanding of relevant trends of current research on Data Science, Technology and Applications, including: Management of Sensor Data, Linked Data, Information Integration, Data Management for Analytics, Data Integrity, Data and Information Quality, Neural Network Applications, Data Science, Social Data Analytics, Data Mining, Deep Learning, Data Structures and Data Management Algorithms, Information Retrieval, Industry 4.0, Feature Selection, Deep Learning and Big Data.

We would like to thank all the authors for their contributions and also the reviewers who have helped to ensure the quality of this publication.

July 2021

Alfredo Cuzzocrea
Oleg Gusikhin
Slimane Hammoudi
Christoph Quix

Organization

Conference Co-chairs

Slimane Hammoudi	ESEO, ERIS, France
Wil van der Aalst (honorary)	RWTH Aachen University, Germany

Program Co-chairs

2021

Christoph Quix	Hochschule Niederrhein University of Applied Sciences and Fraunhofer FIT, Germany

2022

Alfredo Cuzzocrea	University of Calabria, Italy
Oleg Gusikhin	Ford Motor Company, USA

Program Committee

Served in 2021

Ana Fernández Vilas	University of Vigo, Spain
David Kensche	SAP, Germany
Filip Zavoral	Charles University, Czech Republic
Florent Masseglia	Inria, France
Francesco Folino	ICAR-CNR, Italy
Francesco Guerra	University of Modena and Reggio Emilia, Italy
Gabriel Kuper	University of Trento, Italy
George E. Tsekouras	University of the Aegean, Greece
Ivan Ivanov	SUNY Empire State College, USA
Ivo van der Lans	Wageningen University, The Netherlands
Jan Bohacik	University of Žilina, Slovak Republic
Janis Grabis	Riga Technical University, Latvia
Marius Silaghi	Florida Institute of Technology, USA

Martin Krulis — Charles University, Czech Republic
Maurice van Keulen — University of Twente, The Netherlands
Mercedes Ruiz — University of Cadiz, Spain
Miloš Radovanovic — University of Novi Sad, Serbia
Noor Azina Ismail — University of Malaya, Malaysia
Panagiotis Oikonomou — University of Thessaly, Greece
Paola Giannini — University of Piemonte Orientale, Italy
Pawel Kasprowski — Silesian University of Technology, Poland
Pedro Furtado — University of Coimbra, Portugal
Rüdiger Pryss — Ulm University, Germany
Richard Chbeir — Université de Pau et des Pays de l'Adour (UPPA), France
Rihan Hai — RWTH Aachen University, Germany
Sabina Leonelli — University of Exeter, UK
Sandra Geisler — Fraunhofer Institute for Applied Information Technology FIT, Germany
Seongjai Kim — Mississippi State University, USA
Seth Spielman — University of Colorado Boulder, USA
Stavros Simou — University of the Aegean, Greece
Takahiro Kawamura — Japan Science and Technology Agency, Japan
Thanasis Vergoulis — Athena Research and Innovation Center, Greece
Werner Nutt — Free University of Bozen-Bolzano, Italy
Yasser Mohammad — Assiut University, Egypt

Served in 2022

Altan Cakir — Istanbul Technical University, Turkey
Amit Ganatra — Charotar University of Science and Technology, India
Andrea Marrella — Sapienza University of Rome, Italy
Cinzia Cappiello — Politecnico di Milano, Italy
Cristina Sisu — Brunel University London, UK
Dirk Thorleuchter — Fraunhofer Institute for Technological Trend Analysis INT, Germany
Giulio Di Gravio — Sapienza University of Rome, Italy
Gohar Khan — University of Waikato, New Zealand
Jari Veijalainen — University of Jyväskylä, Finland
Jeffrey Ullman — Stanford Univ., USA
M. Tamer Özsu — University of Waterloo, Canada
Mark Hwang — Central Michigan University, USA
Marta Chinnici — Enea, Italy
Mieczyslaw Kokar — Northeastern University, USA

Miguel Martínez-Prieto   University of Valladolid, Spain
Nuno Castro   University of Minho, Portugal
Peter Revesz   University of Nebraska-Lincoln, USA

Served in 2021 and 2022

Alfred Stein   University of Twente, The Netherlands
Allel Hadjali   Lias/Ensma, France
Andreas Gadatsch   Hochschule Bonn-Rhein-Sieg, Germany
Andrzej Skowron   University of Warsaw, Poland
Antonio Corral   University of Almeria, Spain
Antonio Perianes-Rodriguez   Universidad Carlos III de Madrid, Spain
Bruno Defude   Institut Mines-Télécom, France
Christos Anagnostopoulos   University of Glasgow, UK
Christos Makris   University of Patras, Greece
Colette Rolland   Université Paris1 Panthéon-Sorbonne, France
Daniel Martinez-Avila   Universidad Carlos III de Madrid, Spain
Dariusz Jakóbczak   Technical University of Koszalin, Poland
Diego Seco   Universidade da Coruña, Spain
Erich Neuhold   University of Vienna, Austria
Fabien Duchateau   Université Claude Bernard Lyon 1, France
Fabio Schreiber   Politecnico di Milano, Italy
Francesco Buccafurri   University of Reggio Calabria, Italy
George Papastefanatos   Athena Research and Innovation Center, Greece
George Tambouratzis   Institute for Language and Speech Processing, Greece
Gianluigi Viscusi   Linköping University, Sweden
Gianni Costa   ICAR-CNR, Italy
Gloria Bordogna   CNR - National Research Council, Italy
Gunter Saake   Otto-von-Guericke-Universität Magdeburg, Germany
Hai Dong   RMIT University, Australia
Horia-Nicolai Teodorescu   Gheorghe Asachi Technical University of Iasi, Romania
Iulian Sandu Popa   University of Versailles Saint-Quentin-en-Yvelines & INRIA Saclay, France
Jérôme Gensel   Université Grenoble Alpes, France
Jang-Eui Hong   Chungbuk National University, South Korea
Jiakui Zhao   State Grid Big Data Center of China, China
John Easton   University of Birmingham, UK
Jukka Heikkonen   University of Turku, Finland

Karim Benouaret	Université Claude Bernard Lyon 1, France
Kostas Kolomvatsos	National and Kapodistrian University of Athens, Greece
Leandro Wives	Universidade Federal do Rio Grande do Sul, Brazil
Luiz Paulo Fávero	University of São Paulo, Brazil
Marco Villani	University of Modena and Reggio Emilia, Italy
Nieves R. Brisaboa	Universidade de A Coruña, Spain
Nikos Karacapilidis	University of Patras, Greece
Paolino Di Felice	University of L'Aquila, Italy
Pedro G. Ferreira	University of Porto, Portugal
Qingguo Wang	Meharry Medical College, USA
Raimondas Lencevicius	Nuance Communications, USA
Raju Halder	Indian Institute of Technology Patna, India
Riccardo Ortale	ICAR-CNR, Italy
Sergey Stupnikov	IPI RAN, Russian Federation
Sergio Ilarri	University of Zaragoza, Spain
Shaomin Wu	University of Kent, UK
Shengkun Xie	Toronto Metropolitan University, Canada
Spiros Skiadopoulos	University of the Peloponnese, Greece
Stefano Montanelli	Università degli Studi di Milano, Italy
Steven Demurjian	University of Connecticut, USA
Theodore Dalamagas	Athena Research and Innovation Center, Greece
Theodoros Anagnostopoulos	University of West Attica, Greece
Thorsten Schmidt	Emden/Leer University of Applied Sciences, Germany
Vladimir Kurbalija	University of Novi Sad, Serbia
Werner Retschitzegger	Johannes Kepler University Linz, Austria
Yoris Au	Georgia Southern University, USA
Zbigniew Suraj	University of Rzeszow, Poland
Zeev Volkovich	Ort Braude College, Israel

Additional Reviewers

Served in 2021

Sabri Allani	Higher Institute of Management of Tunis, Tunisia
Felix Beierle	University of Würzburg, Germany
Amal Beldi	Tunisia
Anis Tissaoui	Tunisia

Served in 2022

Javier García	Vienna University of Economics and Business, Austria
Stavros Maroulis	Athena RC, Greece
Vassilis Stamatopoulos	Athena RC, Greece
Mihalis Tsoukalos	University of the Peloponnese, Greece

Invited Speakers

2021

Jan Recker	University of Hamburg, Germany
Sandro Bimonte	INRAE, France
Hala Skaf-Molli	Nantes University, France
Volker Markl	German Research Center for Artificial Intelligence (DFKI) and Technische Universität Berlin (TU Berlin), Germany

2022

Dmitry Ivanov	Berlin School of Economics and Law, Germany
Lionel Rigaud	TRIMANE and The Blockchain Group, France

Contents

A Survey-Based Evaluation of the Data Engineering Maturity in Practice

Daniel Tebernum[1]([⊠]), Marcel Altendeitering[1], and Falk Howar[1,2]

[1] Data Business, Fraunhofer ISST, Speicherstraße 6, 44147 Dortmund, Germany
{daniel.tebernum,marcel.altendeitering,
falk.howar}@isst.fraunhofer.de, falk.howar@tu-dortmund.de
[2] Chair for Software Engineering, TU Dortmund University, Otto-Hahn-Strasse 12, 44227 Dortmund, Germany

Abstract. The proliferation of data-intensive applications is continuously growing. Yet, many of these applications remain experimental or insular as they face data challenges that are rooted in a lack of practical engineering practices. To address this shortcoming and fully leverage the data resource, a professionalization of engineering data-intensive applications is necessary. In a previous study, we developed a data engineering reference model (DERM) that outlines the important building-blocks for handling data along the data life cycle. To create the model, we conducted a systematic literature review on data life cycles to find commonalities between these models and derive an abstract meta-model. We validated DERM theoretically by classifying scientific data engineering topics on the model and placed them in their corresponding life cycle phase. This led to the realization that the phases plan, create and destroy, as well as the layers enterprise and metadata are underrepresented in research literature. To strengthen these findings, this work conducts an empirical survey among data engineering professionals to assess the maturity of the model's pillars from a practical perspective. It turns out that the gaps found in theory also prevail in practice. Based on our results, we derived a set of research gaps that need further attention for establishing a practically grounded engineering process.

Keywords: Data engineering · Reference model · DERM · Survey

1 Introduction

Data is an important organizational asset and there is a broad consensus in science and practice that professionally managed data can improve a firms performance by increasing the agility of an organization [27,34]. Well managed and high quality data is the foundation to improve business processes, enhance organizational decision-making, and foster business innovation [4,27]. The fact that data is an asset is shown by the wide variety of works in the literature (e.g., [3,4,27]). A variety of processes, methods, and frameworks emerged from the literature that focus on improving working with data. However, these studies mostly deal with specific types of data (e.g., master data [27] or information governance [34]) and are focused on the managerial level within organizations [3,17]. They lack the global perspective, which is needed to obtain a holistic view of the data engineering landscape.

A. Cuzzocrea et al. (Eds.): DATA 2021/2022, CCIS 1860, pp. 1–23, 2023.
https://doi.org/10.1007/978-3-031-37890-4_1

To close this gap and further professionalize the work with data, we developed DERM (Data Engineering Reference Model) [35]. DERM overcomes the previously mentioned limitations and provides a reference model for the data engineering in organizations. The validation of the model revealed that not all data engineering aspects receive equal or similar attention in the literature. In particular, the phases of planning, creating, and deleting data lacked a theoretical grounding. Also, working with data on an enterprise or metadata level was underrepresented in the scientific literature. To complete the picture, it is necessary to add an empirical perspective to the theoretical overview that DERM provides and offer a theoretically and practically grounded overview of data engineering. To the best of our knowledge, such an overview does not yet exist.

For this purpose, we developed a survey that draws its foundation and structure from DERM. The survey was completed by 28 professionals from the fields of data engineering and data science. The results provide insights into current data engineering practices and allow us to answer the following research questions:

- RQ1: *How mature is data engineering in practice?*
- RQ2: *Do the data engineering (DERM-)phases have a similar maturity in practice as in theory?*
- RQ3: *What urgent research gaps emerge from observing theory and practice?*

The remainder of this paper is structured as follows. In Sect. 2, we describe the DERM model created in our previous work and the results gained during the validation of the model. We then describe the research methodology in Sect. 3, where we go into detail about how we build and evaluate our survey. We present our findings, a discussion, and the derivation of possible further research questions in Sect. 4. We conclude our paper in Sect. 5, where we also address the limitations of our work.

2 Background

In [35], we developed the so-called DERM (Data Engineering Reference Model). The goal of DERM was to provide a data engineering reference model that can serve as the common ground for developing data-intensive applications. DERM is the result of a systematic literature review (SLR) that followed the principles of [19] and [39]. For coding and grouping the papers we used the Grounded Theory Methodology (GTM) [33] as an example. Literature on data life cycles was used as the theoretical foundation for developing the model. The rationale behind this is that data engineering is focussed on data and the data life cycle represents the most concrete general description of data and can, therefore, be used as the basis of a reference model. After applying GTM to receive the most important key topics of the selected literature, the model was iteratively developed (see Fig. 1).

The model consists of six phases that form a cycle. Phases can be skipped, but the order is fixed. The **first** phase deals with the planning of data requirements. It is an organizational phase that deals with issues like policies, copyright and licensing guidelines, data content, data structure, and documentation requirements [10, 27]. The **second** phase is concerned with the creation of data. New data is being created from scratch and

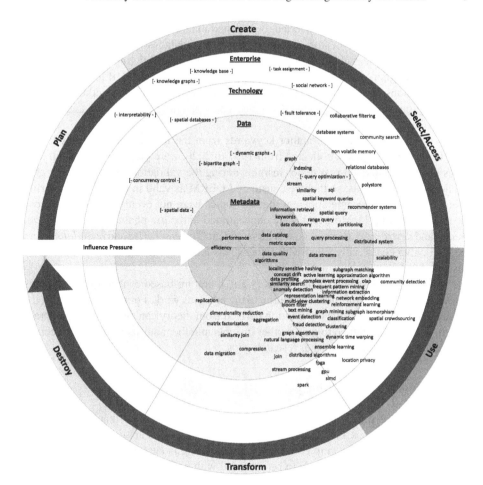

Fig. 1. DERM - A Reference Model for Data Engineering [35].

possible subtasks are triggered (e.g., data quality analysis [1,7] or metadata generation [42]). The **third** phase has selecting and accessing data in its focus. This phase supports users in finding suitable data. For this, technologies such as data catalogs that support the FAIR (Findability, Accessibility, Interoperability, and Reuseability) principles [21] and easy-to-understand user interfaces [14] must exist to meet this requirement. The **fourth** phase deals with the use of data and, thus, comprises all activities that are performed on data. This phase is the most prominent and accordingly receives the most attention. It includes topics such as the integration, analysis, and visualization of data [6,29]. This can provide novel insights into the data and thus generate added value for companies, especially since new approaches for gaining these insights using machine learning and artificial intelligence are available. It is crucial that users make good use of the data and that the results are presented appropriately [22,27]. The **fifth** phase describes the transformation of data. A transformation occurs whenever data is updated, truncated, cleaned, converted, or adjusted in terms of its data quality [3,8,15]. Here, things like long-term storage and preservation of data also play an important role [41]. The **sixth** phase is about destroying or deleting the data. Deleting data makes sense once data of higher-quality is available for the same context [25,26], if it is required by legal regulations (see GDPR [37]), or if the data does not offer any additional value [13]. Deletion ends the life cycle and initiates a new planning phase for data needed for new use cases.

To validate the model, all author keywords from the International Conference on Data Engineering (ICDE), collected from 1997 to 2020, were placed in the model by a focus group. We derived two major insights during the validation. First, we were able to allocate all keywords, so that we considered DERM as valid in the data engineering context. Second, it became apparent that the topics were not evenly distributed across the model (see Fig. 1). Most topics are concentrated in the *use* phase. The phases *plan*, *create*, and *destroy* are represented to a lesser extent. The *enterprise* and *metadata* layers are also only occasionally filled with topics. This led to the formulation of a series of possible future research avenues.

While we had a strong focus on theory and literature-based evaluation in [35], this study aims to add an empirical evaluation to the previous work. For this, we conducted a survey to check whether the distribution derived from theory can also be found in practice. In addition, we aimed to gain further insights into the maturity of data engineering in practice and to identify further research gaps.

3   Research Methodology

The validation of the DERM model (see Sect. 4 in [35]) revealed that the *plan*, *create*, and *destroy* phases and the *enterprise* and *metadata* layers are underrepresented in the scientific data engineering community. This finding is currently solely based on a theoretical perspective and needs to be extended with an empirical evaluation. To gain empirical insights and answer the proposed research questions, we developed a questionnaire to query key informants about the current state of data engineering in practice [20,28]. Based on our previous work and the research questions formulated in Sect. 1, we formulated the following hypotheses a priori:

- H1: *The plan, create, and destroy phases show a low degree of maturity in practice.*
- H2: *The select/access, use, and transform phases show a high degree of maturity in practice.*
- H3: *The enterprise and metadata layers show a low degree of maturity in practice.*

In the following, we will describe how we designed our survey and questionnaire. We will also provide insights into the execution of our survey and how data analysis took place.

3.1   Survey Design and Execution

The six phases known from the DERM model - *plan*, *create*, *access/select*, *use*, *transform* and *destroy* - act as the fundamental basis of the survey. Using this foundation, the authors iteratively developed the overall structure of the questionnaire based on the guidelines by Lietz [23]. In the first iteration, we conducted a brainstorming session in which questions were developed for each phase of the model. This iteration spanned several workshop days due to the broad scope of the topic. In this first run, over 150 questions were collected that we structured in accordance with the phases of the DERM model. In the second iteration, we reviewed the questions and merged similar ones. During this process, we noticed that similar questions were repeatedly asked at each stage. As a result, we decided to standardize these kind of questions and repeat them in each phase. We derived six kinds of recurring questions: "I use/apply standards in phase X", "I can rely on established processes and methods in phase X", "I am using tool support in phase X", "I use some kind of language in phase X", "I consider data quality in phase X", and "I maintain metadata in phase X". We draw on these questions in the evaluation to define the concept of maturity. Only if a phase is positively assessed regarding these topics, we speak of a certain degree of maturity.

Besides these standardized recurring questions, we also added individual questions for each phase, which were discussed among the authors. Most of the questions were designed to be queried on a 5-point Likert scale [24]. We decided on an odd number of points to give the participants the chance to position themselves in the middle. We feared that the participants would otherwise have a bias towards the negative answers given the number of questions and their complexity. As items we chose *never*, *seldom*, *sometimes*, *often*, and *always*. Each phase ends with an optional free-text question in which the participants can describe what they would change from their point of view. We concluded the survey with a section on personal data to allow the differentiation of our results on age, experience, and other factors. In total, our survey consists of 66 content-related questions and 6 questions on personal information.

For the pretest of our questionnaire we asked 3 uninvolved researchers to fill out the survey and provide feedback [28]. As a result, we clarified unclear wordings and merged similar questions. The final version of our survey is attached to this paper (see Appendix).

We used LimeSurvey[1] to implement and distribute our survey online. The survey was active for five month between August and December 2021. We recruited participants from research projects and addressed them via email. We considered participants as suitable if they had a data engineering or data science related job or background. In total, we reached out to 40 candidates this way. After 2 months, we sent a reminder email to all contacts or thanked them for taking part.

3.2 Data Analysis

This section describes the methods we used to analyse and validate the results of the questionnaire [5,32]. All charts were created using Matplotlib[2] and Python. Overall, our data analysis approach included five steps.

First, we generated visualizations for the Likert scale questions (see Fig. 4a, 5a, 6a, 7a, 8a and 9a). We decided to use diverging stacked bar charts as these easily indicate

---

[1] https://www.limesurvey.org/.

[2] https://matplotlib.org/.

positive or negative tendencies. We chose the middle of the neutral responses as the centre of the visualization. We decided to not shift the neutral answers into the negative or positive region. In our case, the shift of a neutral statement towards a certain direction is too dependent on the context of the participant and would not be justifiable. The visualizations are generated for each phase in order to simplify a cross-phase overview.

Second, we use radar charts to evaluate the recurring standard questions for each phase (see Fig. 3). We generated a separate radar chart for each question type with the phases as axes. Since our Likert scale is ordinal, we use the median as a measurement of location. For a simpler and shorter presentation, we have converted the Likert scale into numbers from 1–5. We have also visualized this data for each phase, where the standardized questions are represented in the radar chart (see Fig. 4b, 5b, 6b, 7b, 8b and 9b).

Third, we also utilized radar charts to better compare the maturity of the phases between theory and practice (see Fig. 2). For this, we reused the results of the DERM validation in [35]. The evaluations of theory and practice cannot be taken to the same numerical basis, which is why the charts are scaleless and only allow a comparison of trends. To generate the theory chart, we counted the number of topics that we placed inside the model. Afterwards, we calculated the distribution of topics in these phases. The visualization of the practice is obtained from the standardized questions for the respective phase. Other phase-specific questions were not included because they could undesirably favor or disadvantage a phase. Again, we used the median as measurement of location.

Fourth, to identify correlations between the questions, we applied Spearman's correlation [5, 30]. We chose this non-parametric correlation function for three reasons: we are working with a rather small dataset (see Sect. 4), we use an ordinal scale to receive participants answers, and our data can be best described using the median as measurement of location. Because of these clear properties, no further tests were carried out to identify whether our data is parametric or non-parametric. We considered possible correlations when they exceeded a significance of $+0.6$ and -0.6, which led to 58 correlations for further investigation and discussion [32]. In case of particularly interesting correlations, the *p-value* was determined in order to refute the H_0 hypothesis. We decided for a two-tailed test as we investigated non-specific H_1 hypotheses. We report correlations using the APA format: e.g., $Corr_{Q1,Q2}$ with $r(26) = .60, p = .001$. First, we describe the two variables involved (in our example here Q1 and Q2) and then report the ratios for degrees of freedom, ρ and p-Value. We also interpret these correlations.

Fifth, we analyzed the qualitative answers from the free text fields. These qualitative answers offered us the opportunity to gain an in-depth understanding of data engineering practices. For data analysis we used content analysis as a common approach for analyzing unstructured data like free text [36]. We, hereby, followed an iterative process of dividing the answers into related categories and sub-categories until a dense description of the described aspects emerged. Potential differences in the derived categories were clarified in subsequent discussions among the authors.

4   Results

At the end of the survey period, 28 participants completed the questionnaire. These responses form the basis for our empirical evaluations and results. In the upcoming sections we will present the analytical results from our survey. There we will also test the hypotheses we have previously established and respond to the research questions posed. Whenever we make research recommendations, we always implicitly refer to RQ3. Where appropriate, we conduct an in-depth investigation and interpretation of the results.

4.1   Data Engineering Maturity: Theory vs Practice

To answer RQ2, we created the visualization depicted in Fig. 2. As described in Sect. 3.2, the axes have no scale as they cannot be normalized on a common numerical ground. On the left side of the figure, we can identify the same pattern as in Fig. 1. There is a peak in the *use* phase, followed by *select/access* and *transform*. The phases *plan*, *create* and *destroy* are developed to a lesser extent. In [35] the authors concluded, that these phases are underrepresented in research and need additional work. We therefore wanted to evaluate how these phases are represented in practice. This can be seen on the right side of the figure. Here, we can see a peak in the *transform* phase, followed by all other phases except *destroy*. The *destroy* phase receives the least attention in practice. Based on this, we assume that dealing with the topic of data deletion still has deficiencies, both in theory and in practice. In Sect. 4.3 we will go into more detail about the survey results of the *destroy* phase. The answer to RQ2 is that the maturity of phases is only partially the same. The most prominent example is the *destroy* phase where we can clearly see that it lacks attention in both science and practice. *Transform*, *use*, and *select/access* are well developed to a certain degree, both in theory and in practice. There seem to be minor differences in the *plan* and *create* phases. Here, the survey shows that the participants rated these phases roughly as mature as *use* and *select/access*. It would have to be checked subsequently whether these phases have already reached a high degree of maturity in practice. Another explanation would be that all phases in practice (except *transform*) do not have a high maturity level. We argue for the latter, since the median response was *sometimes*.

4.2   Data Engineering Maturity: Specific Topics

As described in Sect. 3.1, specific questions on standards, processes and methods, tools, languages, data quality, and metadata were asked in the survey in relation to each DERM phase. As a visualization, the results for each type of question were plotted on a radar chart (see Fig 3). Below we will go through the question types individually and try to interpret the results.

Standards are a unified and common way of doing. For example, these are available in the form of DIN standards or RFCs. But also de facto standards play a role here. We perceive standards as something that has an external influence on the technologies and (meta-)data used. Therefore, we see the *enterprise* layer of DERM, which we interpret as a representative of contextual influences, represented here and want to check

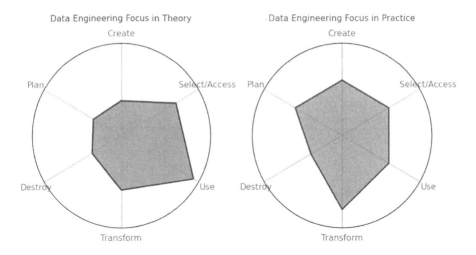

Fig. 2. Data Engineering Focus: Theory vs Practice.

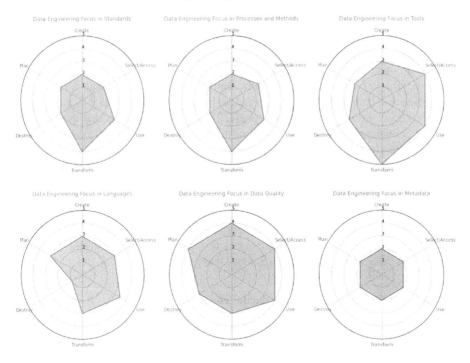

Fig. 3. Visualization of maturity per specific topic.

if hypothesis H3$_{enterprise}$ holds true. Standards are utilized especially in the *use* and *transform* phase. As a result, we argue that in practice standards are needed especially when the data is available and one has to work with them. In the other phases, standards are only very poorly developed. From this point of view, we consider H3$_{enterprise}$ to be confirmed. Even if the use of standards has been established in practice, especially for *use* and *transform*, the other phases should not be neglected. We argue that further standardization of the other phases should be pushed forward. This way, it will be possible to deploy efficient processes, methods, and tools.

Processes and Methods describe things that happen over time or represent a systematic procedure. If we look at the visualization, we can see similarities to the standards category. We assume that the participants perceive processes and methods in the same way as standards. If there are processes and methods, they behave like standards from the user's perspective. The previous interpretations made in standards, therefore, also apply to this category.

Tools support us in the execution of our work. The survey shows that *select/access*, *use*, and *transform* are already well developed in the working lives of the participants. In particular, the transformation of data is very well covered by tools. We assume that many things are nowadays tool-supported because it has been recognized that manual work is very time-consuming. We also believe that the participants of this survey are able to build tools for their tasks that support them in their work. It should be verified for a broader population (e.g., with a non-programming background) if they are also well covered regarding tools.

Languages are used as a common and universal way for conducting data engineering tasks such as searching for data (e.g., SQL) or executing workflows (e.g., Python). We observed that languages are partially developed in all phases but *destroy*. Most participants noted that they either *never* or *seldom* use languages to model or describe the deletion of data. Generally, we derived from the free text answers that languages must be "flexible" and support "auto generation". An interesting positive correlation is $Corr_{Q1,Q59}$ with $r(26) = .72, p < .0001$, which points out that there is a strong link between data standards and the use of languages. Following this, we argue that further research is necessary to support the adoption of existing languages by developing standardized and automated solutions. With regard to the *destroy* phase we call for the development of extensions to existing languages (e.g., SQL or UML) or the creation of novel languages that address the need for describing deletion activities.

Data Quality describes the "fitness for use" of data for data consumers [38]. The respondents consider data quality as an important topic in all six phases of the data life cycle. This indicates that data quality is not a one-time task but rather a continuous effort of different people over the whole life cycle. The same trend can be observed for commercial data quality tools, which increasingly offer functionalities for cooperative data quality work [2]. Notably, we can observe that data quality is slightly more important in the *plan*, *create*, and *select/access* phases. The rationale behind this is that data quality is often still considered as a task in the early stages of data engineering [27]. Data quality solutions should take this aspect into account and provide better integration and automation to support all data engineering phases [1]. An interesting correlation is $Corr_{Q60,Q63}$ with $r(26) = -.68, p = .0001$, which negatively correlates data quality with accidentally deleting data. A high level of data quality is, thus, important to assure data can be used. Overall, we argue that data quality solutions must be further developed in terms of automation, intelligence, and collaborative and integrative capabilities.

Metadata. Our hypothesis $H3_{metadata}$ states that the maturity of metadata use in practice is low. As can be seen from the visualization, the topic of metadata has a very low level of maturity in all phases. We believe that the benefits of metadata maintenance and the use of metadata have not yet been sufficiently adapted in practice. There are several works in the literature that deal with the topic of metadata. Here, the focus lies on improving the understanding of the data with the help of metadata, for example by developing uniform vocabularies for describing the metadata [9,31]. Metadata is also utilized to search and find data using e.g., data catalog systems [12]. The whole topic of metadata in this context is also strongly related to the FAIR principles which are designed "[...] to improve knowledge discovery through assisting both humans, and their computational agents, in the discovery of, access to, and integration and analysis of, task-appropriate [...] data" [40, p.2]. It is, therefore, crucial that work with metadata continues to find its way into practice. All phases are equally affected. Already at the planning stage, thought should be given to metadata so that the data can later be reused in other projects even after their original intended use, which would support the FAIR Principles. On the other end, the deletion phase could benefit from metadata by storing information about which retention periods apply to the data or whether deletion requests from individuals are expected (see GDPR [37]). We also found some interesting correlations regarding the work with metadata. $Corr_{Q23,Q25}$ with $r(26) = .62, p = .0004$ indicates, that automatically generating metadata has a positive correlation with being able to locate the necessary data for one's work. Looking at $Corr_{Q22,Q28}$ with $r(26) = .63, p = .0003$, we see that the ability of the operating system to assist the user in finding data may be dependent on the availability of metadata. The availability of metadata has a positive correlation with the ability to generate metadata automatically (see $Corr_{Q22,Q23}$ with $r(26) = .63, p = .0004$). If we look at the specific answer distribution of Q22, Q23, and Q28 in Fig. 6a, we see that these were answered rather negatively. As a research agenda, we see the automatic generation and maintenance of metadata as an important factor in improving the way we work with data. Overall, we consider the hypothesis $H3_{metadata}$ to be confirmed and see a need for action in practice.

4.3 Data Engineering Maturity: Results per Phase

In the following sections, we will discuss the results for each phase in more detail. Some findings have already been described in the previous sections. If this is the case, we refer to the respective parts.

Plan. The *plan* phase represents the beginning of the data engineering life cycle defined by DERM. Before data is even collected, generated, or purchased, the requirements for the data should be determined. To ensure that the data supports for instance the FAIR principles and has a sufficiently high quality, it is necessary to formulate these properties at an early stage. The participants of the survey are aware of the fact that high data quality is already important at the planning phase and pay attention to it in their work (see Fig. 4). Nevertheless, the use of standards, processes, and tools is very low with a median of 2 and 2.5. The use of languages is somewhat better with a median of 3.

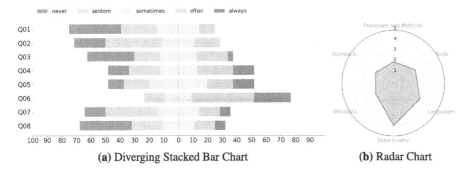

(a) Diverging Stacked Bar Chart   **(b)** Radar Chart

Fig. 4. Plan Phase Visualizations. Q01. I use standards for data or data planning Q02. I can rely on established processes and methods for planning my data needs Q03. I am using tool support in the planning phase Q04. I use modeling languages to describe my data needs Q05. I specify requirements for my data to be generated Q06. I consider data quality as an important aspect in the planning phase Q07. I plan my data demands collaborative Q08. I maintain metadata about the data during the planning phase

Looking at Q7, we can see that planning data is often conducted separately. Therefore, suitable assistant tools should be developed that support the user in the planning process in the same way as another person would do in a collaboration. They should refer to standards, ask follow-up questions, and help by structuring the whole process. This kind of tools would also provide advantages when it collects metadata directly. $Corr_{Q8,Q22}$ with $r(26) = .65, p = .0002$ suggests that the collection of metadata in the *plan* phase would have a positive influence on the retrieval of the data by third parties at a later point in time. When we look at the correlation $Corr_{Q8,Q65}$ with $r(26) = .61, p = .0005$, the *destroy* phase would also benefit if it is already clear at the *plan* phase whether, and if so when and why, the data may have to be deleted again. Overall, the survey results indicate a low level of maturity of the *plan* phase in practice. We, therefore, consider $H1_{plan}$ to be valid.

Create. The creation of data is the second step of the DERM life cycle. After the initial *plan* phase, data is created according to the requirements. The findings for the *create* phase are two-fold. On the one hand, data quality, tools, and languages are well established to create data. On the other hand, there is a lack of standards, processes, and metadata in practice (see Fig. 5). Based on these results, we argue that further research on a standardized and tool-supported creation of metadata is necessary. Several participants noted that a partly automated generation of data, for example by automatically generating the data schema, might be a suitable approach to support the creation of data. One participant also highlighted the use of data quality rules to standardize the creation of data, which is supported by several tools (e.g., [1]). Overall, we consider $H1_{create}$ as partly supported.

Select/Access. A major problem for many who work with data is to find appropriate and existing data for their own projects [12]. Several solutions to support the user in

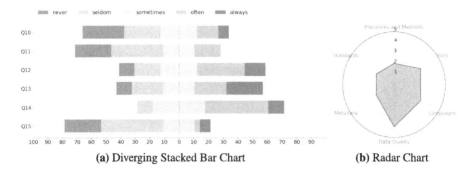

(a) Diverging Stacked Bar Chart   **(b)** Radar Chart

Fig. 5. Create Phase Visualizations. Q10. I use/apply standards that support/restrict my data creation Q11. I can rely on est. processes and methods for creating/buying/acquiring my data Q12. I am using tool support for creating data Q13. I use some kind of standardized language to create data Q14. I consider data quality while creating data Q15. I maintain metadata during data creation

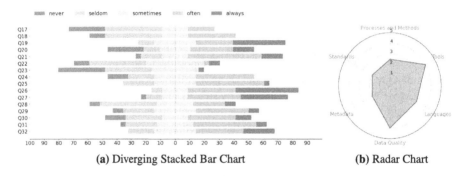

(a) Diverging Stacked Bar Chart   **(b)** Radar Chart

Fig. 6. Select/Access Phase Visualizations. Q17. I use/apply standards for searching and accessing data Q18. I can rely on established processes and methods for searching and accessing data Q19. I am using tool support for searching/accessing data Q20. I use some kind of language to search/access data Q21. I consider data quality while searching/accessing data Q22. Relevant metadata for searching/accessing data is available Q23. Relevant metadata for searching/accessing data is automatically generated Q24. I want to find and access data that my colleagues created Q25. I can find the relevant data for my work Q26. I have data stored on my computer Q27. I can find and access data on my computer without any problems Q28. The operating system provides me with helpful search capabilities Q29. I share data from my computer with others Q30. I use specialized tools to share data with my colleagues Q31. The data I'm searching and accessing is distributed over heterogeneous environments and technical systems Q32. I have the feeling that I spend too much time on searching appropriate data

this work emerged from literature (e.g., Data Civilizer System [11], Data Market Platforms [16]). In particular, data catalogs should be mentioned here. Their main task is "[...] matching data supply and demand" [18, p.9] and, thus, support users in finding, selecting, and accessing data [12].

At first glance, the practice seems well positioned in this phase. There is sufficient support in the form of tools (Q19) and languages (Q20) to find the appropriate data. Despite this, several participants highlighted that they feel they spend too long finding the right data (Q32). As previously described, we believe this is due to a lack of automatically generated metadata which results in a general metadata shortage (see Q22, Q23, and Sect. 4.2 - metadata). We point out that this will be of great importance in the future for working with data.

In this phase, we formulated a particularly large number of questions to gain further insights (see Q24-Q32). It turns out that participants have data in some form stored on their devices (Q26). We therefore wanted to know if the operating system supports the participants in finding the data on their devices (Q28). This was answered rather negatively. Nevertheless, participants are able to find and access the data they are looking for on their device in most times (Q27). We assume that the participants maintain their data and folder structure themselves and thus keep track of the storage locations that are relevant to them. In order to speed up the retrieval of the data being searched for, consideration should be given to migrating previous efforts to develop centralized data catalogs to the operating system level as well. The features that make up a good data catalog (see e.g., [21]) should be anchored and standardized inside the operating system. Such a decentralized data catalog could also be used to make data discoverable among employees and, following this, to make it available in a standardized way without undermining data sovereignty.

If we look at correlations regarding *select/access*, $Corr_{Q18,Q25}$ with $r(26) = .73, p < .0001$ stands out. Established processes and methods are positively correlated with whether one can find the right data to work with. Therefore, we see it as important to further expand the use of processes and methods in practice. With a median of 2.5 (Q18), we still see a lot of potential here. Overall, *select/access* still shows a low degree of maturity in practice. Therefore, we do not consider $H2_{select/access}$ to be confirmed.

Use. The *use* phase is the most prominent phase of the data life cycle as it receives the most attention by the scientific community [35]. Typically, the *use* phase is concerned with the derivation of knowledge from data, which can be used to inform new services, business models, or fuel innovation [4,29]. We, therefore, assumed that the phase receives significant attention in practice as well. Our findings support this assumption and show that the *use* phase is at least medium or well developed in all aspects but metadata (see Fig. 7b). As a result, we consider $H2_{use}$ supported.

The lack of supporting metadata during the usage of data reveals that further research is necessary in this regard. Data catalogs can help to promote and automatically generate and capture metadata [12]. This would also support the further standardization of handling data. Several people noted in the free texts that they wished for "uniform" and "more standardized data set[s]". Another interesting finding is that many participants still use low quality data despite the recognized importance of data quality in earlier phases of the data life cycle. We argue that further research is necessary to allow for a continuous data quality monitoring, for example by using data quality rules [1]).

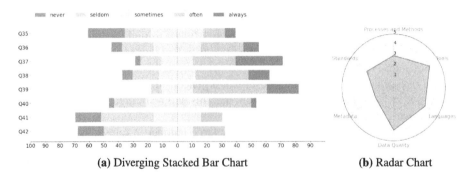

(a) Diverging Stacked Bar Chart   **(b)** Radar Chart

Fig. 7. Use Phase Visualizations. Q35. I use standards that support my data use Q36. I can rely on established processes and methods for utilizing data Q37. I am using tool support for using data Q38. I use languages to make use of my data Q39. I consider data quality as an important aspect for using data Q40. I use data of low quality Q41. Artificial Intelligence or Machine Learning is involved while using data Q42. Metadata supports me in using data

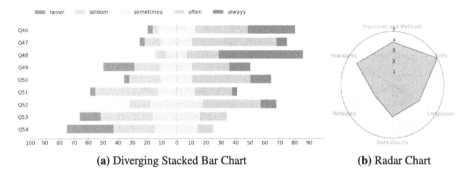

(a) Diverging Stacked Bar Chart   **(b)** Radar Chart

Fig. 8. Transform Phase Visualizations. Q46. I use standards for transforming data Q47. I can rely on established processes and methods for transforming data Q48. I am using tool support for transforming data Q49. I use languages to modell/describe how to transform data Q50. I consider data quality as an important aspect when transforming data Q51. I transform data to improve data quality Q52. I often need to transfer data to another format Q53. Transformations must be developed specifically for the data Q54. Metadata supports me in transforming data

Transform. The transformation of data is the fifth phase of the DERM and occurs when data is changed in one or more of its aspects [35]. In research transformation tasks are often standardized and tool supported, and we were able to draw the same conclusion in our study (see Fig. 7). Most participants noted that they either *often* or *always* use standards for transforming tasks. Only in the metadata category the *transform* phase is below average. Overall, we consider H2$_\text{transform}$ as supported and of high maturity in practice.

Nevertheless, data transforms can be improved. In response to this question one participant noted that the transform should be "invisible" which means more automated and following a standardized process. The fact that participants noted that the transform phase misses metadata support in practice is based on the fact that changes to data are often not tracked and reflected in their corresponding metadata [12,21]. Further research on how metadata can be integrated in data transformation processes could increase the professionalization and automation of data transforms.

(a) Diverging Stacked Bar Chart   **(b)** Radar Chart

Fig. 9. Destroy Phase Visualizations. Q56. I use standards for deleting data Q57. I can rely on established processes and methods for deleting data Q58. I am using tool support for deleting data Q59. I use languages to modell/describe how to delete data Q60. I consider data quality as an important aspect when deleting data. Q61. I delete obsolete data Q62. I know about existing copies of the data that should also be deleted Q63. I delete data by accident Q64. I need to apply legal requirements when deleting data Q65. The deletion of data is reflected in the corresponding metadata

Destroy. The *destroy* phase represents the end of data life cycle. It is important for various reasons that the deletion of data is not ignored. On the one hand, there are legal regulations that enforce or delay the deletion of data. For instance, since May 2018 citizens of the European Union can refer to the right to be forgotten [37]. Companies must be able to search their databases for personal data and provide a requesting person with information about their data. If the data is no longer needed for an agreed on service, a user may have his personal data deleted [37]. Also, data may have a retention period (e.g., tax office related documents) and one is obliged to keep them for decades in some cases. Sometimes data should be deleted to avoid accidental reuse because it is either expired, illegal, or incorrect. Another point why to worry about deleting data is to save storage space. Depending on where the data is located, storage space can be expensive. There is not always the possibility to archive data on cheap storage media like tape. Finally, it is worth mentioning the case that data exchange between companies is becoming more common and formalized (see e.g., IDS³/Gaia-X⁴). It is

---

³ https://internationaldataspaces.org/.

⁴ https://www.gaia-x.eu/.

recommended that "Companies must implement mechanisms to guarantee data security and sovereignty and clarify policies for data usage" [4, p.1789]. Thus, a company could acquire the rights to use data from another company for a fixed period of time. After that, the data may no longer be used and must be deleted.

Our survey reveals a rather negative picture of the *destroy* phase in practice. As can be seen from Fig. 9a, the questions tended to be answered with *never* or *seldom*. Particularly noteworthy are Q56, Q59, and Q65. These were almost entirely answered negatively. We have already reported on Q59 and Q65 in Sect. 4.2. Q56 shows that in practice there is still much to be done in the area of standardization. Here, it would make sense to produce further work that advances standards for deleting data and anchors them in practice. Good standards are a way to develop meaningful processes, methods and tools. There are also positive correlations between the questions that are worth mentioning. First, $Corr_{Q8,Q65}$ with $r(26) = .61, p = .0005$ indicate that there is an effect between maintaining metadata in the planning phase and whether deleting data is reflected in the metadata. Second, $Corr_{Q59,Q65}$ with $r(26) = .62, p = .0004$ indicates that there is also an effect between the use of languages to describe how data should be deleted and whether deleting data is reflected in the metadata. Moreover, the participants agree that they want to interact with the deletion phase as little as possible. One participant wrote: "[...] If it needs to be deleted, it should be deleted on it's own.". Another one wrote: "I don't want to worry about deleting it. Where it is 100% safe, the computer may delete the data itself. [...]".

We, therefore, recommend further research in three directions in particular. First, we see potential in the development of standards and languages that describe and support the deletion of data. In the world of relational databases, for example, we have SQL. Here, the deletion of data can be modeled and linked to conditions. We need to explore how to move these features to a higher level and accommodate the heterogeneity of data. Second, we should explore to what extent metadata can support us in the deletion phase. This includes questions like: *What metadata is relevant to have?*, *How can this metadata be generated?*, and *Where do we ideally store this metadata?*. Here, it is also necessary to explore which metadata can be stored already at the *plan* phase with regard to the deletion of data. Third, automated deletion of data should be further advanced. Where the required information is available, data should be deleted automatically if necessary. Overall, we see $H1_{destroy}$ confirmed.

5   Conclusion

To assess the maturity of data engineering in practice, we extended the theoretical perspective of [35] and conducted a survey among data engineers and data scientists. With regard to RQ1, we can summarize that there are still many areas in practical data engineering that have a low maturity level. In particular, the handling of *metadata* and the *destroy* phase should be mentioned here, which lack a professional management and execution. On the positive side, it can be noted that data quality is considered as important by all participants. If we turn to the comparison between theory and practice, and thus RQ2, we see that there are subject areas that receive little attention in either field. The *destroy* phase stands out here. However, there were also positive results, e.g., the *use* and *transform* phases achieved a high level of attention in theory and practice.

Our work has shown that there is still a lot of potential in the professionalization of data engineering in practice. For the community in theory and practice, this work is intended to provide an impetus to engage more with the less engaged subject areas. Combined with our previous work, this reveals research gaps that need to be addressed in the future. First, the gaps identified should be further consolidated. Our work looks at the issues from a global perspective, which is why we could not capture the state of the art in detail. It is a good idea to conduct dedicated literature research and surveys in the field for individual phases or topics.

At this point we need to address the limitations of this work. The survey is very broad, so we were not able to get detailed insights into the individual data engineering phases. Therefore, this work can only capture an overarching picture of sentiment and does not intend to do more than that. The survey was also completed by only 28 people, which imposes a limited generalizability on our results and findings. We are, thus, careful with our statements in this paper and try to formulate them rather general. Nevertheless, this work has a direct impact on theory and practice. It is obvious that there are still gaps to be filled in order to further professionalize data engineering. As can be seen from the work on DERM [35], some topics also seem to be underrepresented in the academic literature. The research community should focus equally on the *plan*, *create*, and *destroy* phases of data, as well as the use of *metadata* and the impact of an *enterprise* on the data engineering processes. Practitioners should also continue to focus on these topics in their own interest, and benefit from the advantages of a professionalized data engineering environment.

Appendix: Survey

Data Engineering Survey

Thank you very much for taking the time to support us by responding to this survey. Data is a valuable commodity, especially in today's world. Many speak of it as the resource or oil of the 21st century. The right data at the right time, processed and analyzed with the right methods, can make the difference between success and failure of a company. It is therefore all the more important to further professionalize and formalize the handling of data so that the concepts of chance and luck are given no place in the field of data engineering.

Fraunhofer ISST conducts applied research to this end and would like to gain deeper insight into the current state of working with real-world data. Your contribution will enable more targeted modeling of future research priorities. Our applied nature means that our results flow back into industry more quickly.

The survey is divided into 6 sub-areas representing different steps in the data lifecycle, namely **Plan, Create, Access / Search, Use, Transform, and Delete.** Additionally, at the end of the survey we will ask some personal information. Please do not disclose any information that identifies you personally or your employer. Please allow approximately **20 minutes** to complete the survey.

Plan

Before data can be generated and used, it is a good idea to enter a plan phase. Here you can define the structure, meaning and sense of the needed data in advance. We would like to ask you a few questions about your experiences when it comes to plan your data needs.

Please rate the following: *

Please choose the appropriate response for each item:

	never	seldom	sometimes	often	always
Q01: I use standards for data or data planning (e.g. DIN Norms, RFCs, field specific de-facto standards, etc.)	○	○	○	○	○
Q02: I can rely on established proccesses and methods for planning my data needs	○	○	○	○	○
Q03: I am using tool support in the planning phase	○	○	○	○	○
Q04: I use modelling languages to describe my data needs (JSON Schema, XSD, etc.)	○	○	○	○	○
Q05: I specify requirements for my data to be generated (format, size, update cycles, etc.)	○	○	○	○	○
Q06: I consider data quality as an important aspect in the planning phase	○	○	○	○	○
Q07: I plan my data demands collaborative	○	○	○	○	○
Q08: I maintain metadata about the data during the planning phase	○	○	○	○	○

Q09: If you could change the current approach on planning your data needs, what changes would you make?

Create

The creation of the data (e.g. creating a new document) itself is an important step in the overall lifecycle of the data. After all, it is the first step that brings the valuable asset into life. We would therefore like to ask you some questions about this important topic.

Please rate the following: *

Please choose the appropriate response for each item:

	never	seldom	sometimes	often	always
Q10: I use/apply standards that support/restrikt my data creation (e.g. GDPR, dataformats, update intervals, responsibilities, etc.)	○	○	○	○	○
Q11: I can rely on established proccesses and methods for creating/buying/acquiring my data	○	○	○	○	○
Q12: I am using tool support for creating data	○	○	○	○	○
Q13: I use some kind of standardized language to create data (e.g. SQL, Python, etc.)	○	○	○	○	○
Q14: I consider data quality while creating data	○	○	○	○	○
Q15: I maintain metadata during data creation	○	○	○	○	○

Q16: If you could change the current approach to generating data, what changes would you make

If you could change the current state of searching and accessing data, what changes would you make?

Access / Search

Finding and accessing appropriate data concerns most of us. Studies suggest that over 80% of time is spent searching for appropriate data. We'd love to learn more about your personal experiences.

Please rate the following: *

Please choose the appropriate response for each item:

	never	seldom	sometimes	often	always
Q17: I use/apply standards for searching and accessing data (e.g. DIN Norms, RFCs, field specific de-facto standards, etc.)	○	○	○	○	○
Q18: I can rely on established proccesses and methods for searching and accessing data	○	○	○	○	○
Q19: I am using tool support for searching/accessing data. (e.g. Data Catalogs, Search Engines, Web Platforms, ...)	○	○	○	○	○
Q20: I use some kind of language to search/access data. (e.g. SQL, ...)	○	○	○	○	○
Q21: I consider data quality while searching/accessing data	○	○	○	○	○
Q22: Relevant metadata for searching/accessing data is available	○	○	○	○	○
Q23: Relevant metadata for searching/accessing data is automatically generated	○	○	○	○	○
Q24: I want to find and access data that my colleagues created	○	○	○	○	○
Q25: I can find the relevant data for my work	○	○	○	○	○
Q26: I have data stored on my computer	○	○	○	○	○
Q27: I can find and access data on my computer without any problems	○	○	○	○	○
Q28: The operating system provides me with helpful search capabilities	○	○	○	○	○
Q29: I share data from my computer with others	○	○	○	○	○
Q30: I use specialized tools to share data with my colleagues	○	○	○	○	○
Q31: The data I'm searching and accessing is distributed over heterogenous environments and technical systems	○	○	○	○	○
Q32: I have the feeling that I spend too much time on searching appropriate data	○	○	○	○	○

Q33: There is a company-wide data sharing culture *

Choose one of the following answers
Please choose **only one** of the following:

○ no
○ partially
○ yes

Q34: If you could change the current state of searching and accessing data, what changes would you make?

Use

All of us have used data in different ways (e.g. reading a document or analyzing numerical values). We'd like to learn more about how you use your data.

Please rate the following: *

Please choose the appropriate response for each item:

	never	seldom	sometimes	often	always
Q35: I use standards that support my data use (e.g. DIN Norms, RFCs, field specific de-facto standards, etc.)	○	○	○	○	○
Q36: I can rely on established proccesses and methods for utilizing data	○	○	○	○	○
Q37: I am using tool support for using data	○	○	○	○	○
Q38: I use languages to make use of my data (e.g. Python, R, Matlab, ...)	○	○	○	○	○
Q39: I consider data quality as an important aspect for using data	○	○	○	○	○
Q40: I use data of low quality	○	○	○	○	○
Q41: Artifical Intelligence or Machine Learning is involved while using data	○	○	○	○	○
Q42: Metadata supports me in using data	○	○	○	○	○

Q43: Name personal tasks that require the most data

Q44: Name company tasks that require the most data

Q45: If you could change how you use data, what changes would you make?

Transform

Transforming data is an important step in the data lifecycle and includes tasks like adding / removing data, changing data types, or changing the data encoding. How do you usually proceed in data transformation?

Please rate the following: *

Please choose the appropriate response for each item:

	never	seldom	sometimes	often	always
Q46: I use standards for transforming data (e.g JPG to PNG, DOCX to PDF,...)	○	○	○	○	○
Q47: I can rely on established proccesses and methods for transforming data	○	○	○	○	○
Q48: I am using tool support for transforming data	○	○	○	○	○
Q49: I use languages to modell/describe how to transform data (e.g. Python, R, Matlab, ...)	○	○	○	○	○
Q50: I consider data quality as an important aspect when transforming data	○	○	○	○	○
Q51: I transform data to improve data quality	○	○	○	○	○
Q52: I often need to transfer data to another format	○	○	○	○	○
Q53: Transformations must be developed specifically for the data	○	○	○	○	○
Q54: Metadata supports me in transforming data	○	○	○	○	○

Q55: If you could change how you transform data, what changes would you make?

Delete/Destroy

Every one of us has deleted data at one time in our lives. Be it intentionally or unintentionally. On a whim or due to legal requirements. We would like to learn more about your experience on this topic.

Please rate the following: *

Please choose the appropriate response for each item:

	never	seldom	sometimes	often	always
Q56: I use standards for deleting data (e.g. DIN Norms, RFCs, field specific de-facto standards, etc.)	○	○	○	○	○
Q57: I can rely on established proccesses and methods for deleting data	○	○	○	○	○
Q58: I am using tool support for deleting data	○	○	○	○	○
Q59: I use languages to modell/describe how to delete data	○	○	○	○	○
Q60: I consider data quality as an important aspect when deleting data. (e.g. preventing missing references)	○	○	○	○	○
Q61: I delete obsolete data	○	○	○	○	○
Q62: I know about existing copies of the data that should also be deleted	○	○	○	○	○
Q63: I delete data by accident	○	○	○	○	○
Q64: I need to apply legal requirements when deleting data (e.g. GDPR)	○	○	○	○	○
Q65: The deletion of data is reflected in the corresponding metadata	○	○	○	○	○

Q66: If you could change how you delete data, what changes would you make?

Personal

To conclude our survey we would like to gain some personal insights.

Q67: In which industry are you working? (e.g. Software Engineering, Construction, Medical)

Q68: Can you characterize your company more precisely?

Q69: What is your position in the company? (Job Title / Description)

Q70: How long do you work for your current company?

Q71: How many employees work in your company?

Q72: Do you consider your company as "data-driven" (i.e. using data for improving business)?

Choose one of the following answers
Please choose **only one** of the following:

○ not at all
○ little
○ partial
○ a lot
○ absolutely

References

1. Altendeitering, M., Guggenberger, T.: Designing data quality tools: findings from an action design research project at boehringer ingelheim. In: Proceedings of the 29th European Conference on Information Systems, pp. 1–16 (2021)

2. Altendeitering, M., Tomczyk, M.: A functional taxonomy of data quality tools: insights from science and practice. In: Wirtschaftsinformatik 2022 Proceedings (2022)
3. Amadori, A., Altendeitering, M., Otto, B.: Challenges of data management in industry 4.0: a single case study of the material retrieval process. In: Abramowicz, W., Klein, G. (eds.) BIS 2020. LNBIP, vol. 389, pp. 379–390. Springer, Cham (2020). https://doi.org/10.1007/978-3-030-53337-3_28
4. Azkan, C., Iggena, L., Möller, F., Otto, B.: Towards design principles for data-driven services in industrial environments (2021)
5. Bryman, A., Cramer, D.: Quantitative Data Analysis with SPSS 12 and 13: A Guide for Social Scientists. Routledge, Milton Park (2004)
6. Bychkov, I., et al.: Russian-german astroparticle data life cycle initiative. Data 3(4), 56 (2018). https://doi.org/10.3390/data3040056
7. Cheng, X., Hu, C., Li, Y., Lin, W., Zuo, H.: Data evolution analysis of virtual dataspace for managing the big data lifecycle. In: 2013 IEEE International Symposium on Parallel & Distributed Processing, Workshops and Phd Forum, pp. 2054–2063. IEEE (2013)
8. Christopherson, L., Mandal, A., Scott, E., Baldin, I.: Toward a data lifecycle model for NSF large facilities. In: Practice and Experience in Advanced Research Computing, pp. 168–175 (2020). https://doi.org/10.1145/3311790.3396636
9. Data catalog vocabulary (DCAT) (2014)
10. DAMA: DAMA-DMBOK: Data Management Body of Knowledge. Technics Publications (2017). https://books.google.de/books?id=YjacswEACAAJ
11. Deng, D., et al.: The data civilizer system. In: CIDR (2017)
12. Ehrlinger, L., Schrott, J., Melichar, M., Kirchmayr, N., Wöß, W.: Data catalogs: a systematic literature review and guidelines to implementation. In: Kotsis, G., et al. (eds.) DEXA 2021. CCIS, vol. 1479, pp. 148–158. Springer, Cham (2021). https://doi.org/10.1007/978-3-030-87101-7_15
13. El Arass, M., Ouazzani-Touhami, K., Souissi, N.: Data life cycle: towards a reference architecture. Int. J. Adv. Trends Comput. Sci. Eng. 9(4), 5645–5653 (2020)
14. El Arass, M., Souissi, N.: Data lifecycle: from big data to smartdata. In: 2018 IEEE 5th International Congress on Information Science and Technology (CiSt), pp. 80–87. IEEE
15. Emam, I., et al.: Platformtm, a standards-based data custodianship platform for translational medicine research. Sci. Data 149 (2019). https://doi.org/10.1038/s41597-019-0156-9
16. Fernandez, R.C., Subramaniam, P., Franklin, M.J.: Data market platforms: trading data assets to solve data problems. arXiv preprint arXiv:2002.01047 (2020)
17. Khatri, V., Brown, C.V.: Designing data governance. Commun. ACM 53(1), 148–152 (2010)
18. Korte, T., Fadler, M., Spiekermann, M., Legner, C., Otto, B.: Data Catalogs - Integrated Platforms for Matching Data Supply and Demand: Reference Model and Market Analysis (Version 1.0). Fraunhofer Verlag, Stuttgart (2019)
19. Kuhrmann, M., Fernández, D.M., Daneva, M.: On the pragmatic design of literature studies in software engineering: an experience-based guideline. Empir. Softw. Eng. 22(6), 2852–2891 (2017). https://doi.org/10.1007/s10664-016-9492-y
20. Kumar, N., Stern, L.W., Anderson, J.C.: Conducting interorganizational research using key informants. Acad. Manag. J. 36(6), 1633–1651 (1993)
21. Labadie, C., Legner, C., Eurich, M., Fadler, M.: Fair enough? Enhancing the usage of enterprise data with data catalogs. In: 2020 IEEE 22nd Conference on Business Informatics (CBI), vol. 1, pp. 201–210. IEEE (2020)
22. Levitin, A.V., Redman, T.C.: A model of the data (life) cycles with application to quality. Inf. Softw. Technol. 35(4), 217–223 (1993)
23. Lietz, P.: Research into questionnaire design: a summary of the literature. Int. J. Mark. Res. 52(2), 249–272 (2010)

24. Likert, R.: A technique for the measurement of attitudes. Archives of Psychology (1932)
25. Möller, K.: Lifecycle models of data-centric systems and domains. Semant. Web **4**(1), 67–88 (2013). https://doi.org/10.3233/SW-2012-0060
26. Morris, C.: The life cycle of structural biology data. Data Sci. (2018). https://doi.org/10.5334/dsj-2018-026
27. Otto, B.: Quality and value of the data resource in large enterprises. Inf. Syst. Manag. **32**(3), 234–251 (2015)
28. Pinsonneault, A., Kraemer, K.: Survey research methodology in management information systems: an assessment. J. Manag. Inf. Syst. **10**(2), 75–105 (1993)
29. Polyzotis, N., Roy, S., Whang, S.E., Zinkevich, M.: Data lifecycle challenges in production machine learning: a survey. ACM SIGMOD Rec. **47**(2), 17–28 (2018)
30. Spearman, C.: nthe proof and measurement of association between two things, oamerican j (1904)
31. Spiekermann, M., Tebernum, D., Wenzel, S., Otto, B.: A metadata model for data goods. In: Multikonferenz Wirtschaftsinformatik, vol. 2018, pp. 326–337 (2018)
32. Straub, D.W.: Validating instruments in MIS research. MIS Q. **13**(2), 147–169 (1989). http://www.jstor.org/stable/248922
33. Strauss, A., Corbin, J.M.: Grounded Theory in Practice. Sage (1997)
34. Tallon, P.P., Ramirez, R.V., Short, J.E.: The information artifact in it governance: toward a theory of information governance. J. Manag. Inf. Syst. **30**(3), 141–178 (2013)
35. Tebernum, D., Altendeitering, M., Howar, F.: DERM: a reference model for data engineering. In: Quix, C., Hammoudi, S., van der Aalst, W.M.P. (eds.) Proceedings of the 10th International Conference on Data Science, Technology and Applications, DATA 2021, Online Streaming, 6–8 July 2021, pp. 165–175. SCITEPRESS (2021). https://doi.org/10.5220/0010517301650175
36. Vaismoradi, M., Turunen, H., Bondas, T.: Content analysis and thematic analysis: implications for conducting a qualitative descriptive study. Nurs. Health Sci. **15**(3), 398–405 (2013)
37. Voigt, P., Von dem Bussche, A.: The EU General Data Protection Regulation (GDPR). A Practical Guide, 1st edn. Springer, Cham (2017). https://doi.org/10.1007/978-3-319-57959-7
38. Wang, R.Y., Strong, D.M.: Beyond accuracy: what data quality means to data consumers. J. Manag. Inf. Syst. **12**(4), 5–33 (1996)
39. Webster, J., Watson, R.T.: Analyzing the past to prepare for the future: writing a literature review. MIS Q. 13–23 (2002)
40. Wilkinson, M.D., et al.: The fair guiding principles for scientific data management and stewardship. Sci. Data **3**(1), 1–9 (2016)
41. Xianglan, L.I.: Digital construction of coal mine big data for different platforms based on life cycle. In: 2017 IEEE 2nd International Conference on Big Data Analysis (ICBDA), pp. 456–459. IEEE (2017)
42. Yazdi, M.A.: Enabling operational support in the research data life cycle. In: Proceedings of the First International Conference on Process Mining, pp. 1–10 (2019)

Automating Data Quality Monitoring with Reference Data Profiles

Lisa Ehrlinger[1,2(✉)] , Bernhard Werth[3] , and Wolfram Wöß[1]

[1] Johannes Kepler University Linz, Linz, Austria
{lisa.ehrlinger,wolfram.woess}@jku.at
[2] Software Competence Center Hagenberg GmbH, Hagenberg im Mühlkreis, Austria
lisa.ehrlinger@scch.at
[3] Josef Ressel Center for Adaptive Optimization in Dynamic Environments,
University of Applied Sciences Upper Austria, Wels, Austria
bernhard.werth@fh-ooe.at

Abstract. Data quality is of central importance for the qualitative evaluation of decisions taken by AI-based applications. In practice, data from several heterogeneous data sources is integrated, but complete, global domain knowledge is often not available. In such heterogeneous scenarios, it is particularly difficult to monitor data quality (e.g., completeness, accuracy, timeliness) over time. In this paper, we formally introduce a new data-centric method for automated data quality monitoring, which is based on *reference data profiles*. A reference data profile is a set of data profiling statistics that is learned automatically to model the target quality of the data. In contrast to most existing data quality approaches that require domain experts to define rules, our method can be fully automated from initialization to continuous monitoring. This data-centric method has been implemented in our data quality tool DQ-MeeRKat and evaluated with six real-world telematic device data streams.

Keywords: Data quality monitoring · Reference data profiles · Knowledge graphs · Automated quality checks

1 Introduction

Data quality (DQ) is one of the key challenges for applying artificial intelligence (AI) in practice [17]. In a typical AI application, data is integrated from heterogeneous sources into a central repository [37], which is the basis for training and testing of computational models. According to the Seattle Report on Database Research [1], the quality of data in such applications is not stable and cannot be trusted. Despite a precise definition of ETL (extract, transform, load) processes, DQ can vary over time, either in the source systems or in the central repository [5]. It is crucial to monitor DQ, because undetected DQ deterioration affects data analysis results [13]. A further important step is *automation* of DQ assessment, to cope with the speed and volume of data, which quickly overwhelms any DQ monitoring effort [35].

Motivating Example. The COVID-19 dashboard from the Johns Hopkins University [8], in which data (e.g., number of infections, tests, and deaths related to COVID-19) is integrated from numerous media and government reports, facilitates predictions about the pandemic with AI. The main challenge in creating the dashboard was the continuous harmonization and cleaning of newly inserted (e.g., weekly infections) or updated (e.g., corrected) data from different sources [8]. Due to the autonomy of the data providers, the integrated data was highly heterogeneous and data errors, such as invalid numbers, or wrong string encodings were only handled reactively upon discovery[1]. Without a global view on all integrated data sources, it was not possible to *automatically* and *centrally* verify the quality of data modifications.

Contributions. In this paper, we present a novel method for automated DQ monitoring (ADQM) that is based on *reference data profiles* (RDPs). An RDP is a set of data profiling statistics, which is learned automatically and models the target quality of the data. During runtime, modified (inserted, updated, deleted) data can be continuously verified whether the DQ continues to conform to the requirements defined in the RDPs. Our new RDP-based method for ADQM poses a significant advantage for monitoring DQ in heterogeneous real-world settings since it can be fully automated and does (in contrast to existing DQ tools) not require domain experts to manually create DQ rules. The method has been implemented in the DQ tool DQ-MeeRKat (Automated Data Quality Measurement using a Reference-Data-Profile-Annotated Knowledge Graph), where the technical details are described in [9]. DQ-MeeRKat uses a knowledge graph (KG) to automatically create a global view on the local data sources since KGs are a powerful tool for expressing unified data models.

Structure. Section 2 provides an overview on current methods for ADQM, a short background on KGs, and outlines the research gap. We formally introduce our RDP-based method for ADQM in Sect. 3 and describe the DQ tool DQ-MeeRKat, in which the method has been implemented in Sect. 4. We evaluate the method with DQ-MeeRKat on a real-world data set in Sect. 5 and conclude in Sect. 6.

2   Problem Statement and Related Work

Automated DQ monitoring (also "DQ validation" in [33]) describes the calculation and storage of DQ measurements over time to ensure that the qualitative condition of dynamic data remains stable [13,33,35]. More specifically, an ADQM system (formalized in Sect. 3) continuously collects DQ metadata, which is the foundation to derive new insights in the qualitative development of data [13]. According to [13], the following aspects are required to build an ADQM system:

(R1) Defining a DQ measurement strategy
(R2) A DQ repository to store DQ measurement results over time
(R3) The analysis and visualization of the DQ time series
(R4) Automation (i.e., scheduling) of DQ measurement

While (R2–R4) depend on the implementation, the question "how DQ should actually be measured" is not trivial and according to Sebastian-Coleman [35] one of the biggest

---

[1] As pointed out by Lauren Gartner in her keynote at the 2020 MIT CDOIQ Symposium https://www.youtube.com/watch?v=-LOvwtJvIZM (Apr. 2022).

challenges for DQ practitioners. The state-of-the-art offers two different attempts to measure DQ: (1) the *theoretical perspective* which is based on DQ dimensions and metrics, and (2) the *practitioners perspective* which is implemented in most DQ tools. Figure 1 illustrates both perspectives and indicates that DQ measurement is, independently of the perspective, based on different DQ techniques. We discuss the limitations of both perspectives for ADQM below.

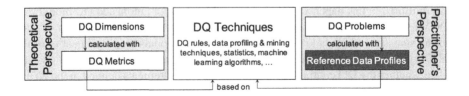

Fig. 1. The Two Different Perspectives on Data Quality Measurement.

2.1   The Theoretical Perspective: DQ Dimensions and Metrics

Data quality is widely perceived as concept with multiple *dimensions*, where each dimension can be objectively measured with one or several DQ *metrics* [22,32,40]. These metrics can be built on the results of defined statistics, DQ rules, or other DQ techniques [32]. Although DQ dimensions are widely considered to be standard in DQ research, a wide variety of definitions and classifications exist for both DQ dimensions (cf. [34,40]) and DQ metrics (cf. [19,22,32]). An overview on possible DQ dimensions and classifications is provided in [28,34]. The following limitations appear with DQ dimensions and metrics for ADQM:

- *Ambiguous definitions.* Due to the wide variety of definitions and classifications, practitioners often find it unclear to decide which DQ dimensions and metrics should be used for DQ measurement in a specific context [35].
- *Gold standard availability.* Many DQ metrics rely on the existence of a perfect reference (or "gold standard"), which, however, is often not available in practice [35]. The absence of such a gold standard impedes a direct application of DQ metrics in practice.
- *Interpretability.* Bronselaer et al. [6] highlight practical issues with the requirements for DQ metrics proposed in [24][2], specifically "normalization", "interval-scaled", and "aggregation". The interpretation of these DQ metrics is often not clear and cannot always be aggregated to higher levels (e.g., from attribute-level to table-level) [6].
- *Ability for evaluation.* Due to the lack of interpretability, also an evaluation of the effectiveness of DQ metrics is not straightforward.

---

[2] The requirements were later refined in [22], but we use here the original source to comply to [6].

In addition to these limitations, the DQ tool survey in [14] reveals that only few tools actually implement DQ metrics as proposed in literature. Some of these metrics have implementation errors, and the majority is applicable on attribute-level only without the possibility to calculate them on higher levels like tables or databases. This circumstance indicates that practitioners (i.e., DQ tool vendors and chief data officers) perceive DQ measurement differently, and not necessarily tied to DQ dimensions and metrics. This different perspective is described below.

2.2 The Practitioners Perspective: DQ Rules and Problems

Current attempts for DQ measurement focus on solving "point problems", that is, algorithms for specific challenges [1]. The major technique implemented in general-purpose DQ tools (e.g., Oracle EDQ, SAS, Talend, Informatica as investigated in [14]) support a domain expert in the creation of rules to resolve specific DQ problems, such as, duplicates or missing values [14,37]. They usually have no or limited capabilities to mine these rules automatically. Thus, in practice, a high manual initialization effort is required to set up all DQ rules, which is a very time-consuming and complex task for domain experts [14]. According to Stonebraker and Ilyas [37], humans can capture at most 500 rules, which is too little for large-scale and data-intensive applications. The manual creation of DQ rules is circumvented with the automatic initialization of RDPs, detailed in Sect. 3.

In addition to rule-based approaches (cf. [21]), there are a number of DQ tools that provide more automated techniques using machine learning to detect DQ problems, e.g., pattern-based error detection [25], duplicate detection [15,36,39], or outlier detection [14]. However, all of these tools focus on specific types of DQ problems or data, i.e., they are domain-specific [14] and do not offer a holistic approach for ADQM. There are two exceptions that can be directly compared to our approach: Heidari et al. [20] with their DQ tool HoloDetect, and the very recent work by Redyuk et al. [33], which has been inspired by our previous work on ADQM [13]. However, both approaches focus on single tabular data files and do not consider non-relational data sources or integration scenarios. We tackle such scenarios with our knowledge graph (cf. Definition 4), which represents heterogeneous data sources with a standardized semantic description such that all data can be further processed the same way. While Redyuk et al. [33] align with our claim that explainability is a core requirement for DQ measurement (to prevent a user from deriving wrong conclusions), Heidari et al. [20] use black box models to learn error representations.

Based on these limitations, Fig. 1 can be completed by adding RDPs as new framework for automated DQ monitoring. An RDP is a composition of different DQ techniques (with a focus on clearly interpretable statistics), which can be learned automatically and represents a quasi-gold-standard that allows to verify whether DQ continues to conform to the requirements modeled in the RDP.

2.3   Knowledge Graphs for Data Integration

KGs have recently gained significant attention with respect to the management of huge amounts of heterogeneous data due to explicit semantics and deductive as well as inductive reasoning techniques to extract new knowledge [23]. While the definition of a KG remains contested (cf. [12, 16, 23]), we summarize the most important aspects in "A knowledge graph acquires and integrates information into an ontology and applies a reasoner to derive new knowledge." [12].

In this paper, a KG is used to store the global domain knowledge (global unified schema), which consists of data source schema descriptions and their annotated RDPs. The data source schemas are semantically described with the data source description (DSD) vocabulary[3] [11], which builds on the W3C standards Resource Description Framework (RDF)[4] and Web Ontology Language (OWL)[5]. The DSD vocabulary guarantees data model independence by mapping each schema to a semantic knowledge-graph-based description. We refer to [11] for details on the DSD vocabulary. This approach allows us to perform paradigm-independent schema integration and consequent annotation of schema elements with data quality information. In other words, the highly general KG description allows us to bridge differences between relational and non relational data models.

3   An Approach for Automated Data Quality Monitoring

To formally describe RDPs, it is initially necessary to formalize an ADQM system as originally introduced in [13].

Definition 1 (ADQM System). *An $ADQM$ system is initialized at t_0 and conducts DQ measurements at subsequent points in time $T = \{t_1, t_2, t_3, ...\}$. For each point in time t, a set of DQ measurement values V_t is obtained for the set of monitored schema elements E. We assume that for every $e \in E$ there exists at least one measurement $v_t(\ldots, e, \ldots)$ that can be considered a "quality" of e at time point t:*
$$\forall_{e \in E} \exists_{v_t \in V_t} v_t(\ldots, e, \ldots) \approx quality(e, t).$$

In a general sense, V_t is not restricted and may provide complex (and possibly aggregated) values of different domains. For the calculation, V_t can take into account one or multiple elements of E as well as additional unmonitored information. Values of V_t may depend on each other. The most important variables are summarized with short descriptions and stand-in data types in Table 1.

---

[3] http://dqm.faw.jku.at/ontologies/dsd (Apr. 2022).

[4] https://www.w3.org/TR/2014/REC-rdf11-concepts-20140225 (Apr. 2022).

[5] https://www.w3.org/TR/2012/REC-owl2-primer-20121211 (Apr. 2022).

Table 1. Summary of Variables for ADQM Formalism.

Variable	Description	Data Type
T	Measurement time points $\{t_1, t_2, t_3, ...\}$	`DateTime`
$e \in E$	Schema element, e.g., table, attribute	`DSD Element`
V_0	DQ measurement values at initialization time	`Double`
$v_t \in V_t$	DQ measurement value at time t	`Double`
$s \in S$	Data profiling statistic	`Function`
$r_t \in R_t$	Data profiling statistic measurement result	`Object`
$p_t(e) \subseteq P_t$	Data profile of e measured at time t	`(Function, Object)`
$p^{ref}(e) \subseteq P^{ref}$	Reference data profile of e	`(Function, Object)`
$cr_t(e) \subseteq CR_t$	Conformance report for e	`(Function, Double)`
$rdpKG$	Knowledge graph containing E and P^{ref}	`RDF Graph`

With rule-based DQ measurement, V_t could be the conformity to the rules. With the classic dimension-oriented DQ measurement, V_t would represent DQ metrics. With the RDP-based method presented in this paper, V_t contains generic statistical descriptors of the data at t as well as composite values obtained by comparing data profiles with each other.

Definition 2 (Data Profile). *Let* $P_t = \{(s, r_t) | s \in S, r_t \in R_t\}$, *where* S *is a set of data profiling statistics and* R_t *a set of results obtained by applying* S *at point t. We call* $p_t(e) \subseteq P_t$ *the "data profile" of e, which is the set of all data profiling statistics pertaining to e.*

Intuitive statistics in S are domain limits, null value percentages, and distribution descriptors (e.g., variance, number of unique values, mean). Some applications might require more sophisticated descriptions of the data, like histograms, distribution estimators, or complex machine learning (ML) models. However, except for very simple aspects of DQ, like counts of null values, a reference or target quality (i.e., a gold standard) is required to assess the quality of e. Here, we suggest the use of a *reference* data profile, which is formally defined as:

Definition 3 (Reference Data Profile). *Let* $P^{ref} = \{(s, r^{ref} | s \in S, r^{ref} \in R^{ref}\}$ *with* R^{ref} *being a set of reference results.* $s(e^{ref}) = r^{ref}$ *is the statistical property s of* e^{ref}, *where* e^{ref} *describes the gold standard (high or perfect quality version) of e. Analogous to Definition 2,* $p^{ref}(e) \subseteq P^{ref}$ *and* $p^{ref}(e) \hat{=} p(e^{ref})$.

There are several ways to obtain r^{ref}. If e^{ref} is available, S can be applied to create its data profile. However, e^{ref} is often not available in practice [35]. If e^{ref} is not available, it is still possible to define r^{ref} directly based on external conditions or domain experts without constructing e^{ref}. As pointed out in [37], such expert-based ratings do not scale for big data environments. Lacking both, e^{ref} and domain-expert-provided r^{ref}, r^{ref} can still be approximated by applying S on earlier iterations of e. In the spirit of automation, we promote and demonstrate the third approach in this paper.

P^{ref} is initially learned at t_0, assuming that the quality of e at time point t_0 is sufficiently high to serve as training data (e.g., after a data audit). Following t_0, we expect the quality of e to deteriorate. Since the reference data profile can change over time (e.g., expected concept drift in variables), $p_x^{ref}(e)$ can be updated at time point $x = t_{last\_update}$. We consider the newest version of $p_x^{ref}(e)$ to be the best descriptor of (the non-existent) e^{ref}. To simplify the notation, we implicitly refer with P^{ref} to P_x^{ref} and with $p^{ref}(e)$ to $p_x^{ref}(e)$ in the following.

An RDP $p^{ref}(e)$ has the same skeletal structure as $p_t(e)$. This structural equality allows for a direct comparison and automated conformance verification of the current state of e, represented with $p_t(e)$, to the target state, represented with $p^{ref}(e)$. This comparison process is explained in Algorithm 1, where the following two phases are distinguished:

1. *Initialization phase* at t_0, where P^{ref} is automatically constructed from E.
2. *Monitoring phase* where P_t is obtained for E at $\{t_1, t_2, t_3, ...\}$.

Algorithm 1. Automated DQ Monitoring with RDPs.

Input: Monitored schema elements E.
Output: Conformance reports CR_t.

1   $x = \text{now}()$;
2   $P_x^{ref} = \text{obtainReferenceDataProfile}(E)$; ;   // Initialization phase
3   **for** t *in* T ;   // Monitoring phase
4   **do**
5   **for** e *in* E **do**
6         $p_t(e) = \text{obtainDataProfile}(e)$;
7         $cr_t(e) = \text{verifyConformance}(p_t(e), p_x^{ref}(e))$;
8   **end**
9   **end**

As shown in Algorithm 1, the ADQM system returns a set of conformance reports $cr_t \in CR_t$, which represent the conformance of P_t to P^{ref} at point t. We would like to point out that the choice of the conformance function can have significant impact when comparing data profiles. A user might benefit from visualizing P_t along with the target state represented in P^{ref}. Automated DQ countermeasures can be implemented depending on the content of CR_t. Such countermeasures (e.g., model-based data cleansing) further increase the degree of automation and elevate DQ monitoring systems to DQ management systems.

In summary, RDP-based DQ monitoring allows to verify whether the data in E continuous to conform to the requirements modeled in P^{ref}. Schema elements in E may display complex structures and relationships and the quality of the elements in E may depend on each other. To tackle this complexity and the heterogeneity of sources with different data models, in DQ-MeeRKat E is modeled as a KG of DSD elements.

Definition 4 (RDP Knowledge Graph). *Let $rdpKG$ be a knowledge graph of DSD schema elements such that $\forall_{e \in E} (e \text{ in } rdpKG)$ and $\forall_{e \in E} \exists_{p^{ref}(e) \subseteq P^{ref}} (p^{ref}(e) \text{ in } rdpKG)$.*

Figure 2 illustrates the entire RDP-based ADQM approach with (1) the initialization phase on the left and (2) the monitoring phase on the right. The input data sources on the left justify the need for the KG: to allow a comparison between these sources and a qualitative evaluation, it is necessary to represent these sources in a single global view, that is, the knowledge graph. During the initialization phase, (a) a semantic description is generated for each schema element e, which is then (b) annotated with a new reference data profile $p^{ref}(e)$.

The right side shows exemplary values for current data profiles P_t. During the monitoring phase, a current data profile $p_t(e)$ is obtained on-the-fly and is compared to its corresponding reference $p^{ref}(e)$ to generate the conformance report $cr_t(e)$. It can be seen that $p_n(e)$ computed at $t = n$ does not conform to its $p^{ref}(e)$ and therefore triggers an alarm.

The advantages of the RDP knowledge graph for DQ monitoring (in contrast to existing methods for ADQM) are summarized in the following:

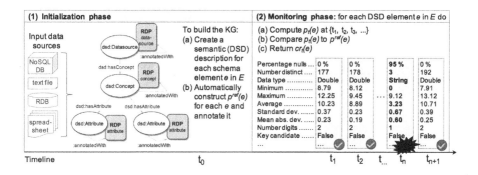

Fig. 2. Illustration of RDP-based DQ Monitoring (based on Fig. 1 in [9]).

– *Improved automation.* The initialization phase (i.e., the creation of $rdpKG$ shown in Fig. 2) can be done fully automatically and therefore replaces the arduous manual creation of DQ rules.
– *Data and domain-independent solution.* While most DQ tools allow DQ measurement on single tabular files (for an overview see [14]; but also specifically Holodetect [20] and the work by Redyuk et al. [33]), the KG allows to investigate multiple heterogeneous data sources at once.
– *DQ dimensions not required.* In contrast to the dimension-oriented view on DQ, it is not necessary to develop DQ metrics and to try to map them to DQ dimensions. The RDP-based approach can be interpreted as a measure-centered view with the aim to measure *what can be measured* automatically.

The statistical methods in S for the current version of DQ-MeeRKat are based on the data profiling (DP) tasks outlined by Abedjan et al. [2, 3]. Details on the statistics and extensions to [3] with respect to ML algorithms are described in the following section.

4   DQ-MeeRKat: Monitoring Data Quality with RDPs

DQ-MeeRKat (Automated Data Quality Measurement using a Reference-Data-Profile-Annotated Knowledge Graph) introduced in [9] implements our new RDP-based method for ADQM. Figure 3 shows the architecture of DQ-MeeRKat with the Java runtime environment in the center. In alignment with the indices, we first describe the components for the initialization phase: (1) data source connectors and DSD elements as the semantic abstraction layer for accessing heterogeneous data sources, (2) the creation of RDPs and how they are annotated to DSD elements, and (3) GraphDB to store the entire KG in Subsect. 4.1. Following, Subsect. 4.2 covers the components to deploy DQ-MeeRKat for ADQM: (4) storage of DQ measurements over time with InfluxDB, and (5) visualization of the DQ time series with Grafana.

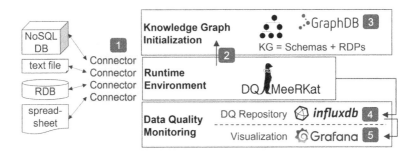

Fig. 3. DQ-MeeRKat Architecture (based on Fig. 2 in [9]).

4.1   Components for Initialization Phase

Connectors and DSD Elements. For populating the KG with semantic schema information from different data sources, e.g., relational DBs, CSV files, or NoSQL databases (DBs), the data source connectors of the DQ tool QuaIIe [10] have been reused. DQ-MeeRKat currently features four different data source connectors for CSV files, MySQL DBs, Cassandra DBs, and Oracle DBs. An additional connector for Neo4J is currently under development. The connectors enable access to heterogeneous data sources and transform their schema to a semantic abstraction layer using the DSD vocabulary (See footnote 3). Here, we list the most important terms and refer for details on the connectors to [10]:

- A dsd:Datasource represents one schema of an information source and has a type (e.g., relational DB, spreadsheet) and an arbitrary number of concepts and associations, which are also referred to as schema elements.
- A dsd:Concept is a real-world object type and can, e.g., be a table in a relational DB or a class in an object-oriented DB.
- A dsd:Attribute is a property of a concept, e.g., "date" may provide information about the day and time a sensor value was recorded.

We refer to these terms jointly as "DSD elements". During the initialization, the KG is created by mapping all data source schemas to their semantic representation in the graph. This step is a prerequisite for comparing the quality of similar elements (e.g., two tables storing customers) from different data sources. To complete the KG, each DSD element is annotated with an RDP, which is explained in the following paragraph. Figure 2 shows a schematic representation of the schema graph with the DSD elements along with their annotated RDPs.

Initialization of Reference Data Profiles. RDPs as well as their corresponding DPs consist of S, a set of DP statistics. These DP statistics are grouped into DP categories and have three properties in common:

- The *label* of a DP statistic is mainly used for identification and visualization.
- The *value* represents the actual value determined by the DP statistic. To support any data types for *value*, the property itself is of data type `Object`. An example value of type `float` would be 1445,26 being the average for the RPM attribute of the telematic device data stream (cf. Subsect. 5.1).
- *valueClass* stores the corresponding Java class to *value*, which allows an automated selection of the correct computation process.

Table 2 outlines all DP statistics that are currently implemented in DQ-MeeRKat. The basis for populating the RDPs was the work on data profiling by Abedjan et al. [2, 3], which we refer to for details on the respective statistics. The current version of DQ-MeeRKat supports all single-column DP statistics from [3], including information like the number of distinct or null values, data types of attributes, or occurring patterns and their frequency (e.g., formatting of telephone numbers) [3]. For attributes of data type `string`, the string length is used to calculate DP statistics like minimum, maximum, or mean. The evaluation of all remaining DP tasks from [3] is part of ongoing research work. In addition to the statistics from [3], we added standard deviation and the more robust mean absolute deviation to consider different variability in the data over time.

Note that extensive data type profiling beyond the currently included basic type and data type is not considered to be part of the DP engine in DQ-MeeRKat. The reasons are that (1) DBMS-specific data types are already considered by the DSD connectors and stored directly with the DSD elements, (2) basic types are inferred for more raw data available in text or CSV files, and (3) data classes and domains, which are also listed in the taxonomy by [3], are covered by the pattern detection implemented in DQ-MeeRKat. Previous research showed that these two DP tasks are commonly implemented with a set of pre-defined patterns [14].

Table 2. Data Profiling Statistics in DQ-MeeRKat.

Category	DP Statistics	DP Statistics Description
Cardinalities	RDP size	Number of rows n for obtaining the data profile
	Number nulls	Number of null values
	Percentage nulls	Percentage of null values
	Number distinct	Number of distinct values
	Uniqueness	Number of distinct values divided by number of rows
Data types, patterns, and domains	Basic type	Generic type, like numeric or alphanumeric
	Data type	DBMS-specific data type (varchar, timestamp, etc.)
	Minimum	Min. value (length) of numeric/textual column
	Maximum	Max. value (length) of numeric/textual column
	Average	Average or arithmetic mean of numeric attribute
	Median	(More robust) Median of numeric attribute
	Standard deviation	Statistics to represent the variance of a numeric attribute (squared deviation from average)
	Mean absolute deviation	Average of all absolute deviations from the arithmetic mean
	Number digits	Maximum number of digits in numeric attribute (also called "size" in [3])
	Number decimals	Maximum number of decimals in numeric attribute
	Patterns	All attribute values that adhere to a pattern represented as regular expression
Histogram	Number of classes	Determined based on Sturge's rule [38] according to $noClasses = 1 + [3.322 * log(n)], n \in \mathbb{N}$
	Class range	Determined based on Sturge's rule [38] according to $range = \frac{max-min}{noClasses}, range \in \mathbb{R}$
	Bucket values	All values that belong to a dedicated bucket (i.e., bin, class)
Dependencies	Key candidate	Indicator: if all attribute values are unique
Outlier detection	Isolation forest	Ensemble method based on isolation trees [30]
	Local outlier factorization	Comparison of the local density of a given point to the local density of its k-nearest neighbors [4]

In terms of dependencies, DQ-MeeRKat is currently restricted to the determination whether an attribute contains only unique values, which is an indicator for a possible candidate key. This DP task is a simplified version of "unique column combinations" as outlined in [3]. While most state-of-the-art DQ tools implement this simple version only (cf. [14]), we plan to extend the dependency category to more sophisticated detection methods.

Two ML models for outlier detection (isolation forest [30] and local outlier factorization [4]) have been recently integrated into the RDPs and are currently under evaluation. Both methods make no hard assumptions on the data and are applicable for high-dimensional data, which was a prerequisite for their inclusion in the RDPs. Isolation forest is an ensemble method based on isolation trees (iTrees). For each iTree, the data points are split until each point is isolated (in a separate rectangle). The less splits are needed for isolation, the more likely a point is an outlier [30]. In the second method, each data point is assigned with a probability score of being an outlier (i.e., the "local outlier factor"). The local outlier factor is obtained by comparing the local density of a given point to the local density of its k-nearest neighbors [4]. With this method, the choice of k influences the results.

Knowledge Graph Store. DQ-MeeRKat stores global domain knowledge in a KG, which consists of DSD schema descriptions and their RDPs. Since RDF and OWL are required to import and process DSD, we use GraphDB[6], formerly "OWLIM" [26], as KG store for DQ-MeeRKat. In contrast to other investigated graph DBs (like Allegro-Graph or Virtuoso), GraphDB meets all requirements for our use case and integrates seamlessly with DQ-MeeRKat and frameworks like RDF4J since it is fully implemented in Java [29].

4.2   Components for DQ Monitoring

After the initialization phase of DQ-MeeRKat, the quality of modified (i.e., inserted, updated, or deleted) data in the data sources can be continuously checked by comparing it to the respective RDP. In each ADQM run, DQ-MeeRKat creates a new current DP for each DSD element in the KG. In addition to the three basic properties (label, value, and valueClass as described in Sect. 4.1), all DP statistics in the current DPs also store a reference to their respective RDP statistic. Thus, each DP statistic can be verified independently.

Based on the foundations for ADQM [13], there are in addition to automation and the selection of a proper DQ measurement method two more requirements for deploying our framework over time: (4) to persist DQ measurements with a timestamp, which indicates when the measurement was taken, and (5) to visualize the measurements to allow human supervision of outliers and tracking the DQ development over time.

Data Quality Repository. We used InfluxDB to store DQ measurements over time, which is the most popular time series DB according to DB-Engines[7] and according to the discussion by [31] suitable for our use case.

Visualization. Since DQ is usually perceived as subjective and domain-dependent concept [40], it is key to visualize the generated time series data for the assessment through domain experts (complementary to automated post-analysis). Although it is possible to use any visualization on top of InfluxDB, we employed the well-known open-source software Grafana[8], which is also recommended by [31]. Grafana offers a customizable user interface that is divided into *dashboards*, which group DP statistics into separate visualization cases.

---

[6] http://graphdb.ontotext.com (Apr. 2022).

[7] https://db-engines.com/de/ranking/time+series+dbms (Apr. 2022).

[8] https://grafana.com (Apr. 2022).

5   Experiments and Results

This section covers the experiments conducted to evaluate our RDP-based method for ADQM with DQ-MeeRKat. Subsect. 5.1 describes the data used for the evaluation and Subsect. 5.2 describes the setup of DQ-MeeRKat used for the experiments. Following, we evaluated our method by means of a qualitative evaluation, where the generated RDPs were investigated by domain experts in Subsect. 5.3, a practical experiment in which batch-loaded data is monitored in Subsect. 5.4, and an experiment in which streaming data is monitored in Subsect. 5.5.

5.1   Evaluation Data

For the experimental evaluation, we used six real-world data streams recorded by an automotive telematic device (Audi A4 CAN bus). The data was provided by Tributech Solutions GmbH[9], an Austrian company that offers a technical solution for the audability of provisioned data streams.

- *Acceleration - braking or forward* (ACC-BoF) contains 23,194 records of a sensor that measures whether the driver pushes the throttle or the brake.
- *Acceleration - side to side* (ACC-StS) contains 23,194 records of a sensor that measures the lateral movement of the car.
- *Acceleration - up or down* (ACC-UoD) contains 23,194 records of a sensor that measures the vertical movement of the car.
- *Device voltage* (D-Voltage) contains 7,275 records of the device voltage.
- *Engine - RPM* (E-RPM) contains 11,316 records that represent the revolutions per minute (RPM) of the car engine.
- *Engine - Speed* (E-Speed) contains 11,316 records of the engine speed.

In addition to the values collected by the sensors, each telematic device data stream contains information about the vehicle in which the device was mounted, a timestamp, a description of the sensor, the source system, the controller, and the device group. Table 3 shows an excerpt of the ACC-BoF data stream, where the variables "Vehicle"

Table 3. Excerpt of the ACC-BoF Data Stream by Tributech.

Vehicle	Date	Description	Value	DeviceGroup
Device1	12/31/19 11:51:40	Forward or braking	3.26561403274536	Driver_Device_1
Device1	12/31/19 11:51:50	Forward or braking	0.00000000000000	Driver_Device_1
Device1	12/31/19 11:51:52	Forward or braking	−1.06892502307892	Driver_Device_1
Device1	12/31/19 11:51:53	Forward or braking	−1.06892502307892	Driver_Device_1
Device1	12/31/19 11:51:53	Forward or braking	−1.24544501304626	Driver_Device_1
Device1	12/31/19 11:51:54	Forward or braking	0.00000000000000	Driver_Device_1
...	...	...	...	...

---

[9] https://www.tributech.io (Apr. 2022).

and "DeviceGroup" were replaced with anonymized values and the variables "Source System" and "Controller" have been omitted for brevity and anonymization. The two RDPs for the values of the streams ACC-BoF and ACC-StS are shown in Table 4 to provide an example on how such an RDP looks like. All other RDPs generated in the course of this evaluation are published on the GitHub repository[10].

Table 4. Reference Data Profiles for Tributech Acceleration Values.

DP Category	DP Statistics	ACC-BoF	ACC-StS
Cardinalities	RDP size	1,000	1,000
	Number nulls	0	0
	Percentage nulls	0%	0%
	Number distinct	200	209
	Uniqueness	20.0%	20.9%
Data types, patterns, and domains	Basic type	Numeric	Numeric
	Data type	Double	Double
	Minimum	-5.5113	-6.3743
	Maximum	4.4424	3.7167
	Average	0.0275	-0.1929
	Median	0.0	0.0
	Standard deviation	1.1805	1.3472
	Mean absolute deviation	0.0	0.0
	Number digits	1	1
	Number decimals	14	14
Histogram	Number of classes	11	11
	Class range	0.9049	0.9173
	Bucket values	[1, 3, 8, 44, 140, 0, 600, 122, 58, 22, 2]	[1, 3, 10, 38, 77, 102, 601, 0, 100, 57, 11]
Dependencies	Key candidate	false	false

5.2 Experimental Setup

The RDP-based method for ADQM has been evaluated with DQ-MeeRKat, which is available on GitHub[11] for repeatability. The architecture and technical details of DQ-MeeRKat are described in Sect. 4 and [9]. For the evaluations outlined in this section, we used InfluxDB[12] version 1.7.7.1 for storing the DQ time series, Grafana[13] version

---

[10] https://github.com/lisehr/dq-meerkat/tree/master/documentation/TributechRDPs/ (Apr. 2022).
[11] https://github.com/lisehr/dq-meerkat (Apr. 2022).
[12] https://www.influxdata.com (Apr. 2022).
[13] https://grafana.com (Apr. 2022).

6.2.5 for visualizing DQ monitoring and GraphDB[14] version 9.4.1 to store the KG[15]. Information on how to install and start the external program requirements to execute the experiments in this section are provided on GitHub (See footnote 11).

For interpretability, we used the following settings to generate the conformance report: two numeric statistic values are conformant if $|a-b| < threshold$. Non-numeric statistics are conformant on equality. The conformance between two data profiles is given by the percentage value of the conformant statistics. The evaluation of more complex conformance functions as well as the outlier detection DP statistics (as included in Table 2) is planned for future work.

5.3   Qualitative Evaluation

To evaluate the quality of automatically generated RDPs and to verify how much refactoring by domain experts is required after the initialization phase, we consulted the data owners from Tributech Solutions GmbH to verify the RDPs for the provided data streams (See footnote 10). The feedback is summarized in the following:

RDP Quality: "After detailed investigation, the automatically generated RDPs were found to be plausible and to fit the provided data very well. No surprising information and none that contradicts the underlying data was found."

Practical Relevance: "Since Tributech deals with the auditability of provisioned data streams (See footnote 9), we see the major benefit of the RDP-based method in the automation of data stream monitoring. From the currently implemented statistics in the RDPs, uniqueness and domain information (such as minimum, maximum, and deviations from the mean) are specifically relevant for this use case."

Generally, practical viability is hard to test without a large user study. However, the feedback from Tributech indicates the practical relevance of our RDP-based method for ADQM. To further increase the utility of DQ-MeeRKat, additional extensions as suggested by the domain experts are discussed in Sect. 6.

5.4   Experiment 1: Monitor the Quality of Batch-Loaded Data

In integration scenarios, data is usually loaded batch-wise (e.g., via an ETL process) in periodic intervals into a data warehouse or data lake [18,37]. The task of an ADQM system in such settings is to verify whether the newly loaded data continues to conform to the requirements modeled in P^{ref}. Thus, the frequency at which DQ should be measured and verified can naturally be defined by the frequency of the ETL process [35]. Sebastian-Coleman [35] points out that periodic measurements for less critical data may also be based on a different schedule, e.g., monthly, quarterly, or annually.

When performing RDP-based ADQM with batch-loaded data, three parameters need to be set: (1) the *threshold* to verify the conformance of P_t to P^{ref}, (2) the *batch*

---

[14] http://graphdb.ontotext.com (Apr. 2022).

[15] Visualizations of the KG in GraphDB are provided on: https://github.com/lisehr/dq-meerkat/tree/master/documentation/kg-visualization/ (Apr. 2022).

size, and (3) the number of records used for learning P^{ref} (*RDP size*). Figure 4 shows the influence of the three parameters on the average RDP conformance reported to the user (CR). To simulate a scenario with batch-loaded data, we grouped single records from the data streams to batches and verified whether the P_t of the batch loaded at time point t conforms to P^{ref}. Note that the transformation of streaming data to batches (with so-called "window functions") is a common technique to compute aggregations and statistics on streams and to analyze them with ML techniques [7].

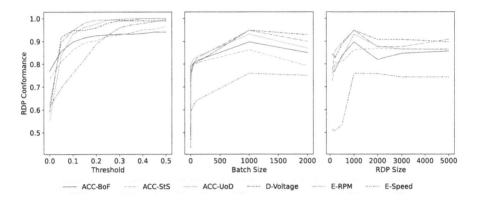

Fig. 4. Parameter Evaluation.

It can be seen that for the Tributech data sets a threshold of 0.1 is sufficient for receiving a very high conformance to P^{ref}, which was expected by the data owners due to the nature of the data. With respect to the batch size and RDP size, 1,000 records turned out to be a good fit for our data. Interestingly, the RDP conformance might deteriorate with an increasing number of records for learning the RDPs or DPs. This shows that the selection of larger batch sizes (time windows) moves the conformance focus from time-local information to time-global information [41]. Table 5 shows the average conformance of all six data streams (all values in %) using the parameter setting determined in Fig. 4. The conformance values in Table 5 are calculated as follows: $cr(e) = $ *number of* $p(e)$ *conforming to* $p_x^{ref}(e)/total$ *number of* $p(e)$, where e is the attribute in the header line and conformance is verified with a deviation less than threshold $= 0.1$.

As outlined in Table 5, all variables except for the sensor value conform perfectly to their corresponding RDP over time. Since the sensor values are the only variables with a relatively high variability, some values exceed the boundaries defined in the RDP when monitoring the entire data. In practice, many attributes (e.g., static string values) yield a high conformance without any deviation from the RDP. This circumstance justifies organization-wide DQ monitoring since these attributes are continuously monitored and not overlooked by domain experts, and rare (unexpected) changes are detected in time. This conformance report can be repeated for different data sets by executing demos\ repeatability\ RDPConformanceTributechData.java from the GitHub repository.

Table 5. RDP Conformance of Batch Data with Threshold = 0.1, Batch Size = 1,000, and RDP Size = 1,000.

CR in %	Vehicle	Date	Description	Source	Controller	Value	DeviceGroup
ACC-BoF	100	100	100	100	100	89.75	100
ACC-StS	100	100	100	100	100	86.34	100
ACC-UoD	100	100	100	100	100	93.17	100
D-Voltage	100	100	100	100	100	94.90	100
E-RPM	100	100	100	100	100	94.81	100
E-Speed	100	100	100	100	100	75.97	100

5.5 Experiment 2: Monitor the Quality of Streaming Data

Handling and analyzing data streams is specifically relevant in Industry 4.0 applications, where sensor data is recorded and analyzed [7]. In addition to quality aspects of static data, additional aspects of DQ, such as the occurrence of repeating patterns need to be considered [27].

Grouping of multiple streaming records (i.e., windowing) allows for the calculation of aggregates and complex statistics [7]. Comparing only single records to their respective $r^{ref}(e)$ precludes the use of some statistics presented in Table 2, because they are either not calculable (e.g., variance) or loose their semantic meaning (e.g., mean).

Table 6. RDP Conformance of Streaming Data with Threshold = 0.1, Batch Size = 1, RDP Size = 1,000, and a Reduced DP Statistics Set.

CR in %	Vehicle	Date	Description	Source	Controller	Value	DeviceGroup
ACC-BoF	100	100	100	100	100	99.99	100
ACC-StS	100	100	100	100	100	99.98	100
ACC-UoD	100	100	100	100	100	94.73	100
D-Voltage	100	100	100	100	100	100	100
E-RPM	100	100	100	100	100	96.87	100
E-Speed	100	100	100	100	100	86.71	100

When comparing Table 5 to Table 6, it can be seen that the overall conformance of the values is higher than with the batch-based conformance checks. Since no aggregation statistics are compared but only (automatically generated) boundaries are checked, the proportion of statistics that do not concern numeric variance (e.g., domain constraints, number of null values) is higher. This data set contains only numeric deviations in DQ with respect to the sensor values.

Both experiments have their application in practice: experiment 1 for ETL-based data integration scenarios and experiment 2 for the conformance verification of sensor or other streaming data that is not preprocessed by window functions. This evaluation shows the differences between the two use cases and that compliance ratings may not be directly comparable between different systems and or parameterizations.

The generation of conformance reports as demonstrated so far is useful for automated post-processing. In other applications, the visualization of the DQ time series to a user might be more interesting. Figure 5 shows an excerpt of the Grafana dashboard, where the green line is the ACC-BoF data stream value and the minimum and maximum boundaries of the RDP are colored red. At $t = 18.54$, several values exceed the maximum boundary. Here, either an automatic alert could trigger subsequent actions or an automated DQ countermeasure can be set in place (e.g., the imputation of a missing value). In less critical cases, a domain expert could trace the origins of the error. Further visualizations are provided in the `documentation\ adqm-screenshots` folder of the GitHub repository (See footnote 11). The visualization dashboard for monitoring data streams can be invoked by executing `demos\ repeatability\ DemoStreamingData.java`.

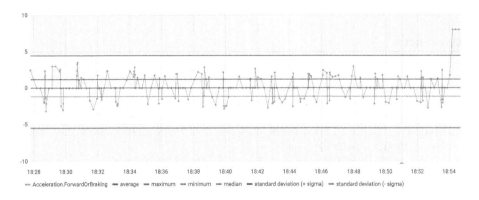

Fig. 5. Visualization of RDP-based Stream DQ Monitoring: ACC-BoF Value.

6 Conclusion and Future Work

In this paper, we presented a novel method for automated DQ monitoring, which is based on *reference data profiles*. We implemented the method in DQ-MeeRKat and demonstrated its applicability by means of two experiments: (1) to monitor the quality of batch-loaded data, and (2) to monitor the quality of streaming data. The two experiments as well as the qualitative evaluation showed the superiority of our RDP-based method (in contrast to existing methods) for application in practice due to the fully automated initialization phase.

In addition to their qualitative evaluation, Tributech Solutions GmbH proposed the following enhancements to continue improving the value of our RDP-based method for deployment in practice: to consider changes in the RDP over time, e.g., when the occupancy rate of a machine depends on the day of the week, and to enhance the interpretability for the end user, e.g., by adding guidelines and clear descriptions of the RDPs for less experienced users. Further, a systematic long-term evaluation in close collaboration with domain experts is planned as follow-up research work. Here, special emphasis should be placed on the newly integrated multi-column DP statistics (cf. [3]) and the two ML models for outlier detection, which have not been evaluated so far.

The overall vision for DQ-MeeRKat is to create a comprehensive "AI-based surveillance state", which characterizes various kinds of data to detect drifts and anomalies in DQ at the earliest possible stage. Thus, we are going to enhance the RDPs with more complex statistics and ML models, such as linear regression and matrix factorization to detect outliers in a high-dimensional space, while still being interpretable. The focus will be on white-box models, since it is crucial that statements about DQ itself are explainable.

Acknowledgements. The research reported in this paper has been funded by BMK, BMDW, and the Province of Upper Austria in the frame of the COMET Programme managed by FFG. The authors also thank Patrick Lamplmair of Tributech Solutions GmbH for providing the data streams as well as Alexander Gindlhumer and Lisa-Marie Huber for their support in the implementation of DQ-MeeRKat.

References

1. Abadi, D., et al.: The Seattle report on database research. ACM SIGMOD Rec. **48**(4), 44–53 (2019)
2. Abedjan, Z., Golab, L., Naumann, F.: Profiling relational data: a survey. VLDB J. **24**(4), 557–581 (2015)
3. Abedjan, Z., Golab, L., Naumann, F., Papenbrock, T.: Data profiling. Synth. Lect. Data Manag. **10**(4), 1–154 (2019)
4. Breunig, M.M., Kriegel, H.P., Ng, R.T., Sander, J.: LOF: identifying density-based local outliers. In: Proceedings of the 2000 ACM SIGMOD International Conference on Management of Data, pp. 93–104 (2000)
5. Bronselaer, A.: Data quality management: an overview of methods and challenges. In: Andreasen, T., De Tré, G., Kacprzyk, J., Legind Larsen, H., Bordogna, G., Zadrożny, S. (eds.) FQAS 2021. LNCS (LNAI), vol. 12871, pp. 127–141. Springer, Cham (2021). https://doi.org/10.1007/978-3-030-86967-0_10
6. Bronselaer, A., De Mol, R., De Tré, G.: A measure-theoretic foundation for data quality. IEEE Trans. Fuzzy Syst. **26**(2), 627–639 (2018)
7. Dell'Aglio, D., Della Valle, E., van Harmelen, F., Bernstein, A.: Stream reasoning: a survey and outlook. Data Sci. **1**(1–2), 59–83 (2017)
8. Dong, E., Du, H., Gardner, L.: An interactive web-based dashboard to track COVID-19 in real time. Lancet. Infect. Dis **20**(5), 533–534 (2020)
9. Ehrlinger, L., Gindlhumer, A., Huber, L., Wöß, W.: DQ-MeeRKat: automating data quality monitoring with a reference-data-profile-annotated knowledge graph. In: Proceedings of the 10th International Conference on Data Science, Technology and Applications - DATA, pp. 215–222. SciTePress (2021)
10. Ehrlinger, L., Werth, B., Wöß, W.: Automated continuous data quality measurement with QualIe. Int. J. Adv. Softw. **11**(3 & 4), 400–417 (2018)
11. Ehrlinger, L., Wöß, W.: Semi-automatically generated hybrid ontologies for information integration. In: SEMANTiCS (Posters & Demos). CEUR Workshop Proceedings, vol. 1481, pp. 100–104. RWTH, Aachen (2015)

12. Ehrlinger, L., Wöß, W.: Towards a definition of knowledge graphs. In: Martin, M., Cuquet, M., Folmer, E. (eds.) Joint Proceedings of the Posters and Demos Track of 12th International Conference on Semantic Systems - SEMANTiCS2016 and 1st International Workshop on Semantic Change & Evolving Semantics (SuCCESS16). CEUR Workshop Proceedings, vol. 1695, pp. 13–16. Technical University of Aachen (RWTH), Aachen, Germany (2016)

13. Ehrlinger, L., Wöß, W.: Automated data quality monitoring. In: Talburt, J.R. (ed.) Proceedings of the 22nd MIT International Conference on Information Quality (MIT ICIQ), UA Little Rock, Arkansas, USA, pp. 15.1–15.9 (2017)

14. Ehrlinger, L., Wöß, W.: A survey of data quality measurement and monitoring tools. Front. Big Data 5(850611) (2022). https://doi.org/10.3389/fdata.2022.850611

15. Elmagarmid, A.K., Ipeirotis, P.G., Verykios, V.S.: Duplicate record detection: a survey. IEEE Trans. Knowl. Data Eng. 19(1), 1–16 (2007)

16. Fensel, D., et al.: Knowledge Graphs. Springer, Cham (2020). https://doi.org/10.1007/978-3-030-37439-6

17. Fischer, L., et al.: AI system engineering-key challenges and lessons learned. Mach. Learn. Knowl. Extr. 3(1), 56–83 (2021)

18. Giebler, C., Gröger, C., Hoos, E., Schwarz, H., Mitschang, B.: Leveraging the data lake: current state and challenges. In: Ordonez, C., Song, I.-Y., Anderst-Kotsis, G., Tjoa, A.M., Khalil, I. (eds.) DaWaK 2019. LNCS, vol. 11708, pp. 179–188. Springer, Cham (2019). https://doi.org/10.1007/978-3-030-27520-4_13

19. Haegemans, T., Snoeck, M., Lemahieu, W.: Towards a precise definition of data accuracy and a justification for its measure. In: Proceedings of the International Conference on Information Quality (ICIQ 2016), Ciudad Real, Spain, pp. 16.1–16.13. Alarcos Research Group (UCLM) (2016)

20. Heidari, A., McGrath, J., Ilyas, I.F., Rekatsinas, T.: Holodetect: few-shot learning for error detection. In: International Conference on Management of Data (SIGMOD 2019), New York, NY, USA, pp. 829–846. ACM (2019)

21. Heine, F., Kleiner, C., Oelsner, T.: Automated detection and monitoring of advanced data quality rules. In: Hartmann, S., Küng, J., Chakravarthy, S., Anderst-Kotsis, G., Tjoa, A.M., Khalil, I. (eds.) DEXA 2019. LNCS, vol. 11706, pp. 238–247. Springer, Cham (2019). https://doi.org/10.1007/978-3-030-27615-7_18

22. Heinrich, B., Hristova, D., Klier, M., Schiller, A., Szubartowicz, M.: Requirements for data quality metrics. J. Data Inf. Qual. 9(2), 12:1–12:32 (2018)

23. Hogan, A., et al.: Knowledge Graphs. CoRR (2020). https://arxiv.org/abs/2003.02320

24. Kaiser, M., Klier, M., Heinrich, B.: How to measure data quality? - a metric-based approach. In: International Conference on Information Systems, Montreal, Canada, pp. 1–15. AIS Electronic Library (AISeL) (2007)

25. Kandel, S., Paepcke, A., Hellerstein, J., Heer, J.: Wrangler: interactive visual specification of data transformation scripts. In: Proceedings of the SIGCHI Conference on Human Factors in Computing Systems, Vancouver, BC, Canada. ACM (2011)

26. Kiryakov, A., Ognyanov, D., Manov, D.: OWLIM – a pragmatic semantic repository for OWL. In: Dean, M., et al. (eds.) WISE 2005. LNCS, vol. 3807, pp. 182–192. Springer, Heidelberg (2005). https://doi.org/10.1007/11581116_19

27. Klein, A., Lehner, W.: Representing data quality in sensor data streaming environments. J. Data Inf. Qual. (JDIQ) 1(2), 1–28 (2009)

28. Laranjeiro, N., Soydemir, S.N., Bernardino, J.: A survey on data quality: classifying poor data. In: Proceedings of the 21st Pacific Rim International Symposium on Dependable Computing (PRDC), Zhangjiajie, China, pp. 179–188. IEEE (2015)

29. Ledvinka, M., Křemen, P.: A comparison of object-triple mapping libraries. Semant. Web 1–43 (2019)

30. Liu, F.T., Ting, K.M., Zhou, Z.H.: Isolation forest. In: 2008 Eighth IEEE International Conference on Data Mining, pp. 413–422. IEEE (2008)
31. Naqvi, S.N.Z., Yfantidou, S., Zimányi, E.: Time Series Databases and InfluxDB. Technical report, Université Libre de Bruxelles (2017)
32. Pipino, L., Wang, R., Kopcso, D., Rybolt, W.: Developing measurement scales for data-quality dimensions. Inf. Qual. **1**, 37–52 (2005)
33. Redyuk, S., Kaoudi, Z., Markl, V., Schelter, S.: Automating data quality validation for dynamic data ingestion. In: Proceedings of the 24th International Conference on Extending Database Technology (EDBT) (2021)
34. Scannapieco, M., Catarci, T.: Data quality under a computer science perspective. Archivi Comput. **2**, 1–15 (2002)
35. Sebastian-Coleman, L.: Measuring Data Quality for Ongoing Improvement: A Data Quality Assessment Framework. Elsevier, Waltham, MA, USA (2013)
36. Stonebraker, M., et al.: Data curation at scale: the data tamer system. In: 6th Biennial Conference on Innovative Data Systems Research (CDIR 2013), Asilomar, California, USA (2013)
37. Stonebraker, M., Ilyas, I.F.: Data integration: the current status and the way forward. Bull. IEEE Comput. Soc. Tech. Committee Data Eng. **41**(2), 3–9 (2018)
38. Sturges, H.A.: The choice of a class interval. J. Am. Stat. Assoc. **21**(153), 65–66 (1926)
39. Talburt, J.R., Al Sarkhi, A.K., Pullen, D., Claassens, L., Wang, R.: An iterative, self-assessing entity resolution system: first steps toward a data washing machine. Int. J. Adv. Comput. Sci. Appl. **11**(12) (2020)
40. Wang, R.Y., Strong, D.: Beyond accuracy: what data quality means to data consumers. J. Manag. Inf. Syst. **12**(4), 5–33 (1996)
41. Zenisek, J., Holzinger, F., Affenzeller, M.: Machine learning based concept drift detection for predictive maintenance. Comput. Ind. Eng. **137**, 106031 (2019)

Towards Comparable Ratings: Quantifying Evaluative Phrases in Physician Reviews

Joschka Kersting[1]([✉]) and Michaela Geierhos[2]

[1] Paderborn University, Paderborn, Germany
joschka.kersting@unibw.de
[2] Bundeswehr University Munich, Research Institute CODE, Munich, Germany
michaela.geierhos@unibw.de

Abstract. We present a concept for quantifying evaluative phrases to later compare rating texts numerically instead of just relying on stars or grades. We achieve this by combining deep learning models in an aspect-based sentiment analysis pipeline along with sentiment weighting, polarity, and correlation analyses that combine deep learning results with metadata. The results provide new insights for the medical field. Our application domain, physician reviews, shows that there are millions of review texts on the Internet that cannot yet be comprehensively analyzed because previous studies have focused on explicit aspects from other domains (e.g., products). We identify, extract, and classify implicit and explicit aspect phrases equally from German-language review texts. To do so, we annotated aspect phrases representing reviews on numerous aspects of a physician, medical practice, or practice staff. We apply the best performing transformer model, XLM-RoBERTa, to a large physician review dataset and correlate the results with existing metadata. As a result, we can show different correlations between the sentiment polarity of certain aspect classes (e.g., friendliness, practice equipment) and physicians' professions (e.g., surgeon, ophthalmologist). As a result, we have individual numerical scores that contain a variety of information based on deep learning algorithms that extract textual (evaluative) information and metadata from the Web.

Keywords: Aspect classification · Rating weight · Physician reviews

1 Introduction

Reviews represent an important form of feedback and have become a kind of quality measure for many goods. The benefits of reviews can be seen, on the one hand, in the fact that they help users to make informed decisions; on the other hand, they also enable organizations to identify customer interests and opinions. In many cases, the reviews are highly individualized in their wording. Evaluation categories, so-called aspect classes, are not always directly addressed. So far, research has neglected data with more suggestive phrases and implicit expressions; this also applies to the weighting of individual statements.

A. Cuzzocrea et al. (Eds.): DATA 2021/2022, CCIS 1860, pp. 45–65, 2023.
https://doi.org/10.1007/978-3-031-37890-4_3

For this purpose, aspect-based sentiment analysis (ABSA) is used to identify and distinguish opinions about evaluated objects, people, or services in unstructured text data [28]. ABSA can serve as a valuable method for quantifying evalutative phrases because it extracts and weights information. This is facilitated by the advances made in natural language processing (NLP) research in recent years, such as transformers like BERT [12,53].

1.1   Use Case: Online Physician Reviews

The aim of this study is to use patient ratings from German-language physician review websites (PRWs) as a sample domain for quantifying evaluative expressions in unstructured text data. Among the investigated PRWs are Jameda.de, Docfinder.at, and Medicosearch.ch. Especially PRWs are suitable because they contain long, complex phrases and implicitly state rating aspects that refer to physicians and their behavior as well as to the staff of a medical practice and the practice as a whole. The latter can be characterized, for example, by both opening hours and equipment. Our previous studies have also built on these data [25–29], but we use them differently here because we aim at quantifying textual data rather than just performing ABSA or specialized evaluations for a particular medical specialty. This study is an extended work based on Kersting and Geierhos [29].

Example 1 (characteristic sample review). 'I want to say here **how well our doctor treated me**. At first, **all appointments are made to according to patients' wishes**, I **never (except once when I was too early there) had to wait long in the offices**. Moreover, I know that the doctor is **always nice with patients**, he also **is confident in what he is doing**. The **rooms are full of light**, while **privacy is maintained**.'

As shown by the bold aspect phrases in this example, identification by human readers is quite easy, while training AI models therefore is a challenging task. However, achieving this is a prerequisite for quantifying evaluative phrases. Previous studies have already investigated different aspect targets [27–29]. In general, these studies were addressing a subset of the existing aspect classes and their targets (physician, staff, office). This study, in contrast, attempts to gain general insights into all classes and aspects. Here, we examine a doctor's office as an evaluation target with the following aspect classes [27]: *"waiting time for an appointment"*, *"waiting time in the practice"*, *"equipment"*, and *"well-being"*[1].

1.2   Unique Feature: Implicit Aspect Mentions

Scholars mostly used exclusively commercial reviews [40,58] for ABSA research, in which nouns often explicitly refer to an aspect by its name or a synonym. Several works take nouns and noun phrases as sufficient representations for aspects [6,41,43,45]. While this may be sufficient when evaluating products, for example, the wording is quite different for many other domains. Adjective-noun constructions are not sufficient because physician reviews capture interpersonal ratings and situations. For example, the

---

[1] Translated from German: *"Wartezeit auf einen Termin"*, *"Wartezeit in der Praxis"*, *"Ausstattung"*, and *"Wohlfühlen"*. The acronym wtwawo sums them up [27].

doctor's friendliness or (subjectively perceived) competence are assessed by phrases such as 'he didn't look at me once while talking' or 'he didn't seem sure what to do next'.

ABSA serves here as a vehicle for data extraction and analysis. First, aspect term extraction (ATE) and aspect category classification (ACC) [6] are performed, i.e., aspect phrases are identified and assigned to their respective aspect class. Second, aspect polarity classification (APC) [6] determines the sentiment polarity of the extracted phrases, i.e., whether they are positive or negative. Third, the relative weight, i.e., the importance of the extracted phrases, is calculated [27]. The result of the pipeline is detailed information, some of which is already available in numerical form. We apply correlation and association methods to combine our results with additional knowledge. Compared to a previous work [29], we do not restrict ourselves to a specific domain. Instead, we draw general conclusions about physicians' specialties, gender, and other matters.

1.3   Course of Action

First, we extend our previous work [27] by focusing on all available PRW data and all specialists. Second, we train and evaluate a set of deep learning models, mainly transformers. Third, we apply our deep learning pipeline [27, 29] to all collected physician ratings from a German PRW. Finally, we correlate and associate our results and obtain numerical scores from which conclusions can be drawn for the health domain. This extends the state of the art.

For this purpose, we organize this study as follows: After introducing the topic, we present the relevant state of the art in the next section. In Sect. 3, we present the raw data underlying the ABSA. For supervised learning in ASBA, the process of data annotation and the aspect classes are shown in Sect. 4. Then, Sect. 5 addresses the deep learning training process and its results, and Sect. 6 describes the application of our text mining pipeline. We also describe the analyses performed, where the text mining results are merged with the existing metadata and analyzed. Finally, we discuss our findings and give an outlook on future projects in Sect. 7.

2   Related Literature

The state of the art relevant to this study consists of (patient) reviews, ABSA and deep learning, as well as correlation and association methods.

2.1   Online Physician Reviews

In the past, various scholars have used physician reviews for their research [5, 24], they also saw them as their primary research target, i.e., they wanted to gain knowledge about physician reviews and PRWs [14–17]. However, physician reviews are less researched compared to commercial reviews [37, 42, 44, 45, 58]. Physician reviews are different because they deal with inter-personal issues and trust is an important factor [24]. Medical treatments are generally the most difficult topic that can be rated [56]. Besides, most ratings are positive [17]. In fact, there are other studies besides ours that dealt with PRWs for ABSA [35].

2.2 Aspect-based Sentiment Analysis

In previous research, we examined implicit aspect mentions [23,25–29]. Most other research focused more on ABSA for commercial data [13,40,58], while we targeted implicit and indirect aspect mentions across phrases. We do not just rely on nouns, seed words, etc., as others do: "An opinion target expression [...] is an explicit reference (mention) to the reviewed entity [...]. This reference can be a named entity, a common noun, or a multi-word expression" [43]. Due to the complexity of natural language, these approaches are not sufficient.

Moreover, most research has dealt with the same review datasets [42,44,45] and ATE is often not conducted [58]. Indeed, it is the data that shape the analyses and subsequent method development, so the data used has an important role in research design, especially in machine learning. Artificial boundaries are disadvantageous because these limits continue to have a wider impact: Most studies use similar approaches for their research design. Most approaches cannot be applied to domains other than commercial reviews, especially not physician reviews. Table 1 demonstrates relevant ABSA datasets considered for our study.

As shown, most ABSA datasets focus on commercial customer reviews and social media content or question-answer data. Most datasets are quite small, use two or three polarity ratings (positive, negative, and neutral) and are unbalanced. Examination of the datasets also reveals that they contain a rather small number of aspect classes [35] or a larger number that are extremely unbalanced [55]. Therefore, we stick to the datasets used in our previous work, especially in the study that is extended by this work [29]: a large PRW dataset containing physician review text and meta information.

2.3 Deep Learning for ABSA

Several studies have used deep learning for ABSA. In our previous work [27–29], we compared multiple neural networks using (bidirectional) long-short term memories ((bi)LSTMs) [21,51] with attention [53] and conditional random fields (CRFs) [32]. We also domain-trained transformers for word representations and fine-tuned them on our tasks, e.g., XLM-RoBERTa [8].

Moreover, we successfully used FastText [4], which creates word representations based on letter vectors. However, FastText is a static embedding computation method. More recent approaches such as transformers [53] compute word representations, embeddings, on-the-fly, based on the context of a word. As mentioned earlier, they can be trained for the domain and later fine-tuned for tasks such as text classification. Nevertheless, transformer research has produced different types of models. We compared several of them to find out which one works best with German physician reviews, given their user-generated and error-prone nature. In previous work, we identified a number of applicable model types [23,27,29], which we also apply here. Among them are available transformers pre-trained on German data, a multilingual transformer, and self-coded neural networks.

Table 1. Tabular overview of sentiment analysis datasets [23].

Ref.	Name	Language(s)[a]	Size & Data[b]	Polarity[c]	Balance
[44]	SemEval-2014	EN	customer reviews (restaurant: 3,800 sentences)	+, −, n, c	no
[42]	SemEval-2015	EN	customer reviews (restaurant: 2,000 sentences)	+, −, n	no
[45]	SemEval-2016	AR, CN, NL, EN, ES, FR, RU, TR	customer reviews (restaurant; EN: 2,700 sentences, NL: 2,300 sentences)	+, −, n	no
[35]	López et al	EN	700 physician reviews	+, −	no
[38]	Mitchell et al.	EN, ES	tweets (EN: 2,300, ES: 7,000)	+, −, n	no
[30]	USAGE	DE, EN	2∗600 customer reviews (products)	+, −, n	no
[47]	GESTALT (2014)	DE	1,800 sentences (political speeches, "STEPS"), 700 customer reviews (products, partly based on Klinger & Cimiano [30])	n/a ; +, −, n	n/a; no
[11]	MPQA	EN	70 texts (news articles, etc.)	+, −	n/a
[48]	SentiHood	EN	5,200 sentences (question-answering platform)	+, −	no
[10]	De Clercq et al.	NL	4,200 texts, customer feedback (baking, trade, recruiting; variable length)	+, −, n	n/a
[55]	GermEval-2017	DE	social media, tweets, news, question-answer platform, transport corporations, 28,000 (short) texts	+, −, n	no
[36]	Maia et al.	EN	500 news articles, 800 tweets (finance)	−1 to +1	n/a

[a] AR = Arabic, CN = Chinese, DE = German, NL = Dutch, EN = English, ES = Spanish, FR = French, RU = Russian, and TR = Turkish
[b] This refers to the aspect phrases or a part of them that can be used for ABSA research. The numbers are rounded, approximate values. When available, the numbers were used for sentences and not for complete texts.
[c] + = positive, − = negative, n = neutral, and c = conflict

2.4 Quantifying Evaluative Phrases

Users of rating platforms assign varying weightings to different aspect classes [18, 34]. The rating weight expresses the importance of an aspect phrase. Previous studies determined evaluation weights quite differently than necessary in the present case, partly because they interpret ABSA differently. Examples include sentence-level weights for aspect classes [18], the use of latent dirichlet allocation (LDA) [19], regression [2], or weighting based on user preferences [34]. Some calculate e.g. relevance scores for whole review texts [57]. Some studies focus on determining a ranking for product features [39, 54]. In this process the main aspects are searched for in connection with polarity [39].

As mentioned, in addition to ABSA, we also calculate the importance of the extracted aspect phrases to make them quantifiable and thus numerically comparable. There are two basic approaches for determining the weighting: First, there is the meta-technique, which assigns weights to evaluative phrases based on external features, such as the frequency of occurrence of the aspect class [39]. Second, there is the individual technique, which analyzes the phrases and determines a weight based on the data-driven features. In a related study [27], we presented and evaluated our algorithm for this. Briefly, the algorithm assigns higher weights to evaluative phrases that contain modifiers. These can be adverbs, comparatives, or superlatives [27]. It has also been successfully applied to PRW data [23, 29]. These examples illustrate the weight differences between evaluative phrases such as 'very pleasant waiting room' as opposed to 'pleasant waiting room'. Comparative adjectives have the same effect, e.g., 'friendlier' and the superlative 'most friendly'. Aspect phrase importance, i.e., an increased weighting describes cases in which reviewers have given greater importance to the things they want to express. Therefore, these aspects are given a greater weight compared to those without other modifying words such as adverbs or superlatives.

2.5   Correlation with Metadata

For the implementation, the results of the weighting techniques must be correlated with metadata. Metadata in the sense of this work are the data that are found in addition to the review texts on PRWs such as medical specialty, opening hours, address, further qualifications, gender of the patient, and the date of publication. The quantitative ratings are also part of the metadata. In short, metadata is the data about the reviews [49].

Since regression does not provide a normalized value that measures the coincidence of data [50], the Spearman's correlation coefficient [52] is used as an alternative. Its scale ranges from -1 to $+1$. A perfect Spearman's ρ of $+1$ or -1 occurs when each of the variables is a perfect monotone function of the other. 0 means no correlation. Correlations do not necessarily indicate a causal relationship. The Spearman's ρ is preferred to the Pearson's r when the data is not normally distributed [46].

To correlate our data, we use the Spearman's correlation coefficient [52] for continuous and discrete ordinal variables (i.e., numbers), and Cramér's V [1] for categorical variables that cannot be represented by numbers. Cramér's V computes a measure of the relationship between two categorical variables. It can only describe the strength, but not the direction, of a relationship [3]. This is different in the case of Spearman's correlation coefficient. It is a standard measure that shows how two columns of data correlate with each other.

3   Underlying Raw Data

The data collection already took place between March and July 2018 [9]. We wanted to avoid that one platform has too much influence on the later analyses, e.g. by only taking aspect classes from the rating classes of the PRWs. Therefore, we crawled three PRWs (`Jameda.de`, `Docfinder.at`, and `Medicosearch.ch`) from three German-speaking countries (Germany, Austria, Switzerland).

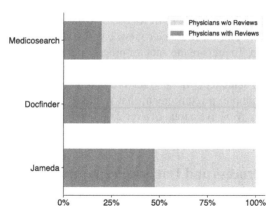

Fig. 1. Proportion of physicians with text ratings in crawled PRWs [23].

Our crawler first collected all physician profile links, then each profile and all associated review texts as well as metadata. There are over 400,000 physician profiles and over 2,000,000 review texts in the database. The rating systems use stars as well as German and Austrian school grades. The largest PRW is Jameda.de. Since the German PRW is by far the largest in terms of available data (reviews, profiles), we apply our analyses to it. Another point that led to the selection of Jameda.de is that almost half of the collected physicians have a textual review, as Fig. 1 shows. Unlike star ratings, German school grades range from 1 to 6, with 1 being the best grade. Moreover, it is important to know that a 5 means insufficient (*"mangelhaft"*), while a 6 means unsatisfactory and is the result of total failure (*"ungenügend"*).

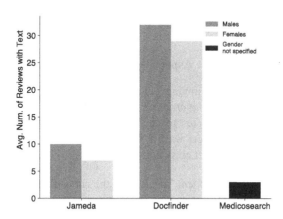

Fig. 2. Average number of ratings with text per physician, separated per gender [23].

Although Jameda.de is the largest PRW, it has fewer reviews with text on average. For Fig. 2, we included all physicians with at least one text rating. However, male physicians are slightly more likely to be rated than female physicians, but there is no significant difference.

In contrast to our previous study [29], we use here all PRW data and not only those of plastic surgeons. We aim for a broader view, e.g., by separating the analyses freely by occupational group. To prepare the data for processing, we split all collected reviews into sentences [25]. We excluded some sentences due to quality concerns. This applies to very short and long sentences. We also set a minimum length for reviews (280 characters) and, as an example, a requirement that multiple grades were assigned to the corresponding reviews. We have a total of over 2,000,000 review texts and are therefore confident that excluding some texts would not hinder the analyses.

4 Annotation Process and Dataset Preparation

The annotation process is necessary to perform supervised machine learning for ABSA, which is a classification task. Therefore, we needed to label aspect phrases in sentences. In this section, we describe the process. Here we build on an earlier dataset [29], which was extended for this work.

For ATE, which is part of ABSA, we need to define aspect classes and mark them in evaluative phrases. To achieve this, we considered and analyzed all available rating categories (so-called aspect classes) from the PRWs [28]. We plan to apply all aspect classes available for physician reviews. Therefore, we describe each class in detail and provide examples. We start with dataset D that deals with a doctor's office. It is preferred here because it was introduced in the study that is extended by this work. The datasets A–C will be described later. We use dataset D to describe the annotation process and the corresponding details [29]. To find aspect classes, all available rating categories from the three crawled PRWs were considered and merged. Examples are those dealing with the competence of the team or waiting time for an appointment. The semantic merging resulted in sets of rating classes [27] that are grouped in different datasets, as the annotators cannot consider about 20 classes at once.

4.1 Annotation Process for the Aspect Terms

Dataset D. Aggregates the following classes: *"equipment"*, *"waiting time for an appointment"*, *"waiting time in the practice"*, and *"well-being"* [29]. Patients are concerned about the time that is takes to get an appointment. They also comment on whether they have a long or short wait if they are already in a doctor's office. The following list explains each aspect class in the dataset D [29]:

- *"Waiting time for an appointment"* deals with the subjectively perceived length of time a patient had to wait to get an appointment:
  → 'I was offered an **appointment in the same week**.'
- *"Waiting time in the practice"* also deals with the perceived waiting time of a patient, but in this case with the waiting time in the doctor's office:
  → 'Even though I had an appointment and told them I was really in a hurry, they **made me sit in the waiting room for two hours**.'
- *"Equipment"* deals with the technical equipment and tools available in a doctor's office:

→ 'All the **equipment seemed to be state of the art**.'
- *Well-Being* deals with the feeling emanating from a doctor's office. That is, the subjective feelings associated with the interiors belong to this class:
  → 'She treated me in a room that felt **very comfortable**.'
  → 'Their office is **warm and flooded with light**, and there are also **drinks** in the waiting areas.'

The annotation process started by splitting review texts into sentences and searching for sentences containing evaluative phrases. Therefore, we binary annotated the sentences with respect to this criterion, trained a classifier model and pre-separated our data for more efficient annotation [27–29].

The annotation process requires manual work. A total of five persons were involved, two external and three internal, all of whom were trained language specialists. The internal members reviewed the annotations made by the externals. In doubt about the quality of the annotation, only the sentences with aspect phrases were kept and reviewed (several hundred), and the other sentences were excluded from further experiments. We applied active learning and consequently had a dramatically smaller number of sentences without aspect phrases in them. This made the annotation process more efficient. Active learning was applied multiple times, as in previous work [28]. We performed a multi-label and multi-class classification to pre-select sentences that had a higher probability of carrying one or more of the desired aspect classes. We justify the use of active learning by the fact that we had to annotate several dozen sentences to find only one that contained an aspect phrase. The resulting dataset D contains 8,000 sentences, of which over 7,000 sentences contain one or more aspect phrase [29].

Annotation data were monitored during annotation, mainly through team discussions. At the end, a final monitoring took place, where over 400 sentences were deleted due to errors or uncertainties in the annotations (e.g., due to different opinions about aspect phrase boundaries). The annotators were asked to include as much information as possible, so it was possible to annotate multiple aspect phrases in one sentence. Most sentences had a user-generated character and were therefore colloquial and unstructured, as patients write as they speak. In addition, they make use of insertions, which complicates annotation: 'I **like the** (except for that one doctor's assistant with blond hair and glasses) **atmosphere**, and I'll always go there when I have an illness.'

The quality of the annotated data is measured by an inter-annotator agreement (IAA). Table 2 shows the IAA results for the detailed representation of dataset D. The physician review domain is challenging for data annotation. We computed the IAAs based on the tagged words as if we were extracting aspect phrases. That is, each word was given a tag indicating the corresponding class (or none-class). We randomly selected 340 sentences (following [25]) and re-annotated them blindly. Then, we compared them with the sentences from the dataset. As Table 2 shows, the Cohen's κ [7] values can be considered as substantial or nearly perfect [33]. The Krippendorff's α scores [31] of all three annotators are considered as good [20]. In summary, the IAAs are satisfactory. The data quality is high and enabled further analyses.

As presented in previous work, the other relevant datasets were annotated and evaluated in the same way as dataset D. Some of the IAAs were even better.

Table 2. Inter-annotator agreement scores for dataset D [29].

Annotators	Cohen's κ	Krippendorff's α
R & Y	**0.710**	**0.768**
R & J	**0.871**	
Y & J	**0.727**	

4.2 Preparation of Further Datasets

Here, we briefly summarize the datasets A–C and present their aspect classes.

Dataset A deals with the physician as an aspect target. It summarizes relevant aspect classes that deal with physician behavior and competence [25, 26, 28]:

- "*Friendliness* deals with the question whether the physician treats his/her patients respectfully (...) Generally, [it] refers to the degree of devotion" [28].
  - → 'He was **really nice**.'
  - → 'He **looks me in the eye** and explains everything.'
- "*Competence* describes the subjectively felt or demonstrated expertise of a physician. (...) It neither asks about the general quality of treatment nor does it cover friendliness or empathy." [28].
  - → 'He **knows what he does**.'
  - → 'She **reduces anxiety** in me.'
- "*Time Taken* refers to the amount of time a physician takes during his/her appointments with patients. (...) When a physician takes sufficient time (...), patients (...) express positive sentiment toward that physician" [28].
  - → 'The doctor **took a lot of time** for me.'
  - → 'The **consultation is very short**, ...'
- "*Explanation* deals with the clarifications a physician uses to explain symptoms, diseases, and (especially) treatments in an understandable manner, because patients naturally need to be informed well." [28].
  - → 'She **explained everything in detail**.'
  - → 'The **clarification was great**, it **helped me better understand** the treatment.'

Dataset B also deals with the physician as an aspect target. It contains six aspect classes, one of which is a general rating that applies to the physician, practice staff, and the office as a whole. The following list describes the aspect classes:

- "*Alternative Healing Methods* describe whether a physician offers alternatives to his/her patients. (...) This does not involve the explanation of a treatment, but rather the general attitude towards alternatives (...)." [28].
  - → 'She also **offers alternative methods**.'
  - → 'He is **absolutely not a single bit open for homeopathy**.'
  - → 'The doctor **deliberately treats alternatively, which I disliked**.'
- "*Treatment* deals with the way a physician treats his/her patients (...)." [28].

   → 'I was **satisfied with the treatment**.'
   → 'She **treats conscientiously**.'
– "*Care/Commitment* includes all evaluations of whether a physician is further interested or involved in caring for and committing to the patient and the treatment." [28].
   → 'After the surgery, the doctor **came by to ask me how I am**.'
   → 'He also **postponed his workday off for me**.'
– "*Overall/Recommendation* indicates that the physician, the team, and the office are generally recommendable so that patients are satisfied and return. If this expressed satisfaction refers solely to the competence of the physician, it would be classified as competence" [28].
   → 'I came here **based on recommendations**.'
   → 'I'**d love to go again**.'
– "*Child-Friendliness* describes how a physician takes care of minors. (...) Physicians are therefore especially required to be able to handle children, which this aspect class investigates" [28].
   → 'She **does not talk to my child at all**.'
   → 'However, he **listens to my son**.'
   → '**Listening to kids: not possible** for her.'
– "*Relationship of Trust* describes the sensitive relationship between patient and physician. It concerns the question whether the patient has confidence in his/her medical service provider (...)." [28].
   → 'I **feel taken seriously**.'
   → 'He **doesn't understand me**.'
   → 'I've been going to Dr. Doe **for 10 years**.'

Dataset C contains all relevant aspect classes identified in the PRW data except those related to physicians. There are comments related to practice staff [27].

– "*Care/Commitment*(...) refers to whether the practice team is (further) involved or interested in the patient's care and treatment" [27].
   → '**Such a demotivated** assistant.'
– "*Friendliness* (...) deals with the friendliness, as in (...) [dataset A], but aims at the team" [27].
   → 'Due to their **very nice manner**, there was no doubt about the team at any time.'
– "*Competence* (...) describes the patient's perception of the team's expertise [as a whole]" [27].
   → 'The staff at the reception makes an **overstrained impression**.'
– "*Accessibility by telephone* [...] indicates how easy it is to reach the team [or not]" [27].
   → 'You have to **try several times before you get someone on the phone**.'

In summary, datasets A–D capture relevant aspects of physicians and their services, but also describe aspects of practice staff and the practice itself. They are used to calculate sentiment polarity based on the annotated aspect phrases [27] because physician reviews are a domain in which aspect phrases and sentiment words cannot be distinguished. The simplest example would be the word 'nice' as in 'He was **nice**.'. In this example, the aspect class "*friendliness*" is specified and the sentiment polarity of the class is positive. Furthermore, evaluative phrases such as 'cold water' would in practice indicate a positive "*Well-Being*" when water is offered in the waiting area. Thus, independent identification of polarity and aspect words is not possible. Therefore, we assigned sentiment polarity scores to a subset of the aspect phrases in each available dataset. A related study shows the evaluation of the polarity dataset [27]. Based on the literature (cf. Table 1) and tests, it was only possible to assign a positive or negative polarity. Finer delineations or a neutral evaluation are not possible [27]. The IAA scores as presented in [27] can be regarded as nearly perfect [33] for Cohen's κ and very good [20] for Krippendorff's α.

5   Model Training

After describing the annotation process and the annotated data, we present here the training process and results for the corresponding ABSA steps. Dataset D [29] serves as an example; the models for datasets A–C and polarity were successfully trained and evaluated in our previous work [29]. We then describe the results of applying them to physician reviews, including polarity classification and phrase importance analysis. After quantifying evaluative phrases using these steps, we are able to correlate the results with metadata.

We trained a set of deep learning models for ATE, ACC, and APC [25–27]. Together with a set of transformers pre-trained for German, we use biLSTM models [28] and XLM-RoBERTa, a multilingual transformer [8]. We trained these transformers domain-specifically, as this leads to better results in aspect term extraction and polarity classification.

Table 3 shows the results for ATE and ACC. Transforms with + denote transforms that were domain-trained on our PRW data. It is noteworthy that FastText vectors can, in part, achieve comparable results to transformer models that have been trained on larger datasets and are context sensitive [12,53].

Domain training of the transformer models was evaluated using the loss scores, as perplexity is not suitable [22]. XLM-RoBERTa (base) performed best with 0.37 after only 4 epochs. The German-specific models achieved a loss of about 1.1–1.3 after 10 epochs. Training for XLM-RoBERTa was discontinued because it performed well from the beginning and did not improve. Electra performed worse with a loss of about 6.7. We tuned the parameters before final testing of the models. The train-test split was 90:10 of the sentences from the raw dataset (cf. Section 3). Table 3 shows that XLM-RoBERTa achieves best results (F1 score of 0.86). This is remarkable since it is a multilingual model that performs better than the models trained with German language data. We used a train-test split of 80:20, which is consistent with other works [23,27,29].

Table 3. Results for ATE and ACC performed in one step for dataset D[a] [29].

Model	Precision	Recall	F1 Score
xlm-roberta-base+	0.81	0.91	**0.86**
∟ biLSTM-CRF+	0.83	0.79	0.81
∟ biLSTM-Attention+	0.84	0.77	0.80
xlm-roberta-base	0.79	0.89	0.83
MedBERT+	0.80	0.90	0.84
MedBERT	0.80	0.89	0.84
electra-base uncased+	0.15	0.20	0.17
electra-base uncased	0.79	0.90	0.84
distilbert-base cased+	0.81	0.89	0.85
distilbert-base cased	0.80	0.88	0.84
dbmdz bert-base uncased+	0.81	0.90	0.85
dbmdz bert-base uncased	0.80	0.90	0.85
dbmdz bert-base cased+	0.82	0.90	0.85
dbmdz bert-base cased	0.80	0.90	0.85
bert-base cased+	0.81	0.90	0.85
bert-base cased	0.80	0.88	0.84
FastText biLSTM-CRF+	0.84	0.75	0.79
FastText biLSTM-Attention+	0.83	0.77	0.79

[a] All pre-trained transformer models are in German and are accessible with their names at https://huggingface.co/models, last accessed 2022-02-07. The BiLSTM-CRF and attention models are based on previous work [28].

Polarity is classified (by APC) using the transformer models that performed best for ATE and ACC [27]. The mode is a binary classification with the classes of positive or negative polarity. For classification, the model was given the aspect phrase and the complete sentence as context. Not surprisingly, very good evaluation results were obtained. XLM-RoBERTa performs best with an F1 score of 0.94 (precision: 0.93, recall: 0.95). Interestingly, XLM-RoBERTa outperforms other transformers trained for German.

In addition to ABSA, we also use an algorithm that weights the importance of aspect phrases. This is achieved by a combination of linguistic features and deep learning. It analyzes the part-of-speech tags of phrases and checks whether adverbs are present. Furthermore, comparatives or superlatives are also considered as important phrases. We also tested statistical approaches that did not yield sufficient results when evaluated by humans, i.e., annotators marked a number of phrases as (not) important [27].

6 Application to Physician Reviews

In this section, we describe the application of the domain-specific deep learning models to the raw data of the physician reviews (cf. Sect. 6.1). Then, the correlation analyses are presented (cf. Sect. 6.2). This completes the quantification of the evaluative phrases.

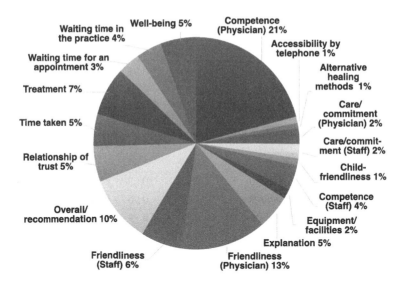

Fig. 3. Relative proportions of aspect classes extracted from raw review sentences [23].

6.1 Recognition of Aspect Classes, Polarity and Importance

Figure 3 shows the relative proportions of all aspect classes extracted from all available review sentences. As it can be seen in Fig. 3, a few aspect classes have quite a large share of all extracted aspect classes. Of all 1.5 million analyzed sentences, 1.4 million contained at least one aspect class. Almost 50% of all extracted aspect classes deal with the *"competence"*, *"friendliness"*, or the *"overall/recommendation"* of the physician. The *"friendliness"* of the staff also reaches a larger proportion. Thus, many aspect classes occur less frequently, but all annotated classes were present in the dataset. This may mean that we constructed and annotated adequate classes.

We also analyzed the polarity and importance of the extracted phrases. Here, we noticed that each class tended to have extreme scores, i.e., overwhelmingly positive/negative polarity or normal/high importance. Figure 4 presents selected aspect classes and their polarity scores. As it can be seen, most of the phrases are very positive, regardless of the aspect target (physician, team). However, the non-specific *"overall/recommendation"* has fewer positive phrases, about 30%. However, this does not true for all aspect classes. The classes of dataset D that target the physician's practice [29] show a different picture here. They are overwhelmingly negative. Reasons for this may lie in the behavior of PRW users. They tend to evaluate interpersonal things positively, non-personal things related to the office negatively. Other conclusions can be drawn by looking at the aspect phrase importance, which is shown in Fig. 5.

As it can be seen, the selected aspect classes have a very high proportion of very important aspect phrases. This true for the *"friendliness"* and *"competence"* of the team. The same classes targeting the physician have a slightly lower proportion of very important phrases, between 20% and 40%. This is also true for the non-specific class of *"overall/recommendation"*. Looking at the selected aspect classes, it seems

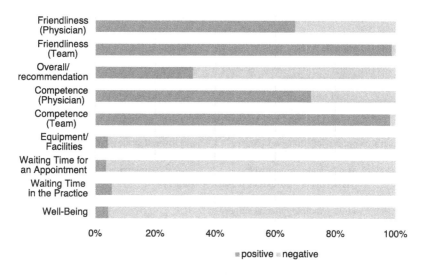

Fig. 4. Selected aspect classes and the relative proportions of phrase polarity values [23].

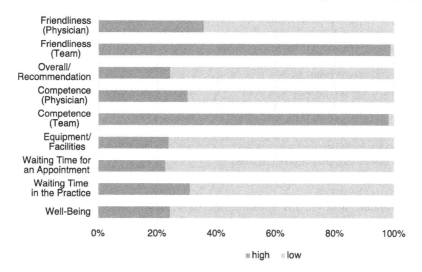

Fig. 5. Selection of aspect classes and proportions of phrase importance values [23].

like patients give significantly higher weight to topics related to the team. That is, they consider the things they write about the team as more important than the things they write about the physicians. Moreover, there is no difference between classes related to physicians and the practice.

6.2 Correlation Analyses

In this section, we merge the results from Sect. 6.1 with metadata. As described in Sect. 2.5, these coefficients analyze data in terms of whether two data series frequently

Table 4. Results of the correlation analyses with metadata[a] [23].

#	Coefficient	Variable X	Variable Y	Result
1	Cramér's V	aspect classes of all extracted phrases	polarities of all extracted phrases	0.59
2	Cramér's V	aspect classes of all extracted phrases	aspect phrase weight	0.51
3	Spearman's ρ	avg. grade reviews with text	avg. overall grade physician	0.52
4	Spearman's ρ	polarity of the aspect phrases extracted for the class "*accessibility by telephone*" separated by physicians in the fields of plastic surgery & aesthetic surgery/radiology/facial surgery	avg. overall grade of physicians in the fields of plastic surgery & aesthetic surgery/radiology/facial surgery	−0.14 / −0.10 / −0.10
5	Spearman' ρ	polarity of the aspect phrases extracted for the class "*accessibility by telephone*" separated by physicians in the fields of pediatrician/veterinarian/urologist	avg. overall grade of physicians in the fields of pediatrician/veterinarian/urologist	0.00 / 0.01 / 0.03
6	Spearman' ρ	polarity of the extracted aspect phrases for the class "*child-friendliness*" separated by physicians in the fields of allergy and pain therapy/vascular surgery/psychiatry	Grades for the child-friendliness per review separated by physicians in the fields of allergy and pain therapy/vascular surgery/psychiatry	−0.31 / 0.34 / 0.04
7	Cramér's V	aspect phrase weight of all extracted phrases, separated by physicians in the fields of pediatrics/nutrition counseling	aspect classes of all extracted phrases, separated by physicians in the fields of pediatrics/nutrition counseling	0.52 / 0.27

[a] The analyses including no specific aspect classes are conducted based on all presented and additional aspects that are not yet introduced.

appear together. However, it is a challenging task to present these analyses in an understandable way. In our previous work [29], we presented analyses that focused on a selected medical profession in textual form. Table 4 shows the results of our correlation analyses based on all data from Jameda.de.

The analyses show that it is possible to combine the recognition results with metadata in a meaningful way. Therefore, we can deviate findings from the presented numbers. The first three rows in Table 4 deal with rather basic associations. We have included here all of the aspect classes presented earlier, as well as other aspects we regarded as necessary. However, as it can be seen, there is a fairly strong relationship between aspect classes and the polarity values they carry. The same is true for the weighting of aspect phrases, i.e., importance. So some aspect classes come with higher importance more often than others. The third row shows that the ratings with text are quite strongly correlated with the physician's overall grade as displayed in the PRW. Positively correlated means that a better grade for ratings with text is associated with a better overall grade per physician. That was comparable in our previous study [29].

Interestingly, we found no differences in ratings by sex, as before. Spearman's correlations in rows four through six are for specific aspect classes and medical specialties. We use the polarity scores of the extracted aspect phrases and the grades. As it can be seen, there are differences between the correlation scores, especially between rows four and five. Row four has (low) correlations, while row five has none. Row six shows that child-friendliness may be important for allergy and pain therapy and vascular surgery, but not for psychiatry. Everything here, of course, is based on the textual reviews. The seventh row shows that the weight (i.e., importance) of the aspect is more strongly associated with pediatricians than with nutrition counseling. These analyses show that it is possible to combine our recognition results with metadata. Thus, we have quantified evaluative phrases from physician review texts in terms of single numerical values that can be used for new insights and decision making.

7 Conclusion

This study extends a previous work [29]. Compared to the previous study, we presented a set of aspect phrase datasets with examples. We domain-trained our deep learning model [27] with the presented aspect classes for ABSA. As a result of our analyses, we not only have structured information, such as evaluative (aspect) phrases, their corresponding classes, sentiment polarity, and phrase weight, but also individual numerical values that provide new insights for comparison between different rating platforms. We also showed that certain aspect classes are more important to medical domains than others. In addition, we plan to further evaluate certain cases of long and implicit phrases, e.g., by excluding all phrases containing nouns.

Acknowledgements. This work was partially supported by the German Research Foundation (DFG) within the Collaborative Research Center On-The-Fly Computing (CRC 901). We thank F. S. Bäumer, M. Cordes, and R. R. Mülfarth for their assistance with data collection and annotation.

References

1. Acock, A.C., Stavig, G.R.: A measure of association for nonparametric statistics. Soc. Forces **57**(4), 1381–1386 (1979)
2. Archak, N., Ghose, A., Ipeirotis, P.G.: Show me the money! Deriving the pricing power of product features by mining consumer reviews. In: Proceedings of the 13th ACM SIGKDD International Conference on Knowledge Discovery and Data Mining, pp. 56–65. ACM, San Jose, CA, USA (2007). https://doi.org/10.1145/1281192.1281202
3. Benning, V.: Cramer's v verstehen, berechnen und interpretieren [Understanding, calculating and interpreting cramer's v]. https://www.scribbr.de/statistik/cramers-v/ (2021). Accessed 20 Apr 2021
4. Bojanowski, P., Grave, E., Joulin, A., Mikolov, T.: Enriching word vectors with subword information. Trans. ACL **5**, 135–146 (2017)
5. Bäumer, F.S., Kersting, J., Kuršelis, V., Geierhos, M.: Rate your physician: findings from a Lithuanian physician rating website. In: Damaševičius, R., Vasiljevienė, G. (eds.) ICIST 2018. CCIS, vol. 920, pp. 43–58. Springer, Cham (2018). https://doi.org/10.1007/978-3-319-99972-2_4

6. Chinsha, T.C., Shibily, J.: A syntactic approach for aspect based opinion mining. In: Proceedings of the 9th IEEE International Conference on Semantic Computing, pp. 24–31. IEEE, Anaheim, CA, USA (2015). https://doi.org/10.1109/icosc.2015.7050774

7. Cohen, J.: A coefficient of agreement for nominal scales. Educ. Psychol. Measure. **20**(1), 37–46 (1960)

8. Conneau, A., et al.: Unsupervised cross-lingual representation learning at scale. In: Proceedings of the 58th Annual Meeting of the ACL, pp. 8440–8451. ACL, July 2020. https://doi.org/10.18653/v1/2020.acl-main.747

9. Cordes, M.: Wie bewerten die anderen? Eine übergreifende Analyse von Arztbewertungsportalen in Europa [How do the others rate? An Overarching Analysis of Physician Rating Portals in Europe]. Master's thesis, Paderborn University (2018)

10. De Clercq, O., Lefever, E., Jacobs, G., Carpels, T., Hoste, V.: Towards an integrated pipeline for aspect-based sentiment analysis in various domains. In: Proceedings of the 8th ACL Workshop on Computational Approaches to Subjectivity, Sentiment and Social Media Analysis, pp. 136–142. ACL, Kopenhagen, Dänemark (2017). https://doi.org/10.18653/v1/w17-5218

11. Deng, L., Wiebe, J.: Mpqa 3.0: an entity/event-level sentiment corpus. In: Proceedings of the 2015 Conference of the North American Chapter of the ACL: Human Language Technologies, pp. 1323–1328. ACL, Denver, CO, USA (2015)

12. Devlin, J., Chang, M.W., Lee, K., Toutanova, K.: BERT: pre-training of deep bidirectional transformers for language understanding. In: Proceedings of NAACL-HLT 2019. pp. 4171–4186. ACL, Minneapolis, MN, USA (2019)

13. Do, H.H., Prasad, P.W.C., Maag, A., Alsadoon, A.: Deep learning for aspect-based sentiment analysis: a comparative review. Expert Syst. Appl. **118**, 272–299 (2019). https://doi.org/10.1016/j.eswa.2018.10.003, Accepted Manuscript

14. Emmert, M., Sander, U., Esslinger, A.S., Maryschok, M., Schöffski, O.: Public reporting in Germany: the content of physician rating websites. Methods Inf. Med. **51**(2), 112–120 (2012)

15. Emmert, M., Meier, F., Heider, A.K., Dürr, C., Sander, U.: What do patients say about their physicians? An analysis of 3000 narrative comments posted on a German physician rating website. Health Policy **118**(1), 66–73 (2014). https://doi.org/10.1016/j.healthpol.2014.04.015

16. Emmert, M., Meier, F., Pisch, F., Sander, U.: Physician choice making and characteristics associated with using physician-rating websites: cross-sectional study. J. Med. Internet Res. **15**(8), e187 (2013)

17. Emmert, M., Sander, U., Pisch, F.: Eight questions about physician-rating websites: a systematic review. J. Med. Internet Res. **15**(2), e24 (2013). https://doi.org/10.2196/jmir.2360

18. Ganu, G., Elhadad, N., Marian, A.: Beyond the stars: Improving rating predictions using review text content. In: Proceedings of the 20th International Workshop on the Web and Databases, vol. 9, pp. 1–6. ACM, Providence, RI, USA (2009)

19. Guo, C., Du, Z., Kou, X.: Products ranking through aspect-based sentiment analysis of online heterogeneous reviews. J. Syst. Sci. Syst. Eng. **27**(5), 542–558 (2018). https://doi.org/10.1007/s11518-018-5388-2

20. Hayes, A.F., Krippendorff, K.: Answering the call for a standard reliability measure for coding data. Commun. Methods Measures **1**(1), 77–89 (2007). https://doi.org/10.1080/19312450709336664

21. Hochreiter, S., Schmidhuber, J.: Long short-term memory. Neural Comput. **9**(8), 1735–1780 (1997). https://doi.org/10.1162/neco.1997.9.8.1735

22. Hugging face: perplexity of fixed-length models - transformers 4.2.0 documentation. https://huggingface.co/transformers/perplexity.html (2021). Accessed 29 Jan 2021

23. Kersting, J.: Identifizierung quantifizierbarer Bewertungsinhalte und -kategorien mittels Text Mining. Dissertation, Universität der Bundeswehr München, Neubiberg (2023)
24. Kersting, J., Bäumer, F., Geierhos, M.: In reviews we trust: but should we? Experiences with physician review websites. In: Proceedings of the 4th International Conference on Internet of Things, Big Data and Security, pp. 147–155. SCITEPRESS, Heraklion, Greece (2019). https://doi.org/10.5220/0007745401470155
25. Kersting, J., Geierhos, M.: Aspect phrase extraction in sentiment analysis with deep learning. In: Proceedings of the 12th International Conference on Agents and Artificial Intelligence: Special Session on Natural Language Processing in Artificial Intelligence, pp. 391–400. SCITEPRESS, Valetta, Malta (2020)
26. Kersting, J., Geierhos, M.: Neural learning for aspect phrase extraction and classification in sentiment analysis. In: Proceedings of the 33rd International Florida Artificial Intelligence Research Symposium (FLAIRS) Conference, pp. 282–285. AAAI, North Miami Beach, FL, USA (2020)
27. Kersting, J., Geierhos, M.: Human language comprehension in aspect phrase extraction with importance weighting. In: Métais, E., Meziane, F., Horacek, H., Kapetanios, E. (eds.) NLDB 2021. LNCS, vol. 12801, pp. 231–242. Springer, Cham (2021). https://doi.org/10.1007/978-3-030-80599-9_21
28. Kersting, J., Geierhos, M.: Towards aspect extraction and classification for opinion mining with deep sequence networks. In: Loukanova, R. (ed.) NLPinAI 2020. SCI, vol. 939, pp. 163–189. Springer, Cham (2021). https://doi.org/10.1007/978-3-030-63787-3_6
29. Kersting, J., Geierhos, M.: Well-being in plastic surgery: deep learning reveals patients' evaluations. In: Proceedings of the 10th International Conference on Data Science, Technology and Applications, pp. 275–284. SCITEPRESS (2021)
30. Klinger, R., Cimiano, P.: The USAGE review corpus for fine grained multi lingual opinion analysis. In: Proceedings of the 9th International Conference on LREC, pp. 2211–2218. LREC, Reykjavik, Iceland (2014). https://www.aclweb.org/anthology/L14-1656/
31. Krippendorff, K.: Computing Krippendorff's alpha-reliability. Technical Report, 1–25-2011, University of Pennsylvania (2011). https://repository.upenn.edu/asc_papers/43
32. Lafferty, J., McCallum, A., Pereira, F.C.N.: Conditional random fields: probabilistic models for segmenting and labeling sequence data. In: Proceedings of the 18th International Conference on Machine Learning, pp. 282–289. ACM, Williamstown, MA, USA (2001)
33. Landis, J.R., Koch, G.G.: The measurement of observer agreement for categorical data. Biometrics **33**(1), 159–174 (1977). https://doi.org/10.2307/2529310
34. Liu, Y., Bi, J.W., Fan, Z.P.: Ranking products through online reviews: a method based on sentiment analysis technique and intuitionistic fuzzy set theory. Inf. Fusion **36**, 149–161 (2017). https://doi.org/10.1016/j.inffus.2016.11.012
35. López, A., Detz, A., Ratanawongsa, N., Sarkar, U.: What patients say about their doctors online: a qualitative content analysis. J. Gen. Internal Med. **27**(6), 685–692 (2012). https://doi.org/10.1007/s11606-011-1958-4
36. Maia, M., Handschuh, S., Freitas, A., Davis, B., McDermott, R., Zarrouk, M., Balahur, A.: WWW'18 open challenge: Financial opinion mining and question answering. In: Companion of the The Web Conference 2018 on The Web Conference 2018, pp. 1941–1942. IW3C2/ACM, Lyon, France (2018). https://doi.org/10.1145/3184558.3192301
37. Mayzlin, D., Dover, Y., Chevalier, J.: Promotional reviews: an empirical investigation of online review manipulation. Am. Econ. Rev. **104**(8), 2421–2455 (2014)
38. Mitchell, M., Aguilar, J., Wilson, T., Van Durme, B.: Open domain targeted sentiment. In: Proceedings of the 2013 Conference on Empirical Methods in Natural Language Processing, pp. 1643–1654. ACL, Seattle, WA, USA (2013)

39. Musto, C., Rossiello, G., de Gemmis, M., Lops, P., Semeraro, G.: Combining text sum-marization and aspect-based sentiment analysis of users' reviews to justify recommenda-tions. In: Proceedings of the 13th ACM Conference on Recommender Systems, pp. 383–387. ACM, Copenhagen, Denmark (2019). https://doi.org/10.1145/3298689.3347024

40. Nazir, A., Rao, Y., Wu, L., Sun, L.: Issues and challenges of aspect-based sentiment analysis: a comprehensive survey. IEEE Trans. Affect. Comput. (2020). https://doi.org/10.1109/taffc.2020.2970399

41. Nguyen, T.H., Shirai, K.: Phrasernn: phrase recursive neural network for aspect-based sen-timent analysis. In: Proceedings of the 2015 Conference on Empirical Methods in Natural Language Processing, pp. 2509–2514. ACL, Lisbon, Portugal (2015)

42. Pontiki, M., Galanis, D., Papageorgiou, H., Manandhar, S., Androutsopoulos, I.: SemEval-2015 task 12: aspect based sentiment analysis. In: Proceedings of the 9th International Work-shop on Semantic Evaluation, pp. 486–495. ACL, Denver, CO, USA (2015). http://aclweb.org/anthology/S15/S15-2082.pdf

43. Pontiki, M., Galanis, D., Papageorgiou, H., Manandhar, S., Androutsopoulos, I.: SemEval 2016 task 5: aspect based sentiment analysis (ABSA-16) annotation guidelines (2016)

44. Pontiki, M., Galanis, D., Pavlopoulos, J., Papageorgiou, H., Androutsopoulos, I., Manand-har, S.: SemEval-2014 task 4: aspect based sentiment analysis. In: Proceedings of the 8th International Workshop on Semantic Evaluation, pp. 27–35. ACL, Dublin, Ireland (2014)

45. Pontiki, M., et al.: SemEval-2016 task 5: aspect based sentiment analysis. In: Proceedings of the 10th International Workshop on Semantic Evaluation, pp. 19–30. ACL, San Diego, CA, USA (2016). http://www.aclweb.org/anthology/S16-1002

46. Rodgers, J.L., Nicewander, W.A.: Thirteen ways to look at the correlation coefficient. Am. Stat. 42(1), 59–66 (1988). https://doi.org/10.1080/00031305.1988.10475524

47. Ruppenhofer, J., Klinger, R., Struß, J.M., Sonntag, J., Wiegand, M.: IGGSA shared tasks on German sentiment analysis GESTALT. In: Proceedings of the 12th KONVENS. pp. 164–173. Hildesheim University, Hildesheim, Germany (2014). http://nbn-resolving.de/urn:nbn:de:gbv:hil2-opus-3196

48. Saeidi, M., Bouchard, G., Liakata, M., Riedel, S.: Sentihood: targeted aspect based sentiment analysis dataset for urban neighbourhoods. In: Proceedings of the 26th International Con-ference on Computational Linguistics: Technical Papers, pp. 1546–1556. COLING/ACL, Osaka, Japan (2016)

49. Schmidt, A., Wiegand, M.: A survey on hate speech detection using natural language pro-cessing. In: Proceedings of the 5th International Workshop on Natural Language Processing for Social Media, pp. 1–10. ACL, Valencia, Spain (2017). https://doi.org/10.18653/v1/W17-1101

50. Schober, P., Boer, C., Schwarte, L.A.: Correlation coefficients. Anesth. Analg. 126(5), 1763–1768 (2018). https://doi.org/10.1213/ane.0000000000002864

51. Schuster, M., Paliwal, K.K.: Bidirectional recurrent neural networks. IEEE Trans. Sig. Pro-cess. 45(11), 2673–2681 (1997). https://doi.org/10.1109/78.650093

52. Spearman, C.: The proof and measurement of association between two things. Am. J. Psy-chol. 15(1), 72–101 (1904). http://www.jstor.org/stable/1412159

53. Vaswani, A., et al.: Attention is all you need. In: Proceedings of the 31st Conference on Neural Information Processing Systems, pp. 5998–6008. Curran Associates, Long Beach, CA, USA (2017)

54. Wang, W., Wang, H., Song, Y.: Ranking product aspects through sentiment analysis of online reviews. J. Exp. Theor. Artif. Intell. 29(2), 227–246 (2017). https://doi.org/10.1080/0952813x.2015.1132270

55. Wojatzki, M., Ruppert, E., Holschneider, S., Zesch, T., Biemann, C.: Germeval 2017: Shared task on aspect-based sentiment in social media customer feedback. In: Proceedings of the

GermEval 2017 - Shared Task on Aspect-based Sentiment in Social Media Customer Feedback, pp. 1–12. Springer, Berlin, Germany (2017)

56. Zeithaml, V.: How consumer evaluation processes differ between goods and services. Market. Serv. **9**(1), 186–190 (1981)

57. Zhang, K., Cheng, Y., keng Liao, W., Choudhary, A.: Mining millions of reviews: a technique to rank products based on importance of reviews. In: Proceedings of the 13th International Conference on Electronic Commerce, pp. 1–8. ACM, Liverpool, UK (2011). https://doi.org/10.1145/2378104.2378116

58. Zhou, J., Huang, J.X., Chen, Q., Hu, Q.V., Wang, T., He, L.: Deep learning for aspect-level sentiment classification: survey, vision, and challenges. IEEE Access **7**, 78454–78483 (2019). https://doi.org/10.1109/access.2019.2920075

SubTempora: A Hybrid Approach for Optimising Subgraph Searching

Chimi Wangmo[(✉)] and Lena Wiese

Goethe University Frankfurt, Robert-Mayer-Str. 10, 60629 Frankfurt am Main, Germany
wangmo@uni-frankfurt.de, lwiese@cs.uni-frankfurt.de

Abstract. Subgraph searching is the problem of determining the presence of a given query graph in either a single or multiple data graph. Due to the wide adoption of graphs in various domains for dataset representation, studies related to graph database management have evolved over the last decades. The subgraph containment query has vast applications in multiple disciplines, particularly for biological datasets that support molecular searching. The classical solution performs expensive one-to-one mapping of the vertices between the query graph and data graph. In the case of multiple data graph settings, also called transactional graph database, the filter-then-verify framework (FTV) adopts specific index structures to represent graph features and to reduce the run-time overheads associated with the one-to-one mapping of the vertices. However, the state-of-the-art approaches mainly suffer from large indexing sizes.

In this paper, we study the problem of subgraph searching in a transactional graph database. We present a new compact representation and faster algorithm to reduce the search space by using (1) a compact data structure for indexing the subgraph patterns, and (2) state-of-the-art compressed inverted and bitmap indexes for maintaining the graph occurrences information. Finally, the candidate graph set, generated after the intersection operation, was verified using the subgraph isomorphism algorithm. Extensive experiments with real datasets show that our compressed inverted and bitmap-based indexes outperform the state-of-the-art algorithm regarding memory usage and filtering time.

Keywords: Subgraph query processing · Subgraph searching · Compressed inverted index · Compressed bitmap index

1 Introduction

Subgraph searching is a well-researched tool for querying subgraphs in the context of graph databases and has been widely used in the biological domains, for instance, by chemists searching for a substructure within chemical compound databases. Since graphs can model complex biological pathways, subgraph containment query, which is subgraph searching in multiple graphs, is used to analyse complex networks. Hence, it is essential to devise a space-efficient and fast algorithm to reduce the query processing time.

A naive approach to search for a pattern within the transactional graph database would be to perform vertex-to-vertex mapping using subgraph isomorphism (also called subgraph matching). Unfortunately, subgraph isomorphism is an NP-complete problem. Therefore, feature (such as paths, tree, or cycles) indexing for the labelled graph has been proposed to alleviate the complexity issue. Such methods follow the filter-then-verify (FTV) framework. However, several challenges in question still remain: (1) how to represent the features in the graphs compactly, (2) how the choice of compression methods impacts the query response time, and (3) which heuristic method can be employed to reduce the number of intersection operations?

The first challenge is associated with the large indexing size of the labelled path traversed from the biological graph. As a result, there is a need for a compact data structure that can sufficiently reduce the indexing size while maintaining the minimal index construction time. Various types of index structures are utilised for storing features (e.g. paths, trees, cycles, etc.), such as *B+tree, R-tree, Hash, Suffix arrays*, and *Tries*. Although a bit slower than *Hash* tables, *Tries* provide a space-efficient approach. In addition, the hash-based method suffers from "collisions", which significantly reduce the filtering power of the algorithm. Given that increases in false-positive candidates during the filtering process can lead to longer verification times, ideally, the choice of access methods should improve the filtering power.

Secondly, another critical issue surrounds speeding up the query response time. In particular, more study is required into examining the composition of filtering time and how to reduce it. Furthermore, properly representing graph occurrences information associated with the labelled path and the graph-id list containing it impacts the candidate graph set and the filtering time. To the best of our knowledge, although both compressed inverted index compression and bitmap compression have been well studied in the context of information retrieval and databases, they have yet to be used in improving the filtering step of subgraph searching. Thus, it would be interesting to analyse the performance of compression-based inverted or bitmap indexes for the filtering step.

To overcome the challenges of slow filtering time and extensive memory consumption of the graph references information, our main contributions are:

- We extend our preliminary work [15] and propose a filtering algorithm for the *Hashmap-based radix tree HRTree* and the *Linkedlist-based radix tree LRTree* to derive the candidate graph set.
- We present a compact representation of the graph occurrences information which is required for enabling a faster filtering process. Furthermore, to balance compression-decompression time and candidate set size, we propose a novel compressed inverted-index, namely *HRTreeIV*.
- We integrate almost all of the state-of-the-art compression techniques into our index structure, thereby creating double-layer subgraph indexes: one for indexing the labelled path and another for maintaining a compact representation of the candidate graph set. To the best of our knowledge, this is the first study done in the design of compression for subgraph searching.
- Finally, we present outcomes of an extensive empirical evaluation of the developed algorithms with the previously existing best algorithms on a large set of representative networks consisting of three real-world datasets. Our new implementation *HRTreeIV* and *HRTreeBM* provides compact representation and speedup to *HRTree*. Compared to *HRTree* and *HRTreeBM*, *HRTreeIV* provides an

improvement of approximately 50% reduced index size. Further, $HRTreeIV$ offers speedup by 83% in terms of filtering time.

The paper is organised as follows. Section 2 provides a brief description of the terminologies associated with graphs. Section 3 presents a detailed discussion of our approach and an extension of our existing work for performing filtering and verification. Section 4 introduces our new space-optimised index structure for subgraph structure. Section 5 discusses the experimental setup and the analysis of the results. Section 6 presents the related works and, finally, Sect. 7 provides the conclusion.

2 Notation, Background, and Problem Statement

In this paper, we consider the undirected, connected, vertex-labelled graph. To enforce clarity, we will uniformly use the term 'vertex' for the vertex in a query or data graph and 'node' for the indexed node in the index tree. The data or query graph (see Definition 1) is used for representing the respective input textual format in the form of the graph structure using an adjacency list. At the same time, an index tree is needed to provide a specialised, compact design to index the specific path lengths from the graph for performing subgraph searching. Notation is shown in Table 1.

Definition 1 (Data Graph). *A data graph is defined as a* $g = \{V_g, E_g, \sigma_g, L_g\}$, *where* V_g *is a set of vertices,* E_g *is a set of edges, and* σ_g *is a set of vertex labels.* $L_g : V_g \to \sigma_g$ *is a labeling function that assigns label* $\sigma_i \in \sigma_g$ *to a vertex* $v_i \in V_g$.

Example 1. In the *transactional database* (see the Definition 3) shown in Fig. 1, $g_0, g_1, ..., g_{40000}$ are labelled, connected *data graphs*. The underlying representation is undirected, containing $|V|$ as $6, 8,$ and 8 for each data graph, respectively. The average number of vertex labels, denoted as $|\sigma|$ is 4.

The paper's main objective is to find the data graph containing a given subgraph within an efficient time and space. Therefore, to provide a theoretical definition, we formally define a *subgraph* as follows:

Definition 2 (Subgraph). *A graph* h *is said to be* subgraph *of the graph* g *if the vertices and edges in* h *are a subset of the vertices in* g, *denoted as* $V_h, \subseteq V_g$ *and* $E_h \subseteq E_g$. *The labeling of the vertices in* h *is the same as the labeling of the corresponding vertices in* g, $L_h \subseteq L_g$.

Example 2. The undirected graph denoted as q_0 in the running example is a subgraph of g_1. Let us denote vertices of g_1 and q_0 as V_{g_1} and V_{q_0}. Further edges of g_1 and q_0 are represented as E_{g_1} and E_{q_0}. We can observe that vertices and edges of q_0, $V_{q_0} = \{v_1, v_5, v_6, v_7\}$ and $E_{q_0} = \{(v_1, v_6), (v_5, v, 6), (v_5, v_7)\}$, exists within V_{g_1} and E_{g_1}. Further, the vertex labels are also the same.

In contrast to the database containing a single large graph, the subgraph search problem contains numerous subgraphs as individual, connected data graphs within a database called the *transactional graph database*. Formally, we define the *transactional graph database* as follows:

Definition 3 (Transactional Graph Database). *A graph database G is defined as a* transaction graph database, *if it contains a set of n medium-sized graphs (with n being the numbers of connected components), $G = \{g_1, g_2, g_3, ..., g_n\}$. The size of the graph database is denoted as $|G| = n$.*

The *subgraph isomorphism* problem can potentially search matching subgraphs in the *transactional graph database*. Nevertheless, in our setting, we initially construct an index graph followed by performing subgraph isomorphism to avoid an expensive one-to-one vertex mapping. Formally, we define the *subgraph isomorphism* as follows:

Definition 4 (Subgraph Isomorphism [9]). *Given a query graph q and data graph g, an embedding of q in g is a mapping $M : V(q) \rightarrow V(g)$, such that: (1) M is injective (i.e. $M(u) \neq M(u')$ for $u \neq u' \in V(q)$), (2) $L_q(u) = L_g(M(u))$ for every $u \in V(q)$, and (3) $(M(u), M(u')) \in E(g)$ for every $(u, u') \in E(q)$. The query graph q is said to be isomorphic to the data graph g, denoted by $q \subseteq g$ if there exists an embedding of q in G.*

Table 1. Notation overview.

Notation	Description
G	transaction graph database
V, E, σ	vertex, edge, and label set
|G|, |E|, |σ|	graph database, edge, and label size
g, q	data graph, and query graph
gIndex, qIndex	graph index and query index
C_q	candidate set for query graph q
HRTree	hashmap-based radix tree
HRTreeIV	inverted-based HRTree
HRTreeBM	bitmap-based HRTree

This leads to the following problem statement addressed in this paper. There are two general approaches, namely (1) subgraph isomorphism and (2) an indexing-based approach to solving the *subgraph searching* problem. In this paper, we focus on approach (2). By building a compact index, we aim to find, efficiently, the matching data graphs within a *transactional graph database*. We begin with the formal definition of *subgraph searching* as follows:

Definition 5 (Subgraph Searching). *Given a transaction graph database, G, and query graph, q, the subgraph search is to find all the graphs $g_{id} \in G$ that contains q, where $1 \leq id \leq n$.*

Example 3. Figure 1 illustrates the subgraph searching in the *transactional graph database*. We use query graph, q_0, and data graphs, g_0, g_1 and g_{40000}.

We shall now introduce the vital parameter used to evaluate *subgraph searching*, based on this we shall iterate why indexing is necessary instead of simply performing *subgraph isomorphism*. The *query response time QRT* is a critical metric to assess the significance of indexing to query processing.

$$QRT = T_{filtering} + |C_q| \cdot T_{verfication} \tag{1}$$

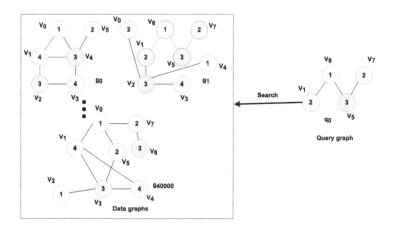

Fig. 1. Running example of subgraph searching in a transactional graph database.

As mentioned previously, *subgraph isomorphism* or verification is an NP-complete problem and, therefore, the indexes can help to reduce the number of graph candidates when performing subgraph isomorphism. However, it has become necessary to enable faster filtering time. We can observe from Eq. 1 that if the number of candidate graphs, $|C_q|$, is large, we would then have to perform multiple verifications. As a result, the QRT would increase substantially. On the other hand, if we build an offline index of the data graphs in the *transactional graph database* for only one time, then, we can then adopt a heuristic filtering algorithm to generate a possible reduced candidate graph set. Hence, we can achieve an overall reduction in the query processing time. Ultimately, we are interested in lowering the filtering time $T_{filtering}$ and the number of candidate graph sets $|C_q|$, which is precisely what our new method achieve (see Sect. 4). We have now established how the filtering power of the indexing reduce the overall query processing time. In the following section, we begin by recollecting some concepts. Then we introduce new definitions and discuss in-depth the newly introduced filtering algorithm for the *Hashmap-based radix tree HRTree* and the *LinkedList-based radix tree LRTree*.

3   Space-Efficient Subgraph Indexing

To enable efficient subgraph searching, we construct indexes on subgraphs using an appropriate data structure. This section briefly describes the design and implementation of subgraph indexing using a suffix tree. In addition, we describe two indexes, namely *HRTree* and *LRTree*. Until recently, the existing studies have mainly discussed decreasing the query response and preprocessing time. In addition to the response time, we also focus on maintaining the labelled path and its occurrences information in static graphs as compactly as possible.

3.1 The Index Graph

As established in Sect. 1, the construction of indexes is a heuristic to support the pruning (also called filtering) of unmatched data graphs, thereby ultimately reducing the number of expensive subgraph isomorphisms (also called verifications). Such a two-phase (filtering and verification) method is particularly significant in a graph database containing many small to medium-sized graphs. We present the visualization of the overall framework in Fig. 2.

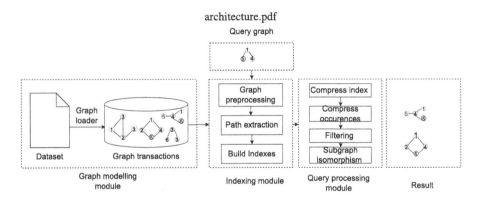

Fig. 2. The *SubTempora* framework.

The filtering phase comprises indexing the labelled path obtained from a graph. This is then followed by performing matching operations between the indexed paths in the graph (see Definition 7) and the query index (see Definition 8), thereby generating a candidate graph set. As for the verification phase, one-to-one mapping of the indexed nodes in the query to the data graph in the candidate graph set is performed.

During filtering, the first step is traversing the labelled path of a particular length from either the data graphs or a query graph using a depth-first search algorithm, known as "Path extraction". The extracted paths are then indexed to a chosen structure; this is defined as *path indexing* (see Definition 6). The labelled path is obtained by concatenating a label associated with a vertex currently traversed from a data or query graph. In contrast, the indexed path is the path in either a graph or a query index (see Definition 9). The first challenge is to represent the traversed, labelled path in a compact manner by primarily choosing an appropriate data structure that is aware of repetitiveness in the prefixes and suffixes of the labelled path. However, the constraint of determining the index structure is ensuring that the occurrences count of each traversed path in each data graph is maintained. Our suffix tree is a radix tree-like structure that compactly contains indexed nodes with node labels and the corresponding path occurrences information (see Definition 10). A compressed suffix tree design ensures that the indexed nodes are merged, based on the common suffixes.

We start by introducing *path indexing*, this is constructed either on the data graphs or the query input. Ultimately, the result of *path indexing* is the index graph. The process of building an index graph is known as "build indexes" in the indexing module of the *SubTempora* (see Fig. 2).

Definition 6 (Path indexing [15]). Path indexing *is the process of building indexes of labelled paths by traversing each vertex* $\{v_1, v_2, ..., v_k\}$ *in each data graph* $\{g_1, g_2, ..., g_n\}$ *using a depth-first search up to a maximum length* l_d.

The generated index graph is of two types: *graph index* and *query index*. The *graph index* is built only once and is then rebuilt upon any changes. Formally, we define the *graph index* as follows:

Definition 7 (Graph Index). *The graph index* $gIndex$ *is defined as an index structure built for the data graphs in the graph transaction database G.*

Example 4. Given the data graphs, g_0, g_1, g_{40000}, in the running example, Fig. 1, we start with the vertex $v_0 \in V_{g_0}$. Consider a preorder traversal from the data graph, g_0, leads to the path, $\{v_0, v_1, v_2, v_3\}$. The corresponding ordered sequence of labels for the vertices, $\{1, 4, 3, 4\}$ is obtained. Further, the number of occurrences count for the given labelled path is maintained in the index graph. The enumeration of all the forward and backward edges for the given data graph is indexed. This is followed by enumerating the rest of the vertices in g_0. The same procedure is carried out with the other data graphs in Definition 3. The generated tree-like structure is the $gIndex$, illustrated in Fig. 3. Note that the nodes in the color 'yellow' are the compressed nodes, resulted from using the heuristic algorithm proposed in our existing work [15].

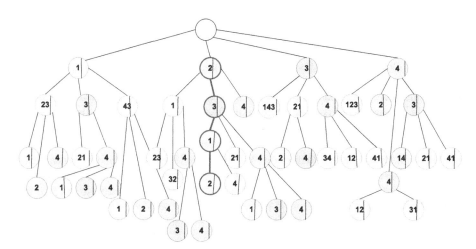

Fig. 3. The graph index $gIndex$ of the running example. (Color figure online)

Similarly to constructing the *graph index*, we build the *query index* by indexing the maximal-length paths obtained from the query graph in the chosen data structure. During the run time, the input query graphs were built individually. Formally, we define the *query index* as follows:

Definition 8 (Query Index). *The* query index *qIndex is defined as an index structure built for the query graph q.*

Internally, the index graph (either *graph index* or *query index*) contains numerous sets of indexed paths (see Definition 9), all of which start with a unique prefix. Intuitively, an *indexed path* consists of the concatenation of node labels obtained by the single traversed path from a root to a leaf node of an *index graph*. Formally, we define the *indexed path* of an *index graph* as follows:

Definition 9 (Indexed path [15]). *An* indexed path, *IP_i, is an ordered sequence of integers of node labels $\lambda = \{\lambda_1, \lambda_2, ..., \lambda_t\}$, where t is the length of the node label, associated with each indexed node γ_r (see Definition 13), where an index path ranges:*

- *in case of qIndex, from a root node, $\mathcal{R}$, to a leaf node, $\mathcal{L}$*
- *in case of gIndex, from a root node, $\mathcal{R}$, to an indexed node, γ_r. γ_r can be either an inner node, $\mathcal{I}$, or a leaf node, $\mathcal{L}$.*

N is the total number of indexed paths in gIndex or qIndex. Here, $IP = \{IP_1, IP_2, IP_3, ..., IP_N\}$ is the set of indexed paths in the gIndex or qIndex. The indexed paths in the qIndex and qIndex are denoted as $IP(gIndex)$ and $IP(qIndex)$ respectively. Formally, we define the IP_i as follows:

$$IP_i = \{\lambda(\gamma_1), \lambda(\gamma_2), ..., \lambda(\gamma_r) \mid 1 \le r \le l_d\} \tag{2}$$

For simplicity, we will use the IP_i in the context of the *qIndex* and IP_j in the context of the *gIndex*, where $1 \le i \le N$ and $1 \le j \le N$. Alternately, we shall also denote using $IP_i(qIndex)$ and $IP_j(gIndex)$.

Example 5. Consider the graph index, *gIndex*, in Fig. 3. *gIndex* is a rooted tree with "white" colored node representing the root, $\mathcal{R}_{gIndex}$. The ending nodes having no children are the leaf nodes, denoted by $\mathcal{L}_{gIndex}$. While, the remaining nodes are the inner nodes, denoted by $\mathcal{I}_{gIndex}$. Now, consider the node label sequences $\{1, 2, 3, 1\}$, it is an *indexed path* with $\mathcal{I}_{qIndex} = 1$ and $\mathcal{L}_{qIndex} = 1$.

Next, we shall introduce the term of *path occurrence*. Recall that we have firstly traversed the labelled path of a fixed length from either a data or query graph and indexing it. Ultimately, we obtain an index graph as a result. Subsequently, the index graph have an indexed paths starting with a unique prefix. However, we are not only interested in storing the labelled paths but also in maintaining their occurrences information. This is because the occurrences of indexed paths is a condition with which we can eliminate the data graphs that may not contain a query graph. Informally, *path occurrence* is the number of times the *indexed path* occurs within a data graph. Consequently, the data structure used for indexed graphs is restricted by (1) the need to index the unique sets of labelled paths and (2) maintaining their occurrences information.

Definition 10 (Path Occurrence). *Given a graph, $g_{id} \in G$, the occurrence count of an indexed path IP_j in G, denoted as $Count(G, IP_j)$, is the sum of the number of times IP_j is observed in each g_{id}. We define $Count(G, IP_j)$ as:*

$$Count(G, IP_j) = \sum_{i=1}^{n} check(IP_j, g_{id}) \tag{3}$$

where,

$$check(IP_j, g_{id}) = \begin{cases} l, & \text{if } IP_j \text{ occurs } l \text{ times in } g_{id}. \\ 0, & \text{otherwise.} \end{cases} \tag{4}$$

Example 6. For instance, the indexed path, $IP_1 = \{1, 4, 3, 4\}$, in Fig. 3, is occurring once in the g_0 (Fig. 1). The occurrences of the IP_i in g_0 is in the vertex sequences, $\{(v_0, v_1), (v_1, v_2), (v_2, v_3)\}$. Hence, $check(IP_1, g_0) = 1$. Additionally, it does not occur in the g_1. However, the IP_1 occurs again once in the g_{40000} (Fig. 1). The occurrences of IP_1 in g_{40000} is in the vertex sequences $\{(v_0, v_1), (v_1, v_3), (v_3, v_4)\}$. Thus, $check(IP_1, g_{40000}) = 1$. Therefore, the occurrence count for the indexed path IP_1, $Count(G, IP_1(gIndex)) = 2$.

The next step is to use the path occurrences information maintained during the construction of the graph and query index in the indexed node to generate a set of candidate graphs. Considering Lemma 1, the process involves searching an indexed path in the data graph index that matches the indexed path in the query graph index, called the *match indexed path*. To clarify, the *match indexed path* results in a matched path similar in concatenated labels to an indexed path in a query graph. This leads us to the *match indexed path* defined as follows:

Definition 11 (Match Indexed Path). *Given the $qIndex$ and $gIndex$, match indexed path, denoted as $MatchPath(IP_i)$, is a function that maps an indexed path IP_i in $qIndex$ to its corresponding matching path IP_j in $gIndex$, where $1 \leq i, j \leq N$. Recall that N is the total number of indexed paths in either $qIndex$ or $gIndex$.*

Example 7. Consider graph index $gIndex$ in Example 4 and query graph q_0 in the running example. Assume the current traversed path in $qIndex$ is $\{2, 3, 1, 2\}$. Its matching indexed path in $gIndex$ is highlighted "red" in Fig. 3.

After obtaining the matching paths to the indexed paths in the query graph, the next step is to evaluate them based on the occurrence information. We are interested in finding if the matching paths in the data graphs contain a similar number of occurrences counts as exist in the corresponding indexed path of the query graph. Ultimately, the result is the candidate graph set, which will be verified using the subgraph isomorphism algorithm. Formally, we define the *matching occurrences* as follows:

Definition 12 (Match Occurrences Information). *For each IP_i that matches the IP_j, a function $MatchGI(IP_i, IP_j)$ is called the* match occurrences information. *It is defined to find all the $g_{id} \in G_I(\gamma_r)$, where $1 \leq r \leq l_d$, that satisfy:*

$$check(IP_j, g_{id}) \geq Count(q, IP_i) \tag{5}$$

Note here that $G_I(\gamma_r)$ is the graph occurrences information (more detail is provided in the Definition 13) associated with the indexed node γ_r in IP_j that matches the $\mathscr{L}(IP_i)$. $\mathscr{L}(IP_i)$ is the leaf-node of the indexed path IP_i. Here, γ_r in IP_j is represented simply as γ_r. Further, recall that we use IP_i and IP_j to denote an indexed path in qIndex and gIndex, respectively.

For the first matching indexed path, denoted as $IP_1(gIndex)$, those $g_{id} \in G_I(\gamma_r)$ that satisfy the condition specified in Eq. 5 are called as the candidate set to the q, denoted as C_q. Subsequently, for each IP_j, C_q is updated to the ordered sequences of $g_{id} \in G_I(\gamma_r)$ that satisfy Eq. 5, denoted as $C_q(IP_j)$, and is present in C_q. As a result, the updated C_q corresponding to $IP_j(gIndex)$, is obtained through an intersection operation between $C_q(IP_j)$ and C_q.

Given C_q, obtained from the matching occurrence of $IP_1(qIndex)$, its matching path $IP_1(gIndex)$ and $C_q(IP_j)$ as an ordered set of graph identifiers for an indexed path IP_j in $gIndex$ satisfying Eq. 5. Formally, the intersection operation to obtain the next candidate set C_q is defined as follows:

$$C_q = C_q(IP_j) \cap C_q = \{g_{id} \mid g_{id} \in C_q(IP_j) \text{ and } g_{id} \in C_q\}. \tag{6}$$

Example 8. Consider the indexed path of $qIndex$, $IP_1(qIndex) = \{2, 3, 1, 2\}$ in the Example 7 again. Assuming that $Count(q_0, IP_1(qIndex)) = 1$, informally, we are interested in finding the data graph containing the equivalent matching path with a similar occurrence count. Notice that in the data graph g_0 and g_{40000}, the $IP_1(qIndex)$ is not present. However, in the data graph g_1, the labelled path $IP_1(qIndex)$ occurs once.

We conclude that the primary filtering cost associated with the *index graph* can be categorized into two parts, firstly, for each indexed path IP_i in $qIndex$, finding the matching indexed path IP_j in $gIndex$, using $MatchPath(IP_i)$. This is then followed by matching the graph occurrences information associated with a leaf node of the $IP_i(qIndex)$, $MatchGI(IP_i, IP_j)$. Note here that, $1 \leq i \leq N$ and $1 \leq j \leq N$. Formally, we define the filtering cost as follows by measuring the runtime of the two functions (runtime measurement is denoted by $\#$):

$$T_{filtering} = \sum_{i=1}^{N} \#MatchPath(IP_i(qIndex))$$
$$+ \#MatchGI(IP_i(qIndex), IP_j(gIndex)) \tag{7}$$

Recall that the index graph is built by indexing labelled paths obtained through preorder traversal of either data or query graph. Lemma 1 provides the property that the compact suffix tree maintains a unique index path.

Lemma 1. *Given an indexed path in a query index $IP_i(qIndex)$, the matching indexed path in a graph index $IP_j(gIndex)$ will appear exactly once.*

Theorems 1 and 2 form the basis for the filtering algorithm. In the following Theorem 1, we show that eliminating non-candidate graphs results in finding the matching indexed path of $qIndex$ in the index graph $gIndex$.

Theorem 1. *Given an index structure of data graphs in a transaction graph database* $gIndex$ *(see Definition 7) and of a query graph q as qIndex (see Definition 8), if q is a subgraph of g, then* $IP(qIndex) \subseteq IP(gIndex)$.

Proof. Assume that q is a subgraph of g, hence $V_q \subseteq V_g$ and $E_q \subseteq E_g$. Therefore, the number of depth-first search traversed, labelled paths of q is always less than the indexed paths obtained by extracting labelled paths from G, $|IP(qIndex)| \leq |IP(gIndex)|$. Furthermore, since the radix-tree index graph contains unique index paths, the index graphs $qIndex$, and $gIndex$ obtained in the process will satisfy Lemma 1. Therefore, each $IP_i(qIndex) \in IP(qIndex)$ is mapped to $IP_j(gIndex) \in IP(gIndex)$, so it follows that $IP(qIndex) \subseteq IP(gIndex)$.

Theorem 2. *Assume that q is a subgraph of data graph(s) in G; given the* $IP_i(qIndex)$ *and its matching indexed path,* $IP_j(gIndex)$, *then it holds that* $Count(G, IP_j(gIndex)) \geq Count(q, IP_i(qIndex))$.

Proof. First, to derive $check(IP_j, g_{id})$ in terms of $Count(q, IP_i(qIndex))$, we use the following argument: If there exists an indexed path $IP_i(qIndex)$ and the number of times it occurs in q is $Count(q, IP_i(qIndex))$, by Lemma 1, we have a matching indexed path in G as $IP_j(gIndex)$. By Definition 10, the number of times $IP_j(gIndex)$ occurs in g_{id} is $check(IP_j, g_{id})$. Assume that in g_{id}, q occurs m_i times. Then, $check(IP_j, g_{id}) = m_i \cdot Count(q, IP_i(qIndex))$. Substituting this into Definition 10, we get:

$$Count(G, IP_j(gIndex)) = n \cdot m_i \cdot Count(q, IP_i(qIndex))) \qquad (8)$$

We have shown that $Count(G, IP_j(gIndex)) \geq Count(q, IP_i(qIndex))$

We have provided an overall discussion on the index graph and presented the composition of the filtering time. In the following subsections, we propose a filtering algorithm based on Theorem 2 for the previously developed *hashmap-based radix tree, HRTree,* and *linkedlist-based radix tree, LRTree.*

3.2   Hashmap-Based Radix Tree (HRTree)

HRTree construction involves the extraction of labelled paths from each data graph and represents them by reducing the repetition of prefix and suffix information. The labelled path is traversed to a specified maximum depth and indexed in a compact suffix tree. A compact suffix tree is a rooted tree with n leaf nodes and $n-1$ inner nodes. In contrast to the Trie-based implementation, the compact suffix tree exploits lazy expansion and path compression; this merges sub-paths with only one child. This leads to a decrease in the number of nodes and pointers. In addition, each indexed node γ_u stores graph occurrences information, G_I, which is represented using key-value pairs. The key refers to the ID of the data graph in the transaction graph database, and the value is the list of occurrences counts associated with each sub-path in the graph. Formally, we define an *indexed node of the hashmap-based radix tree* as follows:

Definition 13 (Indexed node of the Hashmap-based radix tree [15]**).** *An* indexed
node of the hashmap-based radix tree $\gamma_u(HRTree)$ *is a quadruplet* $\langle \lambda, C, G_I, L \rangle$,
which is node γ_u *of a hashmap-based radix tree* $HRTree$. *The element* λ *is a node
label, which consists of an ordered sequence of integers* $\lambda = \{\lambda_1, \lambda_2, ..., \lambda_t\}$, *where
the length of the node label belonging to an indexed node in* $HRTree$, *denoted as*
$length(\gamma_u(HRTree))$, *is* t. *The term "node label" is used in conjunction with an
indexed node of the hashmap-based radix tree, which should not be confused with
the term "label" for a vertex in a graph. The element* Ck *is the set of children keys*
$Ck = \{ck_1, ck_2, ..., ck_m\}$, *where* $ck_k = \{\lambda_1 \in \lambda(child_k(\gamma_u(HRTree))) \mid 1 \leq k \leq
m\}$. $child_k(\gamma_u(HRTree))$ *is the* k^{th} *child of the current indexed node* $\gamma_u(HRTree)$.
Each child key is mapped to the children of the indexed node $M : ck_k \rightarrow
child_k(\gamma_u(HRTree))$, *where* $1 \leq k \leq m$. *The element* G_I *is the graph informa-
tion consisting of graph identifiers* $G_{ID} = \{g_1, g_2, ..., g_{id}\}$, *where* $1 \leq id \leq n$.
Each $g_{id} \in G_{ID}$ *is mapped to its corresponding occurrences count* $c_d \in C$, *where*
$C = \{c_1, c_2, c_3, .., c_d\}$ *and* d *is the maximum number of occurrences in* $\lambda_t(\gamma_u)$. *Here,*
$1 \leq id \leq n$. *The element* L *is a boolean value being* 1 *if and only if the indexed node is
a leaf.*

Algorithm 1. HRTree filtering.

   Input : A queue node Q_u, indexed paths $IP_i(qIndex)$ and $IP_j(gIndex)$, a graph
             database G and a query graph q

   Output: Returns the candidate graph set C_q

1   $gIndex = ConstructOfflineIndex(G)$;

2   $qIndex = ConstructOnlineIndex(q)$;

3   $Q_u.next = (\mathscr{R}_{qIndex}, \mathscr{R}_{gIndex})$;

4   **while** Q_u != *empty* **do**

5       $\gamma_{qIndex} = dequeue(Q_u)$;

6       $\gamma_{gIndex} = dequeue(Q_u)$;

7   **if** $(\gamma_{gIndex}) == \mathscr{L}$ **then**

8           $IP_i(qIndex) = IP_i(qIndex) + \gamma_{qIndex}$;

9           $IP_j(gIndex) = IP_j(gIndex) + \gamma_{gIndex}$;

10         $C_q = MatchGI(IP_i(qIndex), IP_j(gIndex))$;

11   **return** C_q ;

12   **foreach** $child_{qIndex} \in children(\gamma_{qIndex})$ **do**

13           $MChild_{gIndex} = MatchNode(\lambda(child_{qIndex}), \lambda(child_{gIndex}))$;

14           $Q_u.next = (child_{qIndex}, MChild_{gIndex})$;

Algorithm 1 provides an overview of the filtering algorithm of $HRTree$. We consider that an offline index, represented as $gIndex$, based on the $HRTree$ is built for
the graph database G (Line 1). The $HRTree$ index structure for the formulated query
$qIndex$ is built online (Line 2). Let Q_u be a queue node that stores $\mathscr{R}_{qIndex}$ and
$\mathscr{R}_{gIndex}$ in a first-in, first-out (FIFO) manner (Line 3).

Assuming that the queue node Q_u is not empty, we would start by dequeuing
the first node, corresponding to $qIndex$, of the queue node in γ_{qIndex} (Line 5). In

addition, the queue node's second node, associated with the $gIndex$, is also dequeued in the γ_{gIndex} (Line 6). If the current queue node corresponding to $qIndex$, γ_{qIndex}, is a leaf node $\mathscr{L}$, we would retrieve the candidate graph set by matching the graph occurrences information G_I between the $\mathscr{L}(\gamma_{qIndex})$ and its matching node in $gIndex$. Then, we perform an intersection between the candidate set C_q and newly identified data graphs g_{id} in G_I that satisfy condition Eq. 5 (Line 10). Observe that the indexed path $IP_i(qIndex)$ is generated for the $qIndex$ and subsequently, its matching path in $gIndex$, $IP_j(qIndex)$, as a consequence of the breadth-first search traversal. On the other hand, each leaf node of an indexed path in $qIndex$, that is $\mathscr{L}(IP_i(qIndex))$, is matched to the corresponding node of the matched indexed path $IP_j(gIndex)$, denoted as $\gamma_r(IP_j(gIndex))$. The matching child pair is stored in queue node Q_u.

Let us examine the time complexity of finding the matching indexed path in $gIndex$, given the index path $IP_i(qIndex)$.

Lemma 2. *Given an indexed path in a query index $IP_i \in IP(qIndex)$, the matching indexed path in a graph index, $IP_j \in IP(gIndex)$, can be matched in the $O(l_d)$ time complexity based on the first character of each label ($\lambda_1 \in \lambda(\gamma_u)$, $1 \leq u \leq l_d$), where l_d is the maximum depth of the traversed labelled path. The first character of each label is nothing but, $ck \in C(\gamma_r(IP_i))$, where $1 \leq r \leq l_d$.*

Consider the Example 7. We have an indexed path in $qIndex$, $IP_1(qIndex) = \{2, 3, 1, 2\}$. Its mapped indexed path in $gIndex$ highlighted "red" in Fig. 3. We can see that, in the worst-case scenario, we have to traverse l_d indexed nodes.

3.3   LinkedList-Based Radix Tree (LRTree)

The LinkedList-based radix tree $LRTree$ is a compact representation of a Trie data structure. Each indexed node, $\gamma_i(LRTree)$ represents an indexed path, which is a sequence of integers λ from root $\mathscr{R}$ to the current node $\gamma_i(LRTree)$. In addition, an indexed node may contain pointers to its sibling node and child node. As with $HRTree$, $\gamma_i(LRTree)$ contains graph occurrences information G_I. Formally, we define an *indexed node of the linkedlist-based radix tree* as follows:

Definition 14 (Indexed Node of the Linkedlist-based Radix Tree [15]). *An indexed node of the linkedlist-based radix tree $\gamma_u(LRTree)$ is a quadruplet $\langle \lambda, C, S, G_I, L \rangle$, which is node of a Linkedlist-based radix tree $LRTree$. The element λ is a node label, which consists of ordered sequence of integers $\lambda = \{\lambda_1, \lambda_2, ..., \lambda_t\}$, where the length of the node label belonging to an indexed node in LRTree is $length(\gamma_u(LRTree))$, is t. The element Ck is the set of children pointers belonging to the indexed node $\gamma_u(LRTree)$ $Ck = \{child_1(\gamma_u(LRTree)), child_2(\gamma_u(LRTree)), ..., child_m(\gamma_u(LRTree))\}$. The element S is the next sibling pointer associated with the current indexed node. The element G_I is the graph information consisting of graph identifiers $g_{id} \in G_{ID}$ and corresponding occurrences count $c_d \in C$, where $G_{ID} = \{g_1, g_2, ..., g_{id}\}$ and $C = \{c_1, c_2, ..., c_d\}$. Here d is the maximum number of occurrences in γ_u. The element L has a boolean value associated with it; with 1 means that the indexed node is a leaf whereas 0 means it is not.*

In the following discussion, we will derive the time complexity for filtering operation in $LRTree$.

Lemma 3. *Given an indexed path in a query index $IP_i(qIndex)$ and its corresponding matching path in graph index $IP_j(qIndex)$. Let $|IP(qIndex)|$ and $|IP(gIndex)|$ be total number of indexed path in qIndex and gIndex respectively. Additionally, consider n is the total number of data graphs in the G_I and l_d as the maximum path length. Assume that the time complexity for intersecting candidate set is ρ. This leads to the following runtime assessment:*

$$\#MatchPath(IP_i(qIndex)) = \mathcal{O}(|IP(qIndex)| \cdot |IP(gIndex)| + |IP(qIndex)| \cdot l_d) = \mathcal{O}(|IP(qIndex)| \cdot (|IP(gIndex)| + l_d))$$
$$\#MatchGI(IP_i(qIndex), IP_j(qIndex)) = \mathcal{O}(|IP(qIndex)| \cdot (n \cdot \rho)).$$

Then the total time complexity for the filtering in LRTree is,

$$T_{filtering}(LRTree) = \mathcal{O}(|IP(qIndex)| \cdot (|IP(gIndex)| + l_d + (n \cdot \rho))). \quad (9)$$

We must examine each path in $qIndex$ to $gIndex$, one at a time. In the worst case scenario, for each $IP_i(qIndex)$, all the $IP_j(gIndex)$ has to be checked for $MatchPath(IP_i(qIndex))$. This is because $LRTree$ requires the traversal of sibling nodes for prefix matching. Once we find the matching prefix to $IP_i(qIndex)$, we need to descend the $IP_j(qIndex)$ of maximum length l_d until we reach the matching node to $\mathcal{L}(IP_i(qIndex))$. Upon reaching $\gamma_r(IP_j(gIndex))$, where $1 \leq r \leq l_d$, we need to check for the matching occurrence information $MatchGI(IP_i(qIndex), IP_j(gIndex))$. This leads to the examination of all the occurrences count $g_{id} \in G_I(IP_j(gIndex))$, which is $\mathcal{O}(n)$. Moreover, for each n data graphs that satisfy Eq. 5, we have to update C_q as the intersection of existing candidate graph C_q, associated with $\gamma_r(IP_1(gIndex))$, and the newly obtained $C_q(IP_j(gIndex))$.

Apart from developing a filtering algorithm to enable efficient matching, which is discussed in detail in Sect. 3.2 and Sect. 3.3, the second challenge is providing a compact representation of the graph occurrences information. The space-efficient representation of occurrence information influences the index size and filtering time and is tackled in the following Sect. 4.

4   Compact Candidate Graph Set Representation

In this section, we redesign the in-memory data structures to reduce the memory footprints associated with storing candidate graph sets presented in Sect. 3. Generally, the filtering time constitutes the longest time for query response time. Therefore, there is a need to reduce the filtering time by selecting an appropriate representation of the graph reference information. At the same time, the graph occurrences information contains repetitive information, and must be compressed using the relevant compression methods. Consequently, there is a need for a data structure that uses less memory and can enable faster retrieval for low cardinality attributes.

4.1   Compressed Inverted Index

Here, we focus on extending the notion of the well-studied index structure in the information retrieval, inverted index, for the compact representation of the candidate graph sets. Hence, we will define $HRTreeIV$, an inverted index built on top of the GI, which is associated with an indexed node in $HRTree$.

Definition 15 (HRTreeIV). *For all $\lambda(\gamma_u)$ in the gIndex and qIndex, the graph occurrence information of an indexed node in the $HRTreeIV$, denoted as $G_I(\lambda(\gamma_u))$, is a tuple $\langle C, G_L \rangle$. Consider that the sub-path from $\mathscr{R}$ to $\lambda_t(\gamma_u)$ is either IP_j in qIndex (or IP_j in case of qIndex. The count dictionary $C = \{c_1, c_2, ..., c_d\}$ contains the frequency of occurrence of the IP_j in $g_{id} \in G$ (q in case of qIndex). The graph identifier set G_L includes the set of graph identifiers g_{id} containing the IP_j with the mapped count c_d, where d is the maximum number of occurrences of λ_t in indexed node γ_u. In the case of qIndex, $g_{id} \in HRTreeIV = |q|$. Both $c_d \in C$ and its corresponding G_L are sorted in ascending order.*

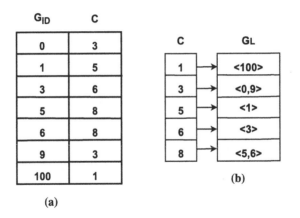

(a)

(b)

Fig. 4. Compressed representation of (a) HRTree graph information with (b) HRTreeIV.

We build an array-based count dictionary C that contains a list of occurrences counts and a compressed linked-list CL for the graph identifier set G_L. Other possible data structures that may be used for building the count dictionary C could be an array, hashing, or trees (such as R-tree, B+tree).

Example 9. Given G in Fig. 1, Fig. 4 shows the simple representation of $GI \in \gamma_u(HRTree)$, in Fig. 4a, with the simple array-based inverted index, in Fig. 4b. We employ compression methods directly on the G_L. Thus, $HRTreeIV$ establishes the mapping from C to the G_L.

The graph identifier sets, G_L, in each indexed node of $HRTree$ and has redundancies in the graph identifiers. Therefore, storing uncompressed G_L would be a waste of storage space, as in the case of GraphGrepSX [1] and GRAPES [5]. This is especially true when only a list intersection of a certain, fewer G_L associated with c_d is required during query processing. Notably, a compact representation of G_L can not only reduce the storage space but can also speed up the list compression operation. The construction of CL would require depth-first traversal of the $HRTree$ and compression of each G_L mapped to c_d. C_L can be organised in a monotonically increasing sequences of $|G_L|$ positive integers drawn from an universe $|m| = 0, 1, 2, .., m - 1$, which are denoted as d-$gaps$. The d-$gaps$ are encoded using the state-of-the-art $S4$-$FastPFor$ [10].

The $S4$-$FastPFor$ is a block-based compression method, which finds the minimum value of integers in G_L so that all the integers are less than and equal to 2^b. The integers that do not fall within the b bits are considered exceptions and stored in a separate array with references to the position of the related block element. In particular, $S4$-$FastPFor$ supports faster decompression of $\mathcal{O}(1)$ per element. The difference in the space-complexity of $S4$-$FastPFor$ and $Partitioned$ $Elias$-$Fano$ are discussed thoroughly in [4].

Now, we shall draw the attention to how the filtering time is affected by the choice of the compression method for the inverted indexes.

Lemma 4. *The upper bound for the filtering time is* $\mathcal{O}(|IP(qIndex)| \cdot (l_d + \rho))$. *Here,* $|IP(qIndex)|$ *is the total number of nodes in all the indexed paths of the qIndex and* ρ *is the time complexity for the intersection operations between the existing candidate set* C_q *and the* $C_q(IP_j)$ *obtained from the graph identifiers-set satisfying Eq. 5.*

Additionally with the usage of a correct compression algorithm ρ can be reduced substantially.

4.2   Compressed Bitmap Index

BM-GGSX, the variant of *GraphGrepSX*, was found to run faster than *GraphGrepSX* but suffers from the following issues: (1) the index size is not compact as the repetition in the labelled indexed paths is not eliminated, while, the number of pointers from the inner nodes grows larger with the maximum path length, (2) the choice of compression algorithm has yet to be thoroughly studied in order to reduce further the compression and intersection time which would then achieve a lower-bound storage size with faster filtering time and, (3) the existing study has yet to study an approach to prune further the candidate graph set. Our paper propose a new nested-indexing structure for subgraph searching using compressed bitmap indexing.

The graph occurrences information $G_I(\lambda(\gamma_u))$ of $HRTreeBM$ is a tuple $\langle C, G_L \rangle$ representation for the graph occurrences information in each indexed node of the $HRTree$. Similar to the $HRTreeIV$, C denotes the count dictionary, which is the occurrence count for the particular indexed sub-path IP_j in data graphs (IP_i in case of query graphs). Meanwhile, G_L indicates the set of graph identifiers of the data graph containing the sub-path IP_j (IP_i in case of q) associated with the current node γ_u.

In order to represent the count dictionary, we used a hash map data structure, while the graph identifier set is represented using the bitset. We have replaced the existing graph occurrences information with the $HRTreeBM$ to support efficient filtering time and compact storage size. In addition, $HRTreeBM$ also supports efficient maintenance due to the nature of its boolean representation. Thus, we have integrated the state-of-the-art $EWAH$ [11] to compress the sorted integer list of graph occurrences G_L.

The candidate data graphs generated at the end of the filtering algorithm are tested using $VF2$ algorithm [3].

5   Evaluation

In this section, we evaluate the performance of our algorithms on real-world datasets. Specifically, our experimental study has achieved three main goals:

- We compared the overall cost, such as the index size and index construction time, of $SubTempora$'s $HRTreeIV$ (discussed in Sect. 4) and $HRTreeBM$ to the existing approaches $HRTree$ and $LRTree$ (discussed in Sect. 3).
- We illustrated the reduction of filtering time.
- We have exhibited the scalability of the $SubTempora$ by varying parameters (such as graph size).

All measurements were carried out on a node of the Lichtenberg cluster at TU Darmstadt. The node consists of four Intel Xeon E2670 and 32 GB of main memory. The sequential codes are run with a fixed clock frequency of 2.6 GHz and disabled HyperThreading.

5.1   System Setup, Datasets and Queries

Biochemical Graphs. We have used three real datasets, namely Antiviral Screen ($AIDS$), Protein Data Bank ($PDBS$), and Protein Contact Maps ($PCMS$) to show the effectiveness of our filtering algorithm. $AIDS$. is an antiviral screen compound dataset published by NCI/NIH. The $AIDS$ dataset is a popular benchmark that contains 40,000 chemical compounds that inhabits the HIV virus. $PDBS$ contains 600 data graphs representing DNA, RNA and proteins. PCMS contains 50 protein contact maps, which is duplicated 4 times to generate 200 data graphs. Table 2 summarizes the real-world datasets.

Table 2. Characteristics of the real-world datasets.

Dataset	$|G|$	$|\Sigma|$	$|V|$	$|E|$	$|G_\Sigma|$
$AIDS$	40,000	62	45	46.95	4.4
$PDBS$	600	10	2,939	3,064	6.4
$PCMS$	200	21	377	4,340	18.9

5.2 Parameter Selection

This research study considered the following evaluation metrics:

- Indexing time: the elapsed time from the beginning to the end of offline index-construction for all the data graphs in the transaction graph database.
- Indexing size: the space consumption by the index graph in the hard disk. The index graph is serialized in binary format.
- Query processing time: the elapsed time from an online-query indexing to obtaining results. It is composed of the filtering and verification times.
- Filtering time: the total amount of time taken for generating the candidate graph set.
- Verification time: the total amount of time taken for performing subgraph isomorphism between the candidate graph set and the query graph.

Another evaluation metric is the false-positive ratio, which is presented below. However, we will not evaluate based on the false-positive ration as the pruning power of all the index graphs is based on the same filtering algorithm, which checks for the Theorem 1 and 2.

- False-positive ratio: the filtering power of an algorithm can be evaluated using the false-positive ratio, which is obtained as follows, where Q refers to all the query graphs in the workload, $|C_q|$ is the set of candidate graphs after filtering, while $|A_q|$ is the set of answer graphs after verification:

$$FP = \frac{1}{|Q|} \sum_{q \in Q} \frac{|C_q - A_q|}{|C_q|}$$

5.3 Performance Comparison

Firstly, we focused on evaluating how our compressed index structure performs in the context of different sizes of data graphs and path lengths. In particular, we have sub-grouped our input datasets as small, medium, and large. The small-sized, medium-sized, and large-sized datasets contained $20\%, 50\%$, and 100% of the original data graphs, respectively. The maximum path length varied from 4 to 8 hops. The results comprise the size of the index structure and the runtime to build the index. Secondly, we considered queries of varying path lengths, as specified above, which were indexed and matched to data graphs in the transaction graph database. When using the *AIDS*, *PDBS*, and *PCMS* datasets, the process to query generation was similar to [7, 14]; this consisted of performing the random-walk and breadth-first search and obtaining a query graphs of sizes: $8, 16, 24$, and 32. Finally, we measured the filtering and query response times. We ran the experiments four times on the datasets and obtained an average of the results to ensure the accuracy of the measurements.

In Fig. 5(a), overall $HRTreeIV$ provides good compression compared to $HRTreeBM$, which resulted in a smaller construction size to $HRTree$, for the *AIDS* dataset. In the case of a small sub-group, we could observe a reduction in the percentage of compressed size for $HRTreeIV$ by approximately 46% and 10% to $HRTree$ and $HRTreeBM$ respectively. However, for the medium-sized dataset, the compression size is reduced to 49% for $HRTreeIV$ instead of $HRTree$ and $HRTreeBM$, respectively. Similarly, for the large-sized dataset, the compression size of $HRTreeIV$ are 53% and 50% lesser than $HRTree$ and $HRTreeBM$. This clearly indicates that as we increase the number of data graphs, the efficiency of compression size increases simultaneously. Interestingly, the index size of $HRTreeBM$ for a small dataset is relatively similar to the $HRTree$. This is likely due to the sparse bitmap caused by fewer data graphs having the same occurrence count. It is clear from this experiment that newly proposed compressed-based index structures $HTreeIV$ and $HRTreeBM$ are the clear winner. In particular, $HRTreeIV$ provides a good compression as the number of data graphs increases. Across all the sizes of *AIDS* dataset, the indexing size of $LRTree$ is considerably huge than the other index structures $HRTree$, $HRTreeIV$, and $HRTreeBM$.

Figure 5(b) showed the index size of different techniques for the small, medium, and large-sized subgroups of the *PDBS* dataset. Observe that for all the subgroups, the reduction in index size is apparent for both $HRTreeIV$ and $HRTreeBM$. In particular for the large-subgroups, $HRTreeIV$ and $HRTreeBM$ achieved a reduction in storage size of approximately 30% and 4% in comparison to $HRTree$.

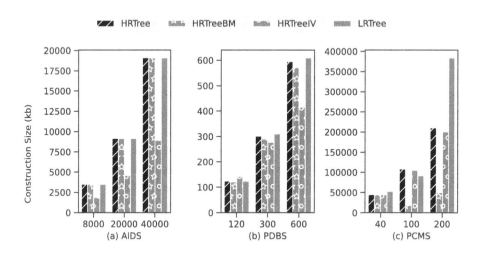

Fig. 5. Comparison of index size (kb) for various techniques ($HRTree$, $HRTreeIV$, and $HRTreeBM$).

In Fig. 6, we plotted the index construction times in seconds (sec) with regard to the number of data graphs and compared the performance of the different strategies proposed in Sect. 4: $HRTreeIV$ and $HRTreeBM$. For the *AIDS* dataset, the index building times were 50, 150, and 300 sec for the small, medium, and large datasets, respectively, when using $HRTree$. Interestingly, the index construction time for the $HRTreeIV$ and the $HRTreeBM$ were approximately similar to the $HRTree$ for all the subgroups of *AIDS* dataset. The general observation is that $LRTree$ takes a shorter time to build the indexes for the transactional graph database, except for the *PCMS* datasets.

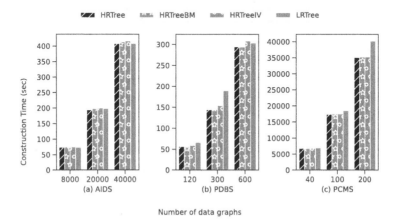

Fig. 6. Comparison of construction time (sec) for various techniques ($HRTree$, $HRTreeIV$, and $HRTreeBM$).

Figure 7 presented the filtering times in seconds of our query execution. We can see the speedup in the filtering time with the compressed index structure. The $HTree$ requires 0, 0.0037, 0.0045, and 0.0275 sec on the *AIDS*, *PDBS* and *PCMS* datasets. This is, however, outperformed by $HRTreeIV$ with approximately 6× speedups for *AIDS* and *PDBS*. $HRTreeBM$ provided a comparable filtering time of 0.0039, 0.004, 0.0200 seconds respectively for the *AIDS*, *PDBS*, and *PCMS* datasets.

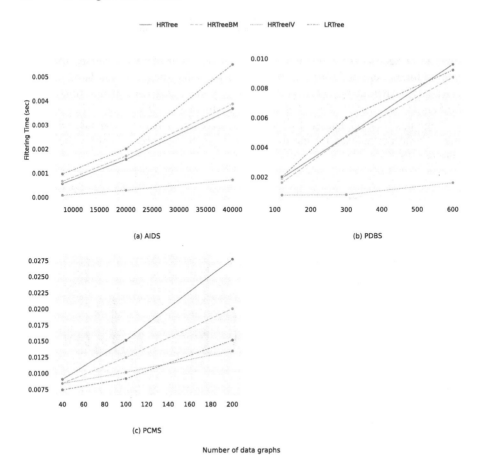

Fig. 7. Comparison of filtering time (sec) for various techniques ($HRTree$, $HRTreeIV$, and $HRTreeBM$).

6   Related Work

The primary motivation for graph indexing is to reduce the costly pairwise graph pattern matching. The methods of solving the subgraph matching problem are seen to be categorised into filter-then-verify (FTV) approaches and non-filter (using sub graph isomorphism (SI)) paradigms. As mentioned previously, the FTV methods generally target numerous small graphs while the SI methods are typically tested on single large graphs. Filter-then-verify approaches first filter the data graphs that do not match the query graph and then verify only those pruned, candidate graphs by using various SI algorithms. Although the recent approaches show improvements to the subgraph matching algorithm to solve subgraph searching problems, as discussed in [12] the performance of subgraph isomorphism methods may deteriorate as the number of data graphs increases. Furthermore, [8] proposed hybrid methods that use state-of-the-art subgraph indexing and subgraph matching methods.

The filter-then-verify approach can be further classified as mining-based or non-mining-based approaches. As discussed in [13], the mining-based approach generates frequent features by using graph mining methods; these consist of a candidate generation phase using either an a apriori-based approach or a pattern growth approach, a pruning phase to remove redundant features, and a support counting phase to measure the occurrences of the features in the graph(s). Typically, the last step for counting the support of the features differs concerning the graph setting. It is important to note here that the frequent features are generated based on the fulfilment of the downward closure property. The downward closure property states that if a graph is frequent, then all of its subgraphs must also be frequent. On the other hand, the non-mining-based approaches require the exhaustive enumeration of all the features and then are required to store them within the indexes.

Filter-then-verify (FTV) methods like GraphGrep [6], GraphGrepSX [1], and GRAPES [5] are all path-based exhaustive enumeration methods. In contrast to the non-mining based methods, approaches such as CP-Index [16], gIndex [17], FG*-Index [2] and, Lindex+ [18] use mining-based methods to enumerate graph-based frequent patterns. [14] clearly pointed out that for mining-based FTV methods, there is a trade-off between the frequent feature extraction and the filtering power of the indexes. As a result, the time taken to construct the indexes will be long although the query response time can be fast. While the non-mining-based FTV methods can be constructed quickly, they may lack pruning ability, and, hence, consume a large amount of memory for construction and the size of the indexes can become exponential to the graph size.

Based on our empirical study, building a mining-based index incurs considerable overheads without gaining higher filtering power for most queries, an observation that has already been confirmed by [8]; Indeed, several benchmarks have shown that existing indexing methods followed by frequent subgraph mining are inefficient in query processing on widely-used datasets such as *PDBS*, *PCMS*, and *PPI*. Therefore, we used a non-mining-based index which supported a compact and faster query processing for all the enumerations of paths from a transactional graph database.

7   Conclusions

In this paper we proposed $SubTempora$, a novel hybridising approach that combines space-time efficient subgraph indexing with subgraph isomorphism. Hence, our subgraph indexing supports a compact indexing size for large datasets and an efficient filtering time in contrast to the state-of-the-art implementations. In addition, we have deepened the evaluation obtained in our previous work by using additional dataset and by varying the characteristics of the graph to study its effect on the various metrics. In future work, we plan to integrate $SubTempora$ for an efficient indexing to support Visual Exploratory Subgraph Searching and further develop a maintenance algorithm for $SubTempora$ to assist continuous query processing. To the best of our knowledge, $SubTempora$ is the first approach in the literature that supports nested subgraph indexing based on succinct data structure.

Acknowledgements. The authors would like to thank Deutscher Akademischer Austauschdienst (DAAD) for providing funds for research on this project. Extensive calculations were conducted on the Lichtenberg high-performance computer of the TU Darmstadt for this research under project ID P0020213. Furthermore, the authors would like to thank Prof. Dr. Daniel Lemire, for the insightful discussion during the preparation of this work.

References

1. Bonnici, V., Ferro, A., Giugno, R., Pulvirenti, A., Shasha, D.: Enhancing graph database indexing by suffix tree structure. In: Dijkstra, T.M.H., Tsivtsivadze, E., Marchiori, E., Heskes, T. (eds.) PRIB 2010. LNCS, vol. 6282, pp. 195–203. Springer, Heidelberg (2010). https://doi.org/10.1007/978-3-642-16001-1_17

2. Cheng, J., Ke, Y., Ng, W.: Efficient query processing on graph databases. ACM Trans. Database Syst. **34**(1), 2:1–2:48 (2009). https://doi.org/10.1145/1508857.1508859

3. Cordella, L.P., Foggia, P., Sansone, C., Vento, M.: A (sub) graph isomorphism algorithm for matching large graphs. IEEE Trans. Pattern Anal. Mach. Intell. **26**(10), 1367–1372 (2004)

4. Fuentes-Sepúlveda, J., Ladra, S.: Energy consumption in compact integer vectors: a study case. IEEE Access **7**, 155625–155636 (2019). https://doi.org/10.1109/ACCESS.2019.2949655

5. Giugno, R., Bonnici, V., Bombieri, N., Pulvirenti, A., Ferro, A., Shasha, D.: GRAPES: a software for parallel searching on biological graphs targeting multi-core architectures. PLoS ONE **8**(10), e76911 (2013)

6. Giugno, R., Shasha, D.E.: GraphGrep: a fast and universal method for querying graphs. In: 16th International Conference on Pattern Recognition, ICPR 2002, Quebec, Canada, 11–15 August 2002, pp. 112–115. IEEE Computer Society (2002). https://doi.org/10.1109/ICPR.2002.1048250

7. Katsarou, F.: Improving the performance and scalability of pattern subgraph queries. Ph.D. thesis, University of Glasgow, UK (2018)

8. Katsarou, F., Ntarmos, N., Triantafillou, P.: Hybrid algorithms for subgraph pattern queries in graph databases. In: Nie, J., et al. (eds.) 2017 IEEE International Conference on Big Data (IEEE BigData 2017), Boston, MA, USA, 11–14 December 2017, pp. 656–665. IEEE Computer Society (2017). https://doi.org/10.1109/BigData.2017.8257981

9. Kim, H., Choi, Y., Park, K., Lin, X., Hong, S., Han, W.: Versatile equivalences: speeding up subgraph query processing and subgraph matching. In: Li, G., Li, Z., Idreos, S., Srivastava, D. (eds.) SIGMOD 2021: International Conference on Management of Data, Virtual Event, China, 20–25 June 2021, pp. 925–937. ACM (2021). https://doi.org/10.1145/3448016.3457265

10. Lemire, D., Boytsov, L., Kurz, N.: SIMD compression and the intersection of sorted integers. Softw. Pract. Exp. **46**(6), 723–749 (2016). https://doi.org/10.1002/spe.2326

11. Lemire, D., Kaser, O., Aouiche, K.: Sorting improves word-aligned bitmap indexes. Data Knowl. Eng. **69**(1), 3–28 (2010). https://doi.org/10.1016/j.datak.2009.08.006

12. Licheri, N., Bonnici, V., Beccuti, M., Giugno, R.: GRAPES-DD: exploiting decision diagrams for index-driven search in biological graph databases. BMC Bioinform. **22**(1), 209 (2021). https://doi.org/10.1186/s12859-021-04129-0

13. Mrzic, A., et al.: Grasping frequent subgraph mining for bioinformatics applications. BioData Min. **11**(1), 20:1–20:24 (2018)

14. Sun, S., Luo, Q.: Scaling up subgraph query processing with efficient subgraph matching. In: 35th IEEE International Conference on Data Engineering, ICDE 2019, Macao, China, 8–11 April 2019, pp. 220–231. IEEE (2019). https://doi.org/10.1109/ICDE.2019.00028

15. Wangmo, C., Wiese, L.: Efficient subgraph indexing for biochemical graphs. In: Cuzzocrea, A., Gusikhin, O., van der Aalst, W.M.P., Hammoudi, S. (eds.) Proceedings of the 11th International Conference on Data Science, Technology and Applications, DATA 2022, Lisbon, Portugal, 11–13 July 2022, pp. 533–540. SCITEPRESS (2022). https://doi.org/10.5220/0011350100003269

16. Xie, Y., Yu, P.S.: CP-index: on the efficient indexing of large graphs. In: Macdonald, C., Ounis, I., Ruthven, I. (eds.) Proceedings of the 20th ACM Conference on Information and Knowledge Management, CIKM 2011, Glasgow, United Kingdom, 24–28 October 2011, pp. 1795–1804. ACM (2011). https://doi.org/10.1145/2063576.2063835

17. Yan, X., Yu, P.S., Han, J.: Graph indexing: a frequent structure-based approach. In: Weikum, G., König, A.C., Deßloch, S. (eds.) Proceedings of the ACM SIGMOD International Conference on Management of Data, Paris, France, 13–18 June 2004, pp. 335–346. ACM (2004). https://doi.org/10.1145/1007568.1007607

18. Yuan, D., Mitra, P.: Lindex: a lattice-based index for graph databases. VLDB J. **22**(2), 229–252 (2013). https://doi.org/10.1007/s00778-012-0284-8

Exploring Instagram and Youtube Data
to Extract User Insights: The Greek Paradigm

Stefanos Vlachos, Dimitris Linarakis, Nikos Platis, and Paraskevi Raftopoulou[✉]

Dept. of Informatics and Telecommunications, University of the Peloponnese,
GR-22131 Tripoli, Greece
{nplatis,praftop}@uop.gr
https://dit.uop.gr/

Abstract. In an era when the word "digital" is more significant than ever, companies, following the boom of social media platforms, are giving up traditional advertising practices and use new policies of diffusion for engaging potential customers online. This shift encapsulates numerous modern marketing strategies, with the most popular one being influencer marketing, which forms the subject of our research. In more detail, for the work presented in this paper, tools and techniques were used to scrape public Instagram and YouTube profiles and collect data uploaded by users during 2020. This data was explored and analyzed in order to extract information concerning the digital behaviour and preferences of the Greek Instagram and YouTube communities, the activity of Greek companies on social media, as well as the social and commercial impact of the emerging COVID-19 pandemic during 2020 on Greek users' digital behaviour. The work presented in this paper is an extension of our work in [32] and is the first study in the literature to perform an analysis on the behaviour of the Greek community of the two aforementioned social media platforms.

Keywords: Web scraping · Data exploration · Social media · Influencer marketing · User activity patterns · User preferences · COVID-19

1 Introduction

Over the past twenty years, the number of social media users has been steadily rising, with 190 million of them joining social media during the last 12 months, summing up to 4.74 billion social media users globally until October 2022 (almost 60% of the global population, 4.2% growth per year, 6 new users every single second on average) [3,5,6]. Moreover, the typical social media user actively uses or visits an average of 7.2 different social platforms each month and spends approximately 2.5 h per day browsing. Specifically, six social media platforms claim one billion or more monthly active users, who engage with and are affected by a multitude of posts [22,35]. Hence, social network platforms hold, without doubt, a central role in interpersonal relationships, in the dissemination of information, knowledge and technology, in the formation of trends, and in the adoption of opinions. This massive use of social media platforms, along with the

This work was supported by project ENIRISST+.

A. Cuzzocrea et al. (Eds.): DATA 2021/2022, CCIS 1860, pp. 90–113, 2023.
https://doi.org/10.1007/978-3-031-37890-4_5

fact that the majority of online content is user-generated, has prompted many businesses not only to develop their digital presence on social media, but also to give up traditional advertising practices and use new policies, fitting the customers' engagement with the social platforms, for promoting their products and services. In this context, the potential advertising reach for the most popular social media platforms is given in Table 1.

Table 1. Potential advertising reach per platform [3].

Platform	Users (bn.)
Facebook	2.934
YouTube	2.515
WhatsApp	2
Instagram	1.386
WeChat	1.299
TikTok	1

Given the aforementioned phenomena, in order for a business to pursue its growth in the digital era it should adapt to the modern needs of the market and implement modernised marketing strategies, including, among others, brand storytelling, digital PR, the surround sound method, video marketing, and community building [1]. These techniques, that aim at increasing user awareness and attracting engagement, are the foundation of the *Influencer Marketing* (IM) approach. IM is a process of diffusion over social networks [41], according to which a company that wants to market a product or service, cost- and time-effectively, identifies a small number of users with high social network impact (known as *influencers*[1]) and whose social network presence tallies with their products. These users become the initial adopters of the product and recommend it to their social media friends (also called *followers*), expecting that they will be influenced to purchase it and, in turn, recommend it to their friends. This chain of influence among influencers and social media users causes an *influence dissemination* (through the social network) and can eventually lead to the wide adoption of the product. In fact, recent surveys [4, 8] show that 80% of consumers in 2019 made purchases recommended by influencers, while 93% of marketers stated they would use IM within their overall marketing strategy.

Taking into consideration these observations, in the context of the Greek project "Intelligent Research Infrastructure for Shipping, Supply Chain, Transport and Logistics+" (ENIRISST+)[2], we started investigating whether transportation businesses (i.e., ferry companies, airlines, etc.) use modern practices for promoting their services on social media. The fact that no relative study was available thus far concerning the Greek community in total, in addition to the increasing rate of Greek businesses entering social media and the huge impact of the 2020 COVID-19 outbreak on social relationships as well, led to the expansion of our research to include all kind of Greek businesses

---

[1] https://www.simplilearn.com/types-of-influencers-article.
[2] https://enirisst-plus.gr.

and social media users. Since the work in [16] shows that the consumers' purchase behaviour is significantly affected by the characteristics of each platform, we decided to base our research on Instagram and YouTube, a decision made considering the popularity of these platforms during the year 2020 in Greece, their different characteristics and the continuously increasing commercial interest in them.

Therefore, in this work we study and analyse the interplay of commerce with Instagram and YouTube regarding three fundamental axes: (a) the users' digital behaviour and preferences, (b) the influencers' digital behaviour, and (c) the interest of companies to draw marketing policies grounded on these behaviours. This paper further extends our work presented in [32] with new content (including sections, descriptions, and tables) to better explain the way used to approach the domain under investigation and new observations to shed more light on the Greek Instagram and Youtube community. In more detail, (i) we present a *qualitative analysis* of the activity of the *Greek community* on Instagram and YouTube for the year 2020, (ii) we identify *marketing policies and behavioural patterns* in the two platforms, (iii) we compare the *observations* made on these two significantly different (in terms of content and interaction) social platforms, and, finally, (iv) we examine the *social and commercial impact of COVID-19* on social media users' *activity*. This work could be the first step to inter-temporally study and decode the activity of users and businesses on social media, both in Greece and globally, gaining some useful insights that can help businesses to better approach their audience.

The rest of the paper is organised as follows. Firstly, we present studies most relevant to our work in Sect. 2. Next, we present the methodology used both for the data collection/storage and data analysis processes in Sect. 3. The results of our research are presented in Sect. 4. Finally, Sect. 5 concludes the paper and gives future directions.

2 Related Work

A large number of studies address influence dissemination and marketing under different perspectives, attempting to understand this complex phenomenon (detailed surveys can be found in [9, 15, 27]). The work in [16] shows that platform characteristics affect consumers' purchase behaviour, while [40] is a systematic review that identifies the key themes and the dominant concepts of social media IM. In more detail, this work reveals five research themes: (i) influencers' characteristics and how they impact consumers, (ii) psychological-related influential factors, (iii) quality of influencer content and the resulting consequences, (iv) the effects of sponsorship disclosure, and (v) the implemented marketing techniques. On a similar basis, [25] studies data from 281 followers of social media influencers and examines the effectiveness of IM mechanisms, while [18] puts great emphasis on the impact of the COVID-19 pandemic on various growth strategies, including IM. The COVID-19 factor is also addressed in [34], where the relevant to the pandemic behaviours of social media influencers are dissected, in relation to their audience response.

Instagram is a social media platform that focuses on the use of images and videos, making it the most used application for IM [43]. Numerous studies [10, 28, 30, 31, 39] have explored the potential motives for following influencers on Instagram, as well as the factors that affect the users' engagement with influencers. In the same context, two programmatic approaches are presented in [26] and [24], attempting to predict content popularity, based on factors such as image quality and time of upload, and to analyse the role of nano-influencers. As also referred in [2], nano-influencers[3] offer a surprising amount of value for today's brands, since the relatively small target group means that their audiences tend to be more active and loyal and their recommendations are perceived as more genuine. The study presented in [11] aims to gain insights into the level of persuasion knowledge of IM on Instagram and the cues people use to identify IM. In addition, [14] indicates and discovers key antecedents and consequences of IM in Instagram and suggests that influencers' originality and uniqueness, as well as the fit in personalities among influencers and consumers, are crucial factors to impact consumers behaviour. The work in [20] investigates the impact of Instagram upon source credibility, consumer buying intention, and social identification with different types of celebrities. The findings of this research show that celebrities on Instagram are influential in the purchase behaviour of young female users, although non-traditional celebrities are considered more credible. Finally, the most effective types of Instagram marketing tools in purchasing behaviour are also studied in [19] and [10] in the context of UK and German influencers, correspondingly, indicating that there are significant gender differences in relation to impulse purchasing behaviour on Instagram.

The last couple of years, the YouTube platform has also evolved as a primary marketing selection for brands promotion, with a plethora of studies having attempted to investigate the behaviour of users on the platform and the rate of commercial influence exerted by influencers. To this end, a multidimensional analysis of the top 1700 YouTube channels during 2022 was performed in [33] in order to explore correlations between the domain of a YouTube channel and the performance of its videos. Concerning brand awareness, [37] studies the role of YouTube as a social media platform and its impact on creating visibility for brands. Similarly, the way YouTube IM can help improve future marketing strategies for international companies is examined in [13]. The work in [42] employs a heuristic-systematic model to investigate how cues influence credibility evaluations of information posted by YouTube influencers, while [7] reveals that combined entertainment and informativeness are the key factors that make YouTube influencers popular in the new era market. In the context of product placement in videos, [36] emphasizes the importance of consumer-to-consumer product reviews in influencing consumer outcomes through para-social interaction. Some studies are country-bound, such as [38] which attempts to quantify product promotion by German YouTube channels between 2009 and 2017, and [23] which analyses and explains the influence of YouTube beauty vloggers on Indonesian Muslim Consumer's Purchase Intention of Halal Cosmetic Products. Finally, some works focus on specific age groups: since YouTube is a popular platform among children, [12, 17] identify how vloggers target and may affect young children; on the other hand, in an attempt to study how older adult viewers use YouTube, [29] reveals that older adults are eager to watch videos on YouTube because they believe this information to be unbiased compared to other media sources.

---

[3] Nano-influencers are content creators within a social media platform, with anywhere from 100 to 10,000 followers.

As it can be perceived, there are several works aiming to identify or quantify the factors of IM in social media. However, the communities of each country share different social characteristics and consumer habits, factors that distinctly shape the users' behaviour on social media and provide space for new observations. However, the majority of the studies cited above, either focus on specific platforms and IM aspects, or are based on a small amount of data. For these reasons, we decided to utilize the knowledge provided by the aforementioned literature and carry out the first (to the best of our knowledge) analysis concerning Greek IM on both Instagram and Youtube.

3 Methodology

Our research process is unfolded in three stages: (i) problem identification and preparation, (ii) data collection and storage and (iii) data exploration and analysis. In this section, we explain the strategies and tools that were employed at each stage.

3.1 Problem Identification and Preparation

The very first step of our study was to investigate the selected domain and identify the areas of interest that provide space for more extensive research. Stating a set of fundamental questions could help us identify the main concepts and transfuse a goal-oriented character to our work. The questions that guided the research process of the present work are:

- Which are the underlying factors that drive users to actively interact with the uploaded content in social media platforms on a daily basis?
- Which were the preferences of the Greek social media community during 2020? Are these preferences age- or gender-related?
- Which were the thematic categories and types of content that obtained significant attention by Greek social media users during 2020? Which of these categories strived in 2020, in terms of content production?
- What is the role of businesses in social media and which are the potential relationships developed between the various categories of content creators?

The year 2020 was the period during which COVID-19 broke out. The pandemic brought radical changes to people's daily lives, prompting us to also examine the impact of COVID-19 on the Greek social media community.

After setting the fundamental axes of our study, a preliminary search was conducted in order to locate the available data and determine the fields that would best serve our needs. As a result, the collection of Greek public accounts that maintained a non-zero activity rate during 2020 and at least 1K followers on Instagram / 5K subscribers on YouTube was deemed necessary.[4] These guidelines were set based on the facts that: (i) public accounts house publicly accessible data and can potentially promote a product or service [21] and (ii) we wanted to study the activity of influencers of the whole spectrum, from nano to mega influencers.

---

[4] These thresholds do not hold for Greek business accounts, due to their limited and recent presence on social media platforms.

3.2   Data Collection and Storage

For data collection, we considered a wide range of approaches and tools, including auto-mated scraping techniques, authorised APIs provided by the platforms, or even questionnaires given out to the users of social networks. The requirements and limitations of the data collection process led us to use every one of the aforementioned methods. We expand on our choices below.

Location of Appropriate Profiles. In order to define the set of profiles on which our study would be based, we firstly located credible web sources which compile lists of popular Greek social media creators and businesses. More specifically, we leveraged:

- **starngage:**[5] a marketplace that connects brands with content creators from different media
- **stats.videos:**[6] a site that includes YouTube statistics for popular video creators per region
- **socialbakers:**[7] a site that includes social media insights per industry or region

Subsequently, we developed two web scraping mechanisms (one for starngage and one for stats.video), using the **Scrapy framework,**[8] and collected numerous key-value pairs of profile names and profile/channel IDs related to popular content creators. Additionally, we hand-picked the names of Greek businesses having digital presence in social media from socialbakers and manually searched for the corresponding profile/channel IDs on the social media platforms of interest. Eventually, we collected several public accounts as shown in Table 2.[9] These accounts will later be used as the feed sample of our data collection algorithms.

Table 2. Number of collected profiles.

Platform	Male	Female	Business	Uncategorised/Other	Total
Instagram	784	926	806	249	2,766
YouTube	782	318	314	654	2,068

Instagram Dataset. An Instagram (IG) account includes a plethora of valuable fields. However, our research focused on a subset of collectable attributes. Despite the fact that IG provides an authorized API for collecting these fields, the complexity of setting up and using this API led to the use of scraping software. In more detail, an automated web scraping mechanism was developed, using the Scrapy framework and the Python programming language, which (i) gains access to the usernames of IG accounts that were

---

[5] https://starngage.com/app/global.

[6] https://stats.video/top/most-subscribed/youtube-channels/greece/of-all-time.

[7] https://www.socialbakers.com/statistics/youtube/channels/greece.

[8] https://scrapy.org/.

[9] Note that profiles shown as "Uncategorised/Other" correspond to accounts administrated by groups of people (e.g., tv channels, magazines, etc.) and are less prone to seeking for promotion through IM.

initially collected, (ii) extracts the required fields from each IG account and, finally, (iii) groups the data related to each account and stores them as documents in a **MongoDB database**[10] (see Listings 1.1 and 1.2). The source code of our IG scraping mechanism is available on GitHub[11].

```
1  "personal_info": {
2      "user_id": "an ID",
3      "account_type": "a type set by the user",
4      "account_category": "a category set by the user",
5      "owned_by": "Male, Female, Business or Other",
6      "followers": "number of followers",
7      "following": "number of following",
8      "posts": "number of posts",
9      "videos": "number of videos",
10     "avg_erpost": "average Engagement Rate Post",
11     "avg_erview": "average Engagement Rate View",
12     "avg_likes": "average likes per post",
13     "avg_comments": "average comments per post",
14     "avg_engagement": "average ER Comments Post"
15     "avg_days_between_posts": "avg. days between successive
           uploads"
16 },
17 "tagged_users": ["user1ID", "user2ID", "etc"],
18 "hashtags": ["hashtag1", "hashtag2", "etc"]
```

Listing 1.1. IG dataset example: Personal information.

```
1  "user_posts": [{
2      "post_id": "an ID",
3      "post_date_timestamp": "upload date of the post",
4      "post_type": "Photo, Video or Slideshow",
5      "likes": "number of post likes",
6      "comments": "number of post comments",
7      "views": "number of views (for videos)",
8      "er_post": "Engagement Rate Post",
9      "er_comments_post": "Engagement Rate Comments Post",
10     "er_views": "Engagement Rate Views (for videos)",
11     "post_tagged_users": ["user1ID", "user2ID", etc],
12     "post_hashtags": ["hashtag1", "hashtag2", etc],
13     "slide_posts" (for slideshows): [{
14         "slide_id": "an ID",
15         "slide_type": "Photo or Video"
16         "slide_views": "number of views (for videos)"
17     }]
18 }]
```

Listing 1.2. IG dataset example: User posts.

---

[10] https://www.mongodb.com/.
[11] https://github.com/stefanos-vlachos/Instagram_Scrapy_Scraper.

YouTube Dataset. Similarly, a YouTube (YT) channel consists of numerous fields, but we based our analysis on a subset of the available attributes. In the case of YT, the YT Data API provided access to a wide variety of metadata related to YT creators and content. The communication with the YT Data API was established via an automated mechanism that was developed using the Scrapy framework. This mechanism, after (i) being provided with the channel ID of each YT channel, (ii) requests the required fields from YT Data API and (iii) stores them as documents in the MongoDB database (see Listings 1.3 and 1.4). The source code of our YT scraping mechanism is available on GitHub[12].

```
 1  "channel_data": {
 2      "id": "an ID",
 3      "keywords": ["keyword1", "keyword2", "etc"],
 4      "creation_date": "creation date of the channel",
 5      "view_count": "total number of views",
 6      "subscriber_count": "number of subscribers",
 7      "video_count": "number of 2020 videos",
 8      "owned_by": "Male, Female, Business or Other",
 9      "avg_days_between_videos": "avg. days between successive
        uploads"
10  }
```

Listing 1.3. YT dataset example: Channel data.

```
 1  "video": {
 2      "video_id": "an ID",
 3      "title": "title of the video",
 4      "video_category": "category given by YT",
 5      "upload_date": "upload date of video",
 6      "duration": "duration of video in ms",
 7      "view_count": "number of video views",
 8      "like_count": "number of video likes",
 9      "comment_count": "number of video comments",
10      "dislikes": "number of video dislikes"
11      "tags": ["tag1", "tag2", "etc"]
12  }
```

Listing 1.4. YT dataset example: Video information.

Questionnaire. The restrictive privacy policies of IG and YT, in addition to our interest in exploring the social media users' preferences in more depth, led to the creation and distribution of a questionnaire, using Google Forms.[13] The answers to the posed questions could help us better interpret the already collected data, since they comprise a more informative tool for assessing the users' sympathy or indifference towards certain types of content, taking also into account the age and gender factors. Therefore, our questionnaire aimed at various categories of Greek IG and YT users, in terms of age and

---

[12] https://github.com/stefanos-vlachos/Youtube_Scrapy_Scraper.
[13] https://www.google.com/forms/about/.

social characteristics. In particular, the questionnaire consisted of 4 introductory questions, 23 questions related to IG and 20 questions related to YT, and it was answered by 270 people. Table 3 gives the demographic details of the people that participated in our research.

Table 3. Demographic information of the questionnaire participants.

	Gender			Age				
	Male	Female	Non-Binary	(18-24)	(25-43)	(35-44)	(45-54)	(>50)
Participants	82	187	1	128	53	66	20	3

3.3 Data Exploration and Analysis

As was mentioned in Sect. 3.1, the main purpose of this research is to investigate and address the various factors that may affect the performance of an uploaded post, and, thus, the rate of the exerted influence. Thus, at this stage, the collected data, retrieved via both the scraping mechanisms and the questionnaire, will be explored and analysed, in order to answer the fundamental questions set at the beginning of the research process.

Starting with, we explore (i) the popularity of an account by counting the number of its followers/subscribers, (ii) content dynamics by the number of "Like" reactions, the number of comments, and the number of views on IG/YT uploads, and (iii) the negative feelings of the audience for the content by the number of "Dislike" reactions. To this end, we also investigate the data for potential correlations between influence rate and factors such as (i) the used keywords/hashtags, (ii) the topic and type of uploaded content, or (iii) the gender of the creator, by calculating, plotting and, finally, examining the distribution of count and mean aggregations of the simpler metrics.

The combination of the measurements and, then, the creation of new derivative ones help us better assess the performance of posts in relation to their reach or their creator's popularity (also referred as the *engagement* of the community with the uploaded content) and enhance the accuracy of the primary observations. A list of the derivative performance metrics used in this work is presented in Table 4[14]. Notice that, although both platforms offer visual content, we use different engagement measures since they support different posting options. Finally, by comparing and enhancing our measurements with the questionnaire answers, we manage to reinforce our understanding of the role of IM in the Greek IG and YT communities and wrap up the findings of the present work. Our findings are presented in detail in Chap. 4.

Outliers Management. During the analysis stage of the data, there were accounts and posts that gathered a huge amount of reactions, steering the measurements away from the actual picture. In order to prevent this phenomenon, the distribution of all the available measures are thoroughly examined. This process highlighted the outliers in the dataset, which are then excluded to ensure the representativeness of the final conclusions.

---

[14] ER stands for Engagement Rate.

Table 4. Performance metrics.

Platform	Metric Name	Mathematical Expression	Range
Instagram	ER Post	$\frac{PostLikes}{AccountFollowers} \cdot 100$	$[0, \infty)$
	ER Comments Post	$\frac{PostLikes+PostComments}{AccountFollowers} \cdot 100$	$[0, \infty)$
	ER Views	$\frac{VideoLikes}{VideoViews} \cdot 100$	$[0, \infty)$
YouTube	Video Engagement	$\frac{VideoLikes+VideoComments}{VideoViews} \cdot 100$	$[0, \infty)$
	Dislikes Ratio	$\frac{VideoDislikes}{VideoLikes+VideoDislikes} \cdot 100$	$[0, \infty)$
	Views/Subscribers Ratio	$\frac{VideoViews}{ChannelSubscribers} \cdot 100$	$[0, \infty)$

Tools Used. The tools that gave us the ability to successfully carry out the exploration and analysis of the collected data are **MongoDB Compass**[15] and **MongoDB Charts**,[16] for querying our data and visualizing the results, and **Google Sheets**,[17] for analysing the questionnaire results.

4 Results

The conclusions of the present research were drawn in a process governed by our research goals (presented in Sect. 3.1) and can be categorized into four thematic axes: (i) Instagram community, (ii) YouTube community, (iii) Businesses & Influencer Marketing and, finally, (iv) the impact of COVID-19.

4.1 Instagram Results

Starting with IG, our main objective is to address the factors that boosted the community's engagement with the uploaded content, as well as the productivity of social media creators, in 2020. Initially, the Greek community maintains a high level of familiarity with IG. This holds especially true for the younger users of the platform, who stated that they have been active on the platform for more than two years (point of reference is the year 2020) and have been using it on a daily basis. However, the ongoing integration of older users into the platform indicates its overall absorption by the Greek community. Detailed results are omitted due to space constraints.

In addition, Figs. 1 and 2 indicate that female users gathered the largest number of followers within 2020. On the other hand, Fig. 3 shows that male users are characterized by a higher following tendency, when compared to female creators and businesses. Overall, a higher engagement rate was marked by male and female users, implying that content uploaded by individual creators exert a higher rate of influence (Fig. 4).

---

[15] https://www.mongodb.com/products/compass.
[16] https://www.mongodb.com/docs/charts/.
[17] https://www.google.com/sheets/about/.

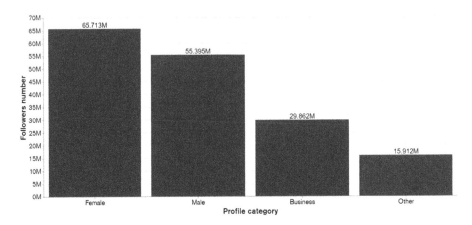

Fig. 1. Number of followers per account category (IG).

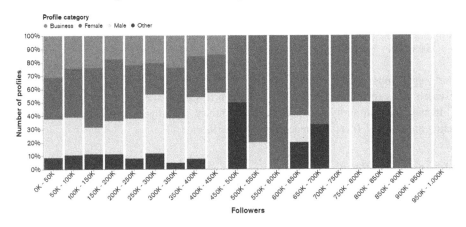

Fig. 2. Number of profiles per range of followers (IG).

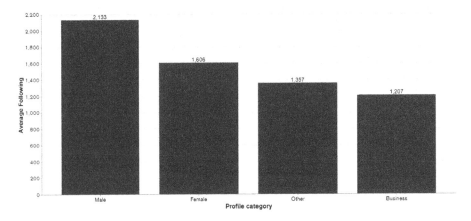

Fig. 3. Average following per account category (IG).

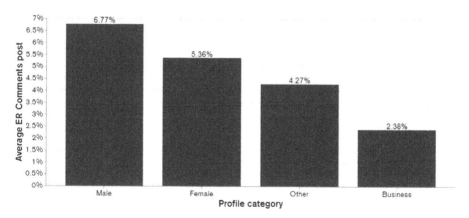

Fig. 4. Average engagement per account category (IG).

In terms of content quantity, business and female accounts were by far leading in number of produced posts within 2020 (Fig. 5). Taking a closer look at the overall production of content throughout the year, summer of 2020 was marked by a significant boost in productivity of male and female creators, revealing the increased activity on IG during this period of the year. It is also worth noticing that the majority of hashtags used by female creators and businesses were related to *Fashion* and *Lifestyle*, proving that IG provides a fertile ground for these types of content (Figs. 6 and 7).

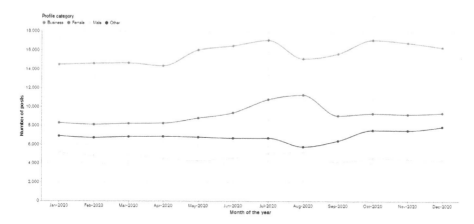

Fig. 5. Number of posts per month and account category (IG).

Taking into consideration the hashtags used by the majority of Greek users, in addition to the answers given to our survey, we conclude that the Greek community is particularly interested in *lifestyle*, *arts*, *travelling*, and *entertainment*. However, male users also expressed their preference towards *sports* and *technology*, while female users seemed to also be keen on *fashion/beauty* and *cooking*.

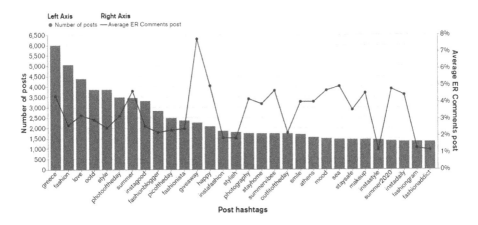

Fig. 6. Most used hashtags by female creators (IG).

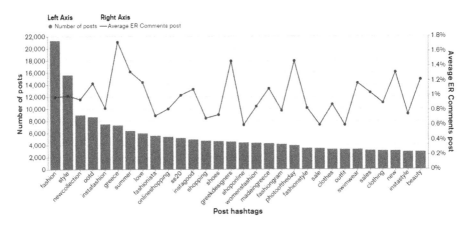

Fig. 7. Most used hashtags by businesses (IG).

Finally, the effect of upload frequency to engagement is investigated. In more detail, Fig. 8 may indicate that the bombarding of the platform with numerous posts, as well as infrequent uploads, lead to lower engagements rates, compared to more moderate upload frequencies.

4.2 YouTube Results

Concerning YT, a similar approach with IG is adopted in order to examine the specific points of interest. To start with, the Greek audience seems to be even more familiar with the character of YT related to IG, something that meets our intuition since YT pre-existed IG. Our questionnaire highlights that users of all ages have been using it for more than two years (point of reference is the year 2020). However, despite the wide absorption of YT, a partial shift of the users towards the weekly use of the platform was inferred from the answers to our questionnaire. Detailed results are omitted due to space constraints.

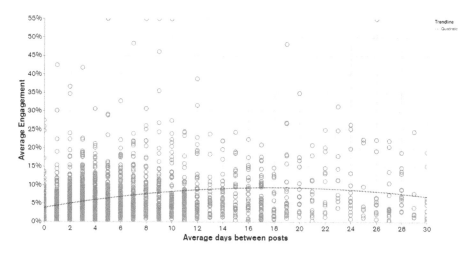

Fig. 8. Average engagement compared to upload frequency (IG).

In contrast to IG, male video creators and uncategorized channels have a stronger presence on the YT platform, based both on the number of channels and number of uploaded videos in 2020 (Figs. 9 and 10). The dominance of male creators and uncategorized channels in YT can also be inferred from the relatively wide audiences maintained by these categories of channels (Fig. 11). Overall, a higher engagement rate was marked on YT by male and female users (Fig. 12). Supplementarily, newly created channels also marked high engagement rates, implying that new content creators on the platform cover the modern needs of the Greek YT community more effectively (Fig. 13). It is worth highlighting that videos uploaded by channels created in 2020 were mostly related to *Gaming*, *Entertainment* and *People & Blogs* (Figs. 14 and 15).

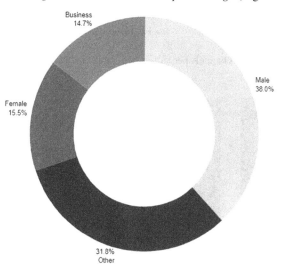

Fig. 9. Number of channels per channel category (YT).

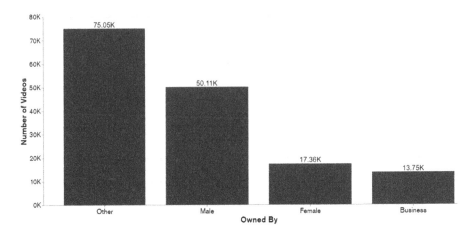

Fig. 10. Number of videos per channel category (YT).

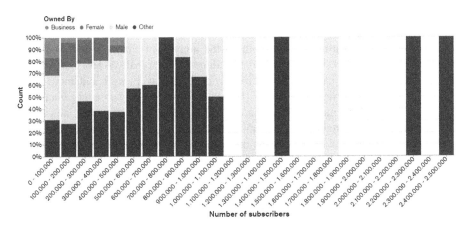

Fig. 11. Number of channels per subscribers range and channel category(YT).

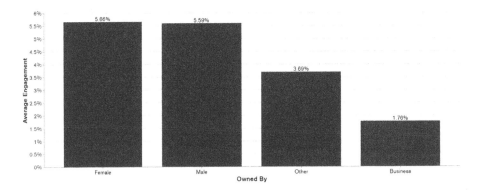

Fig. 12. Average engagement per channel category(YT).

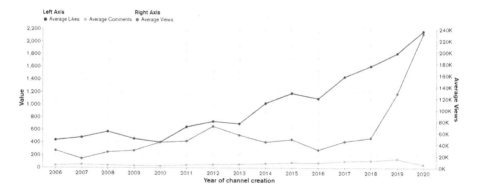

Fig. 13. Average engagement per year of channel creation (YT).

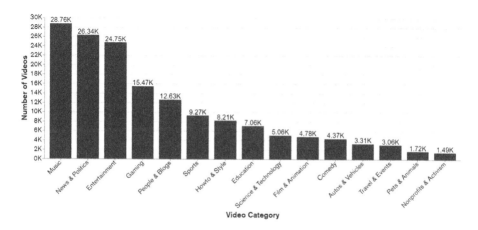

Fig. 14. Number of videos per video category(YT).

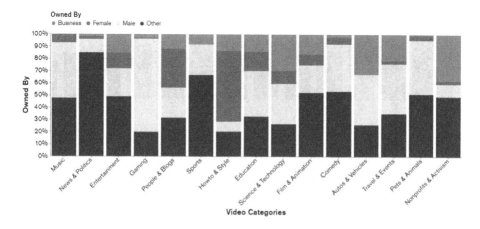

Fig. 15. Number of videos per channel category and video category(YT).

Concerning the community's engagement with the various thematic categories within 2020, it is observed that *gaming, comedy, entertainment, arts* and *educational content* are poles of great interest, with the first three marking the highest average number of views. Taking also into consideration the questionnaire results, male users also expressed their preference towards *gaming* and *sports*, while female viewers gravitated towards *lifestyle, fashion/beauty,* and *cooking.* On the other hand, *News and politics* videos seem to causes negative feelings, holding the record for the highest average number of "Dislike" reactions (Fig. 16). Finally, videos that include the active participation of viewers (e.g., QnAs, challenges, "We're reacting to your stories"), as well as exhibition of products (e.g., reviews, haul, unboxing) obtained significant attention in 2020, while remarkably popular are also proved to be videos that feature highlights from the creator's daily life (Vlog) (Fig. 17).

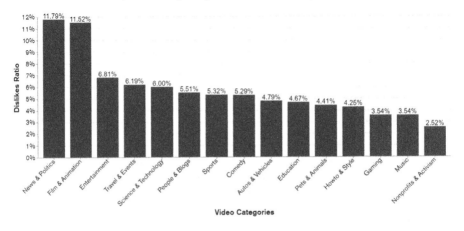

Fig. 16. Average Likes-Dislike ratio per video category (YT).

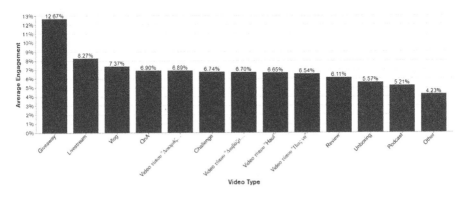

Fig. 17. Average engagement per video type (YT).

4.3   Business and Influencer Marketing

A large number of businesses have been found to be active on social media. Generally, businesses are characterized by a conservative and professional character on IG and YT, since they tend to properly schedule their activity throughout the week and keep a strict following strategy (Figs. 3 and 18). However, IG seems to be a preferable option for the development of commercial relationships, based on the number of businesses and their posts on this platform.

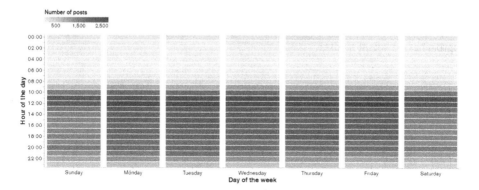

Fig. 18. IG posts per day and hour (Businesses).

After analysing the hashtags used by businesses on social media and taking also into consideration the number of business posts uploaded within 2020, an increase in the activity of businesses during holidays, celebrations and anniversaries, such as Easter, summer, Christmas or Valentine's Day, is noticed, uncovering the significance of these periods for businesses in terms of commerciality (Figs. 5 and 19). Nevertheless, businesses seem to encounter difficulties approaching effectively their audience and, thus, establishing a committed community. In addition, the interference of monetized posts/advertisements with users' regular feed is proved to be inadequate to drive traffic into the page of the advertised businesses. In fact, the answers to our questionnaire show that such techniques are probably connected with feelings of annoyance.

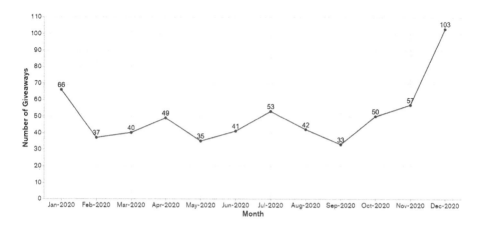

Fig. 19. Number of YT Giveaways throughout 2020.

On the other hand, IM was proved to be a more effective practice of promoting a service or product. Posts that include the exhibition of a product by a content creator are related to much higher engagement rates (Fig. 20). Admittedly, the headliners of 2020 in the Greek social media community were *Giveaway* posts, since they gathered an eminent amount of reactions on both platforms under research. Additionally, the fact that younger users are more prone to follow social media influencers (based on the questionnaire answers) may position the younger age groups in the spotlight of IM approaches on social media.

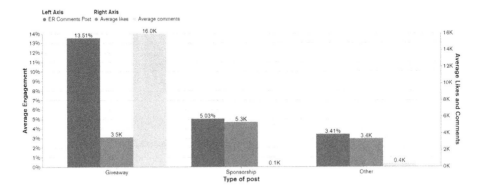

Fig. 20. Performance of Giveaways on IG.

The different dynamics of creators on IG and YT have also shaped the business strategies, with them being adjusted to the needs and particularities of each platform. Our findings show that businesses on IG during 2020 aimed at female content creators and posts related to *fashion*, *beauty* and *lifestyle*. Respectively, *gaming*, *science/technology*, *fashion/beauty* and *travelling* are identified as video categories with increased commercial interest in YT (see Fig. 21).

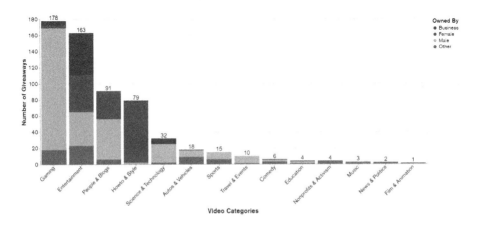

Fig. 21. YT Giveaways per video category.

4.4 Impact of COVID-19

The year 2020 was marked by the COVID-19 outbreak, which brought radical changes to peoples' daily lives. The state of lockdown that followed led to a major shift of users towards social media, a phenomenon whose effect is investigated as a final step of the present study. A preliminary indicator of people's emotional state during this period, as shown in Figs. 22 and 23, is the emerge of numerous hashtags explicitly referring to the pandemic, such as #stayhome, #staysafe, #staystrong, #quarantinelife or #covid_19. It is worth highlighting that a few hashtags that were widely used during the quarantine actually expressed feelings of nostalgia and reminiscence (e.g., #throwback, #memories). The significant raise in the number of uploaded YT videos that was marked in 2020 could also comprise another sign of the users resorting to social media as the only means of communication during the lockdown (Fig. 24).

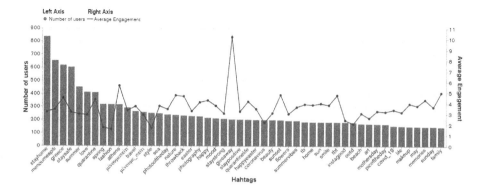

Fig. 22. Most used IG hashtags during March 2020-May 2020.

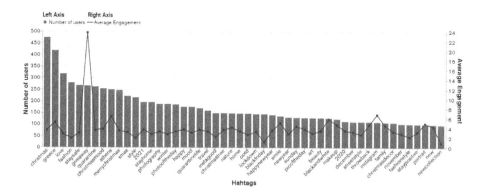

Fig. 23. Most used IG hashtags during November 2020-December 2020.

The increased presence of users on social media appear to have provided an opportunity for businesses to enhance, or even build from scratch, their digital presence on social media platforms, as a quite intensive use of quarantine-related keywords was marked on behalf of them. Finally, certain categories of YT videos, including *gaming, entertainment, comedy* and *news & politics*, also met an increase in the amount of produced content, possibly uncovering the users' need for such content during the pandemic.

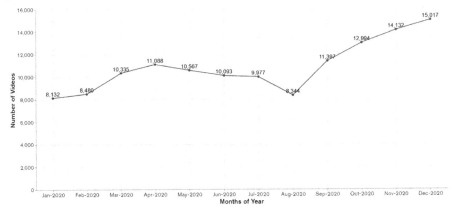

Fig. 24. YT videos per month.

5   Conclusions and Future Work

In this work, we have presented a study concerning the interference of commerce and IM with the Greek communities of Instagram and YouTube. Our research process is based on three fundamental axes: (i) activity and preferences within the Instagram community, (ii) activity and preferences within the YouTube community, (iii) businesses & IM and, finally, (iv) the impact of COVID-19.

This work could be the first step to inter-temporally study and decode the activity of users and businesses on social media, both in Greece and globally, gaining some useful insights that can help businesses to better approach their audience. The results of the study could be enriched by expanding the under-examination datasets with a wider range of fields that were not used in this work (e.g., IG stories, text of uploaded comments) or even with data from other popular social media platforms (e.g., TikTok, Twitter, Facebook). In a more technical context, the data collection mechanisms built for this work could be improved, in terms of time-efficiency, data management and anti-scraping techniques avoidance. Finally, the integration of machine learning could also add another dimension to our study and provide valuable knowledge, training a model with the collected datasets and mining potential behavioral patterns of users and trends.

Acknowledgements. This work was supported by project ENIRISST+ under grant agreement No. MIS 5047041 from the General Secretary for ERDF & CF, under Operational Programme Competitiveness, Entrepreneurship and Innovation 2014-2020 (EPAnEK) of the Greek Ministry of Economy and Development (co-financed by Greece and the EU through the ERDF).

References

1. 18 of the best marketing techniques for 2022. https://blog.hubspot.com/marketing/marketing-techniques (2021). Accessed 25 Nov 2022
2. What you need to know about working with Nano influencers. https://www.forbes.com/sites/forbesagencycouncil/2021/03/08/what-you-need-to-know-about-working-with-nano-influencers/?sh=2f249cb16851 (2021). Accessed 2 Dec 2022
3. https://datareportal.com/social-media-users (2022). Accessed 25 Nov 2022
4. 28 essential influencer marketing statistics you need to know in 2022. https://thesocialshepherd.com/blog/influencer-marketing-statistics (2022). Accessed 2 Dec 2022
5. Number of social media users worldwide from 2018 to 2027. https://www.statista.com/statistics/278414/number-of-worldwide-social-network-users/ (2022). Accessed 9 Dec 2022
6. Social media usage statistics for digital marketers in 2022. https://www.searchenginejournal.com/top-social-media-statistics/418826/ (2022). Accessed 9 Dec 2022
7. Acikgoz, F., Burnaz, S.: The influence of 'influencer marketing' on YouTube influencers. Int. J. Internet Mark. Advert. **15**(2), 201–219 (2021)
8. Advertising, R.: Rakuten marketing 2019 influencer marketing global survey. https://www.iab.com/wp-content/uploads/2019/03/Rakuten-2019-Influencer-Marketing-Report-Rakuten-Marketing.pdf (2019). Accessed 24 Jan 2022
9. AlSumaidan, L., Ykhlef, M.: Toward information diffusion model for viral marketing in business. Int. J. Adv. Comput. Sci. Appl. (IJACSA) **7**(2), 637–646 (2016)
10. Asdecker, B., Landwehrjohann, M., Vornberger, K., Vogel, Y.: Influencer marketing on Instagram: exploring the role of travel and other factors on a post's success. In: Proceeding of the 50th European Marketing Academy Conference (EMAC), May 2021
11. Boerman, S., Müller, C.: Understanding which cues people use to identify influencer marketing on Instagram: an eye tracking study and experiment. Int. J. Advert. 1–24 (2021). https://doi.org/10.1080/02650487.2021.1986256
12. Boerman, S., van Reijmersdal, E.: Disclosing influencer marketing on YouTube to children: the moderating role of para-social relationship. Front. Psycol. (2020)
13. Carreon, N.: YouTube Influencer Marketing: A Qualitative Research of Danish YouTube Influencers In An International Perspective. Master's thesis, Copenhagen Business School, May 2019
14. Casaló, L.V., Flavián, C., Ibáñez-Sánchez, S.: Influencers on Instagram: antecedents and consequences of opinion leadership. J. Bus. Res. **117**, 510–519 (2020). https://doi.org/10.1016/j.jbusres.2018.07.005
15. Chen, W., Lakshmanan, L., Castillo, C.: Information and Influence Propagation in Social Networks. Morgan & Claypool Publishers, California (2013)
16. Chen, Z., Lu, H., Li, L.: How new media marketing influence consumers' purchase behavior in the era of big data. In: Proceedings of the International Conference on Cyber Security Intelligence and Analytics (CSIA), pp. 601–606, March 2021
17. Coates, A., Hardman, C., Halford, J., Christiansen, P., Boyland, E.: It's just addictive people that make addictive videos: children's understanding of and attitudes towards influencer marketing of food and beverages by YouTube video bloggers. Int. J. Environ. Res. Public Health. **17**(2) (2020). https://doi.org/10.3390/ijerph17020449
18. Coll-Rubio, P., Carbonell, J.M.: Growth communication strategies in the digital age. Am. Behav. Sci. **56**, 16 (2022). https://doi.org/10.1177/00027642221132798X
19. Djafarova, E., Bowes, T.: 'Instagram made me buy it': generation z impulse purchases in fashion industry. J. Retail. Consum. Serv. **59** (2021). https://doi.org/10.1016/j.jretconser.2020.102345

20. Djafarova, E., Rushworth, C.: Exploring the credibility of online celebrities' Instagram profiles in influencing the purchase decisions of young female users. Comput. Hum. Behav. **68**, 1–7 (2017). https://doi.org/10.1016/j.chb.2016.11.009

21. Dreghorn, B.: What is the difference between the 3 Instagram profile types. https://www.business2community.com/instagram/what-is-the-difference-between-the-3-instagram-profile-types-02300390 (2020). Accessed 28 Jan 2022

22. Eirinaki, M., Gao, J., Varlamis, I., Tserpes, K.: Recommender systems for large-scale social networks: a review of challenges and solutions. Futur. Gener. Comput. Syst. **78**, 413–418 (2018). https://doi.org/10.1016/j.future.2017.09.015

23. Elvira, M.: The influence of YouTube beauty vloggers on Indonesian Muslim consumers purchase intention of halal cosmetic products. Nusantara Islamic Econ. J. **1**(2) (2022). https://doi.org/10.34001/nuiej.v1i2.250

24. Himelboim, I., Golan, G.J.: A social network approach to social media influencers on Instagram: the strength of being a Nano-influencer in cause communities. J. Interact. Advert. (2022). https://doi.org/10.1080/15252019.2022.2139653

25. Hugh, D.C., Dolan, R., Harrigan, P., Gray, H.: Influencer marketing effectiveness: the mechanisms that matter. Eur. J. Market. **56**, 3485–3515 (2022). https://doi.org/10.1108/ejm-09-2020-0703

26. Purb, K.R., Murugesan, R.K.: Instagram post popularity trend analysis and prediction using hashtag, image assessment, and user history features. Int. Arab J. Inf. Technol. **18**(1) (2021). https://doi.org/10.34028/iajit/18/1/10

27. Kempe, D., Kleinberg, J., Tardos, E.: Maximising the spread of influence through a social network. Theory Comput. **11**(4), 105–147 (2015)

28. Kim, H.: Keeping up with influencers: exploring the impact of social presence and parasocial interactions on Instagram. Int. J. Advert. **41** (2022). https://doi.org/10.1080/02650487.2021.1886477

29. Lee, J., et al.: Exploring the community of older adult viewers on YouTube. Univ. Access Inf. Soc. (2022). https://doi.org/10.1007/s10209-022-00918-3

30. Lee, J.A., Sudarshan, S., Sussman, K.L., Bright, L.F., Eastin, M.S.: Why are consumers following social media influencers on Instagram? Exploration of consumers' motives for following influencers and the role of materialism. Int. J. Advert. **41**, 78–100 (2022). https://doi.org/10.1080/02650487.2021.1964226

31. Lin, R.H., Jan, C., Chuang, C.L.: Influencer marketing on Instagram. Int. J. Innov. Manage. **7**(1), 33–41 (2019)

32. Linarakis, D., Vlachos, S., Raftopoulou, P.: From digital footprints to facts: mining marketing policies of the Greek community on Instagram and YouTube. In: Proceedings of the 11th International Conference on Data Science, Technology and Applications (DATA). Lisbon, Portugal, 11–13 July 2022

33. Lupsa-Tătaru, D.A., Lixăndroiu, R.: YouTube channels, subscribers, uploads and views: a multidimensional analysis of the first 1700 channels from July 2022. Sustainability (2022). https://doi.org/10.3390/su142013112

34. Morteo, I.: Influencer Marketing in an Uncertain Economic Climate: A Wasted Opportunity. CRC Press, Apple Academic Press (2023)

35. Peng, S., Zhou, Y., Cao, L., Yu, S., Niu, J., Jia, W.: Influence analysis in social networks: a survey. J. Netw. Comput. Appl. **106**, 17–32 (2018). https://doi.org/10.1016/j.jnca.2018.01.005

36. Penttinen, V., Ciuchita, R., Caic, M.: YouTube it before you buy it: the role of ParaSocial interaction in consumer-to-consumer video reviews. J. Interact. Market. **57** (2022). https://doi.org/10.1177/10949968221102825

37. Prasad, R.: YouTube videos as an effective medium in branding - a study among urban women in mysuru city. Int. J. Mech. Eng. Technol. ("IJMET"). **9**(7), 397–408 (2018)

38. Schwemmer, C., Ziewiecki, S.: Social media sellout: the increasing role of product promotion on YouTube. Soc. Med. Soc. (2018)

39. Tafesse, W., Wood, B.P.: Followers' engagement with Instagram influencers: The role of influencers' content and engagement strategy. J. Retail. Consum. Serv. **58** (2021). https://doi.org/10.1016/j.jretconser.2020.102303

40. Vrontis, D., Makrides, A., Christofi, M., Thrassou, A.: Social media influencer marketing: a systematic review, integrative framework and future research agenda. Int. J. Consum. Stud. **45** (2021). https://doi.org/10.1111/ijcs.12647

41. Wang, W., Street, W.N.: Modeling and maximizing influence diffusion in social networks for viral marketing. Appl. Netw. Sci. **3**(1), 1–26 (2018). https://doi.org/10.1007/s41109-018-0062-7

42. Xiao, M., Wang, R., Chan-Olmsted, S.M.: Factors affecting YouTube influencer marketing credibility: a heuristic-systematic model. J. Med. Bus. Stud. **15**, 188–213 (2018)

43. Yuliati, A., Huda, S.: Analysis of influencer's influence as digital marketing. Eduvest J. Univ. Stud. **2**(11) (2022). https://doi.org/10.36418/eduvest.v2i11.643

Automatic Detection of Facial Landmarks for Denture Models

Ashwinee Mehta[1] (ID), Richard Bi[3] (ID), Sheba Moamen[2] (ID), Maged Abdelaal[2] (ID),

and Nic Herndon[1(✉)] (ID)

[1] Department of Computer Science, East Carolina University, Greenville, NC, USA
herndonn19@ecu.edu
[2] School of Dental Medicine, East Carolina University, Greenville, NC, USA
[3] Department of Electrical and Computer Engineering, University of Illinois
Urbana-Champaign, Champaign, IL, USA

Abstract. The neoclassical canon proportions for face evaluation were defined by artists and anatomists in the 17th and 18th centuries. These proportions are used as a reference for planning facial or dental reconstruction treatments. However, the vertical canon assumption that the face is divided vertically into three equal thirds, which was adopted a long time ago, has not been verified yet. We used 2D photos freely available online and annotated them with anthropometric landmarks using machine learning to verify this hypothesis. Our results indicate that the vertical dimensions of the face are not always divided into equal thirds. Thus, this vertical canon should be used with caution in cosmetic, plastic, or dental surgeries, and reconstruction procedures. In addition, when working with 2D images, we observed that landmarking 2D images can be inaccurate due to pose sensitivity. To address this problem we proposed the use of 3D face landmarking. Our results indicate that regardless of the 3D face scan pose, we were able to annotate the face scans with close to accurate landmarks.

Keywords: Vertical canon · Facial and dental reconstruction · Anthropometric landmarks · Machine learning · Face recognition · Geometric descriptors · Face scans

1 Introduction

A person's face influences their perceived physical appearance, and facial proportions are used for assessing attractiveness, for recommending hairstyles, jewelry, eyeglasses, etc. Face landmarks also have a wide range of applications within the medical field. For instance, they have been used to analyze patients with sleep apnea [11] and to diagnose fetal alcohol syndrome [25]. In dentistry, the facial proportions are used to create a denture of suitable shape, size, and position.

The neoclassical canons that were developed in the 17th and 18th centuries to evaluate the shape of a face. These canons are based on the assumption that certain fixed ratios exist between different parts of a human face. One of these eight neoclassical canons, the vertical canon, states that the face is divided into three equal sections: from

The first two authors, Ashwinee Mehta and Richard Bi, contributed equally to this article.

© The Author(s), under exclusive license to Springer Nature Switzerland AG 2023
A. Cuzzocrea et al. (Eds.): DATA 2021/2022, CCIS 1860, pp. 114–133, 2023.
https://doi.org/10.1007/978-3-031-37890-4_6

the top of the forehead (Trichion) to the bridge of the nose (Glabella), from the bridge of the nose to the base of the nose (Subnasale), and from base of the nose to the chin (Menton), as shown in Fig. 1. This canon is widely used in facial surgeries and dental reconstruction procedures.

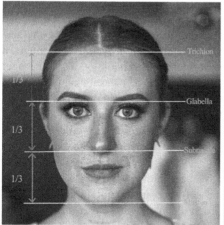

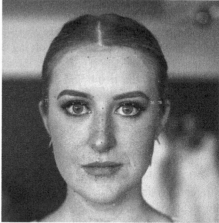

(a) The neoclassical vertical canon states that the face is divided into three equal thirds.

(b) To test this hypothesis we used the Dlib-81 library to automatically place facial landmarks on an image.

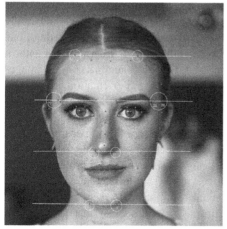

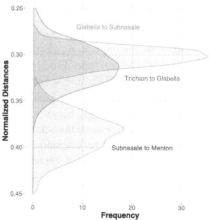

(c) Out of the landmarks generated by the Dlib-81 library we used the ten circled landmarks to place the four lines.

(d) The density distributions of the three distances using annotated images from LFW, MUCT, and CUHK datasets seem to invalidate this hypothesis.

Fig. 1. Facial landmarks used to automatically place the lines for Trichion, Glabella, Subnasale, and Menton. These lines were used in one of the neoclassical canons, the vertical canon, to surmise that each face is divided into three equal sections. However, evidence shows that these distances are not equal. (Note: this image is adapted from [23]).

Missing teeth with age causes a person's face to collapse. While fixing the patient's teeth, it is also important to consider restoring the patient's facial shape. With a collapsed face, only the bottom one third of the face, i.e., from Subnasale to Menton is affected and needs to be restored. This facial restoration also needs a reference face for comparing the facial shape proportions to convert the collapsed face into a non-collapsed face shape. Inclusion and evaluation of facial aesthetics is important while planning for facial or dental reconstruction treatment. Many clinical textbooks and journal articles recommend to use these neoclassical canons for evaluating the aesthetics. However, before blindly applying these recommended neoclassical formulae, it is important to validate them. With the advancements in technology, it is no longer required to use the traditional anthropometric tools to take measurements from the human face. We can use machine learning to train a model to automatically identify the different anthropometric landmarks of the human face and thus avoid the need for direct contact with patients. The objective of this study is to verify the vertical canon by using automated methods that eliminate the need to take the measurements manually using different anthropometric tools.

All the canon validation methods that have been previously proposed have used different physical instruments [2,4,7,20] and software applications for taking measurements of the face [5]. Some of the proposed techniques have used a ready-made database that had images with the anthropometric landmarks annotated [28,29]. However, none of the techniques have used automated tools for getting the measurements and validating the vertical canon. These techniques are discussed in Sect. 4.

Our proposed method used large volume of photos available online, annotated them with automated machine learning tools, and verified this hypothesis. We have performed the automatic validation of the vertical canon by annotating the images from three freely available image datasets using machine learning. By using the proposed method, one can validate the vertical canon automatically without the need to use traditional anthropometric tools or instruments directly on the patient. However, landmarking 2D images could be inaccurate due to the sensitivity to face position and orientation. To address this, we propose using 3D face landmarking. 3D face scans mitigate the issues associated with 2D face images because the extra geometric information available in 3D face scans can help improve the accuracy of landmark placement and because 3D face scans are inherently not pose sensitive. Our proposed method is designed to be used for landmarking 3D face scans for improving the design and visualization of dentures.

Note that this work was previously published in [23]. In this extended version we included the analysis of using three-dimensional facial scans to annotate with facial landmarks. Using 3D scans instead of 2D images should address the measurement issues due to face position and orientation.

2 Materials and Methods

2.1 2D Facial Landmarks Annotation

We evaluated the vertical neoclassical canon using face images from the following three freely available datasets:

- Labeled Faces in the Wild (LFW) [16], a database of face photographs designed for studying the problem of unconstrained face recognition with 13,233 images of 5,749 individuals collected from the web. All images have a resolution of 250×250 pixels.
- The Milborrow/University of Cape Town (MUCT) face database [24], with 3,755 images of 276 individuals sampled from students, parents attending graduation ceremonies, high school teachers attending a conference, and employees of the university at the University Of Cape Town campus in December 2008. This diverse population includes a wide range of subjects, with approximately equal numbers of males and females, and a cross section of ages and races. All images have a resolution of 480×640 pixels.
- The Chinese University of Hong Kong (CUHK) [35], a student database for research on face sketch synthesis and face sketch recognition, with 188 images of 188 individuals. All images have a resolution of 1024×768 pixels.

All images from these databases are not labeled with any anthropometric landmarks.

We processed these images using the following workflow:

1. Facial Annotation: place the anthropometric landmarks on these images. We initially evaluated the Dlib's 68-point facial landmark detector [18], the most popular facial landmark detector, which places 68 different facial landmark points. Since this library does not provide facial landmarks for the forehead, we used an extended version of this library, 81 Facial Landmarks Shape Predictor, which includes landmarks that delineate the forehead. Out of these 81 landmarks, we used only the following ones, as shown in Fig. 1c:

- The left- and right-forehead, used for the placement of the Trichion line.
- The left-temple, left-exterior eyebrow, right-exterior eyebrow, and right-temple, used for the placement of the Glabella line, since none of the 81 landmarks are placed at the position for the bridge of the nose. We used the mid-vertical distance between these landmarks as anchors for the Glabella line.
- The left- and right-base of the nose, used for the Subnasale line.
- The left- and right-side of the chin, respectively, used for the Menton line.

2. Evaluate the Annotation: visually inspect the placement of the four lines mentioned above. We noticed that the predictor placed the landmarks in the correct positions in images that had eyeglasses, beard, bald heads, hats, as well as for people of different age groups and races, and to different background colors and patterns. However, some of the lines were incorrectly placed for images that did not have a front profile view, as shown in Fig. 2.

3. Choose Images: select about 500 images with correctly positioned landmarks. We chose 464 images from the LFW dataset, 86 images from the MUCT dataset, and 29 images from the CUHK dataset, for a total of 579 images.

4. Measure Distances: between Trichion and Glabella, between Glabella and Subnasale, and between Subnasale and Menton, using the 579 selected images. Since the images have different resolutions, we normalized the three distances using Eq. 1.

$$d'_i = \frac{d_i}{\sum\limits_{j=1}^{3} d_j} \qquad (1)$$

where d'_i is the normalized distance of d_i, and d_j is one of the three distances.

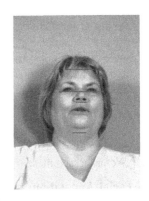

Fig. 2. Incorrect placement of landmarks observed on some images from the MUCT database due to shift in face positions. The left and middle images have the Glabella line misplaced, and the right image has the Glabella and Menton lines misplaced. (Note: this image is adapted from [23].)

5. Visualize the Density Distributions of These Distances: using density plots. These are shown in Fig. 1d for the 579 combined images, and in Figs. 3b, 3d, and 3f, for the 464 images from the LFW database, the 86 images from the MUCT database, and the 29 images from the CUHK database, respectively.

2.2   3D Facial Landmarks Annotation

An overview of the process for locating landmarks on 3D face scans is shown in Fig. 4, and has the following steps.

1. Orient the Face Scan. The standard orientation for face scans within this project is shown in Fig. 5a, with the x-axis horizontal with respect to the face, and the y-axis vertical with respect to the face. The z-axis is the axis orthogonal to both the x and y axes that comes out of the sheet. To orient the face into the standard position, we first assumed the target face scan is a PyVista PolyData object [30] without occlusions whose points can be described by the $3 \times n$ matrix F_1, where n is the number of points in the target face scan. This target face scan may potentially be rotated into an arbitrary orientation. Let the $3 \times n$ matrix F_0 represent the points of the face scan after it has been rotated into the standard position. Then, if we let T be the linear transformation that rotates the points of F_0 into the points of F_1, we have $F_1 = \left[T(\vec{e_1})\ T(\vec{e_2})\ T(\vec{e_3}) \right] F_0$ or

$$F_0 = \left[T(\vec{e_1})\ T(\vec{e_2})\ T(\vec{e_3}) \right]^{-1} F_1, \qquad (2)$$

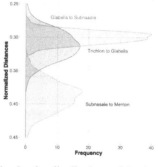

(a) Sample image from the LFW dataset. The images in this dataset have a size of 250×250 pixels.

(b) The density distributions of the three distances for the 464 images used from the LFW dataset.

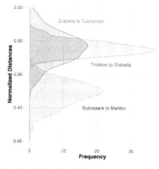

(c) Sample image from the MUCT dataset. The images in this dataset have a size of 480×640 pixels.

(d) The density distributions of the three distances for the 86 images used from the MUCT dataset.

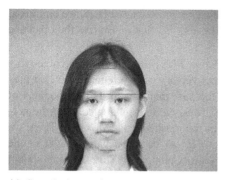

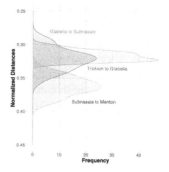

(e) Sample image from the CUHK dataset. The images in this dataset have a size of 1024×768 pixels.

(f) The density distributions of the three distances for the 29 images used from the CUHK dataset.

Fig. 3. Images used in this analysis, shown to scale, along with their corresponding distance distributions. The distributions for each dataset indicate that the neoclassical vertical cannon is not valid. (Note: this image is adapted from [23]).

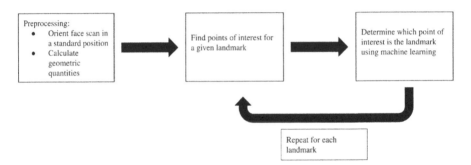

Fig. 4. Overview of the process for locating landmarks on 3D face scans. The first step is preprocessing. During this step, the target face scan is oriented into a standard position, and the relevant geometric descriptors for the points within the scan were calculated. After preprocessing, the location of each landmark is determined. To do so, points of interest are first located for each landmark. Then, a combination of a regression model and clustering is employed to predict the final location of each landmark.

where $\vec{e_1} = [1, 0, 0]^T$ is the vector that points in the positive x-direction, $\vec{e_2} = [0, 1, 0]^T$ is the vector that points in the positive y-direction, and $\vec{e_3} = [0, 0, 1]^T$ is the vector that points in the positive z-direction. Thus, to determine F_0, we determined $T(\vec{e_1})$, $T(\vec{e_2})$, and $T(\vec{e_3})$. To determine $T(\vec{e_1})$, we noted that when $T(\vec{e_1}) = \vec{e_1}$, the components of the face mesh's unit normal vectors along $\vec{e_1}$ generally formed the bowl-shaped distribution seen in Fig. 5b. This was due to the symmetry of a face scan in the standard orientation about the yz-plane and the large, flat sides of the face. Thus, to find $T(\vec{e_1})$, we created an objective function whose input was a vector $\vec{v} \in \mathbb{R}^3$. This objective function should be minimized when $\frac{\vec{v}}{|\vec{v}|} = T(\vec{e_1})$. For this project, we used an objective function that calculated the sum of squared residuals between a histogram generated using the components of the unit normal vectors of the target face scan along $\frac{\vec{v}}{|\vec{v}|}$ and an idealized distribution of a vertically and horizontally scaled secant function. Then, we employed SciPy's optimize module to determine the vector $\vec{v} \in \mathbb{R}^3$ that minimizes the objective function, and let $T(\vec{e_1}) = \frac{\vec{v}}{|\vec{v}|}$.

A similar process was undertaken to determine $T(\vec{e_3})$. In particular, we noted that when $T(\vec{e_3}) = \vec{e_3}$ and when the mesh's normal vectors were oriented such that they point away from the mesh's center of mass, the vast majority of the components of the normal vectors along $T(\vec{e_3})$ were positive. Thus, we first guaranteed that the normal vectors of the face mesh point away from the mesh's center of mass. Then, we defined our objective function with input $\vec{v} \in \mathbb{R}^3$ to be the negative mean of the components of the face mesh's unit normal vectors along $\frac{\vec{v}}{|\vec{v}|}$. This function should be minimized when $\frac{\vec{v}}{|\vec{v}|} = T(\vec{e_3})$. Once again, we used SciPy's optimize module to determine the vector $\vec{v} \in \mathbb{R}^3$ that minimized our objective function. Additionally, when determining $T(\vec{e_3})$, we also enforced the fact that $\left[T(\vec{e_1})\, T(\vec{e_3})\right]$ is a set of orthonormal vectors. To do so, we let $\vec{u} = \vec{v} - comp_{T(\vec{e_1})}\vec{v}$ and let $T(\vec{e_3}) = \frac{\vec{u}}{|\vec{u}|}$. Finally, since $\left[T(\vec{e_1})\, T(\vec{e_2})\, T(\vec{e_3})\right]$ forms an orthonormal set of vectors, we knew that $T(\vec{e_2}) = T(\vec{e_1}) \times T(\vec{e_3})$ or $T(\vec{e_2}) = T(\vec{e_3}) \times T(\vec{e_1})$. To complete the construction of $\left[T(\vec{e_1})\, T(\vec{e_2})\, T(\vec{e_3})\right]^{-1}$, we initially chose $T(\vec{e_2}) = T(\vec{e_1}) \times T(\vec{e_3})$. After determining

$\left[T(\vec{e_1})\ T(\vec{e_2})\ T(\vec{e_3}) \right]^{-1}$, we found F_0. The results for this rotation from F_1 back to F_0 were not always satisfactory after a single iteration. Accordingly, we repeated the process for finding $\left[T(\vec{e_1})\ T(\vec{e_2})\ T(\vec{e_3}) \right]^{-1}$ outlined above until we reached an iteration where each of $T(\vec{e_1})$, $T(\vec{e_2})$, and $T(\vec{e_3})$ laid on approximately the same lines as the $\vec{e_1}$, $\vec{e_2}$, and $\vec{e_3}$. More concretely, if we let M be the element-wise absolute value of $\left[T(\vec{e_1})\ T(\vec{e_2})\ T(\vec{e_3}) \right]^{-1}$, we iterated until the norm of $M - I_{3,3}$ was within a certain tolerance of 0. Finally, to complete the process of orienting the target face scan into a standard position, we corrected for the arbitrary choice of $T(\vec{e_2})$ we made earlier. In particular, we first located the tip of the nose or pronasal as the point with the largest z-value from all the points within the face scan. Then, we examined the set of points in the neighborhood of the pronasal, dividing this set of points into two subsets: the set of points with a larger y-value than the pronasal and the set of points with a smaller y-value than the pronasal. We then approximated the derivative of z with respect to y (z_y) at each of these points using the unit normal vectors. In particular, if the unit normal vector at a given point $\vec{n} = [n_x, n_y, n_z]^T$, we found that $z_y = -\frac{n_y}{n_z}$. Using z_y calculated at each point, we calculated the mean magnitude of z_y, $|z_y|$, for both the points with larger y-values than the pronasal and the points with smaller y-values than the pronasal. If our choice for $T(\vec{e_2})$ was correct, we should find that $|z_y|$ for the points below the pronasal is larger than $|z_y|$ for the points above the pronasal. When $|z_y|$ for the points above the pronasal was larger than $|z_y|$ for the points below the pronasal, we flipped the face mesh we obtained after finding $\left[T(\vec{e_1})\ T(\vec{e_2})\ T(\vec{e_3}) \right]^{-1}$ about the xz-plane.

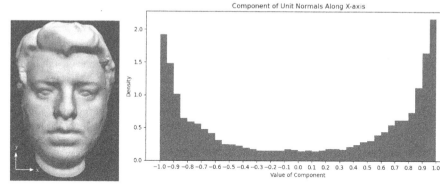

(a) The orientation of x and y axes for face scans.

(b) The distribution of unit normal components along $T(\boldsymbol{e_1})$.

Fig. 5. To orient the face into the standard position we used a linear transformation that rotates the points of the 3D scan. To determine the vector that points in the positive x-direction we used the fact that the components of the face mesh's unit normal vectors along $\vec{e_1}$ generally formed a bowl-shaped distribution.

2. Identify Geometric Descriptors. After a target face scan was rotated into the standard orientation, geometric descriptors of the target face that were needed for locating landmarks were calculated. Specifically, the following geometric descriptors were calculated: the first derivatives of z; the second derivatives of z; the coefficients of the first fundamental form, E, F, and G; the coefficients of the second fundamental form, L, M, N; the first derivatives of the coefficients of the first and second fundamental forms; the second derivatives of the coefficients of the first and second fundamental forms; the Gaussian curvature, K; the mean curvature, H; the maximum and minimum principal curvatures; the curvedness index, C; and the shape index, S. A detailed description of the geometric descriptors excluding C and S can be found in [26]. The descriptors C and S are detailed in [19]. Of the descriptors that may be unfamiliar, the descriptor S deserved special attention. The descriptor S can vary within the range $[-1, 1]$, and different values within this range specify different shapes of the surface. In particular, if $S \approx -1$ for a point, the shape of the surface at that point is a cup or a depression. On the other hand, if $S \approx 1$ at a point, the surface at that point is a dome. If $S \approx 0$ at a point, the surface at that point is a saddle. To calculate the first and second derivatives, we first stored the z-values of the points within the face scan as a data array of a PyVista PolyData object [30] that represented the face scan. Then, we projected the mesh onto the xy-plane and applied PyVista's `compute_derivative` function [30] on our stored z-values to calculate the first derivatives of z. To compute the second derivatives of z, we simply applied the `compute_derivative` function to our calculated first derivatives. All the remaining geometric descriptors were calculated by simply applying their respective formulas after the first and second derivatives of z were calculated. Finally, after all the geometric descriptors were calculated, a second PyVista PolyData object [30] was created as a deep copy of the face scan. For this PolyData object, the values for each geometric descriptor were scaled such that a given value was replaced by that value's z-score. This is the "scaled face mesh," and the geometric descriptors for this mesh are the "scaled geometric descriptors."

3. Find Landmarks of Interest. After the geometric descriptors were calculated for the target face mesh in standard orientation, the points of interest for each landmark could be located. Given a landmark, that landmark's points of interest are the set of points whose geometric descriptors were highly similar to the geometric descriptors of the landmark. To search for points of interest, we outlined a set of criteria involving the geometric descriptors (step 2, above), and we selected the following points of interest.

- **Pronasal.** The pronasal is unique in that it had only one point of interest. We specify that the point in the oriented target face scan with the largest z-value is the point of interest for the pronasal. Because there was only one point of interest, this point was automatically the predicted location of the pronasal landmark.
- **Endocanthions.** To find the points of interest for the endocanthions or the inner eye corners, we first filtered the points within the face scan using the following two requirements. First, the shape indices, S, for points of interest must be within the range $[-1, -0.375)$, and second, the points of interest for the endocanthions must be above the pronasal, with a distance from the pronasal between 7.5% and 20% of the range of y-values for the points within the mesh. After the points have been filtered by these initial two requirements, we calculated $z_x^2 + z_y^2$ for every remaining point and kept only the 10% of the points that passed through the initial filter with the smallest values for $z_x^2 + z_y^2$. Then, we partitioned the remaining points into two sets: points with x-values smaller than that of the pronasal (i.e. points to the left of the pronasal) and points with x-values larger than that of the pronasal (i.e. points to

the right of the pronasal). Finally, for each of these two sets of points, we selected the $\frac{1}{1000}n$ points with the largest Gaussian curvatures, K, where n is the number of points in the mesh (which had possibly been clipped during the calculation of geometric descriptors). Finally, we returned these two sets of selected points as the points of interest for the endocanthions. An example of the points of interest (POIs) for the endocanthions is shown in Fig. 6a.

– **Cheilions.** To find the points of interest for the cheilions or the corners of the mouth, we first filtered the points within the face on the basis of their position relative to the pronasal. In particular, we only considered points whose distances along the x-axis from the pronasal exceeded 10% of the range of the x-values in the face mesh. Additionally, we required that points of interest had smaller y-values than the pronasal and that points of interest were at least a distance of 10% of the range of the y-values in the face mesh from the pronasal in the y-direction. We also required that the distance between points of interest and the pronasal in the z-direction was no more than 25% of the range of the z-values in the face mesh. Next, of the points whose positions relative to the pronasal were valid, we selected only the points whose shape indices were in the range $(-1, 0)$. We then partitioned the remaining points based on whether they lie to the left (smaller x-values than the pronasal) or to the right (larger x-values than the pronasal) of the pronasal. Finally, we selected the 50% of points within each of the two sets with the largest curvedness indices, C, and returned these points as points of interest for the cheilions. An example of the points of interest (POIs) for the cheilions is shown in Fig. 6b.

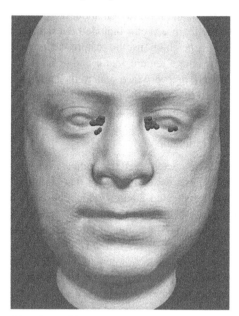 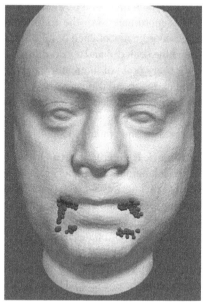

(a) Points of interest for the endocanthions or the inner eye corners.

(b) Points of interest for the cheilions or the corners of the mouth.

Fig. 6. Since many points fit the criteria set forth, it is necessary to refine them to obtain the final predicted location of the landmark.

4. Landmark Refinement. After finding the points of interest for a given landmark, it's generally necessary to refine these points of interest to obtain the final predicted location of the landmark. The first step in refining a given landmark's location was the use of a regression model that predicts each point of interest's distance from the actual location of the landmark. After this regression was complete, the results of the regression model and the results of an application of clustering to the points of interest were combined to deduce the final predicated location of the landmark.

5. Regression Model Training. To conduct landmark refinement as described above, it was necessary to train a regression model for each landmark that can predict the Euclidean distance between the actual location of the landmark and a given point of interest for this landmark. The first step in creating these regression models for landmark refinement was the acquisition of a dataset with labelled landmarks. We used the Texas 3D Face Recognition Database (Texas3DFRD) [14, 15]. In particular, the 2D representations of 3D face scans from the Texas3DFRD were converted to 3D face scans using 3DDFA_V2 [12,13]. Then, the face landmarks for the faces in the database were extracted by projecting the landmarks generated by 3DDFA_V2 onto the surface of the face meshes. After the acquisition of a dataset of annotated 3D face scans, the training of the regression models for each landmark could commence. First, the points of interest for a target landmark were found on each face within the database of annotated 3D face scans. Then, for each point of interest, a feature vector was generated. This feature vector contained the scaled geometric descriptors associated with this point of interest, the Euclidean distance from this point of interest to the target landmark's location on the face from which this point of interest was extracted, and information about the point of interest's coordinates. For the endocanthions, the feature vector included the scaled x, y, and z coordinates of each point of interest. For the cheilions, the feature vector only included the scaled x and z coordinates. Finally, after a feature vector had been generated for every point of interest for a given landmark on every face scan in the annotated face database, an AdaBoost regressor was trained to regress the target variable, which is the Euclidean distance between a point of interest and the actual landmark location. This AdaBoost regressor used a decision tree regressor of maximum depth 20 as its base regressor and contained an ensemble of 50 estimators.

6. Landmark Refinement on a Query Face. Having determined the points of interests for a given landmark on a query face and trained a regression model for that landmark, the points of interests were refined into a final predicated landmark location by first predicting the Euclidean distance from each point of interest to the actual landmark location using the regression model. Then, we clustered the points of interest based on their x, y, and z coordinates using the OPTICS algorithm. The minimum cluster size we used with OPTICS was $\frac{1}{2}m$, where m is the number of points of interest. Next, for each cluster, we determined the median predicted Euclidean distance between the points of interest within the cluster and the actual landmark. We then selected the cluster with the minimum median predicted Euclidean distance between the points of interest within the cluster and the actual landmark. Finally, the predicted location of the landmark on the query face was determined by calculating the median x, y, and z coordinates for the points of interest in the selected cluster and then projecting the point composed of the median coordinates onto the query face using a nearest-neighbor search.

3   Results and Discussion

3.1   2D Facial Landmarks Annotation

Figure 1d shows the distribution of the three distances across the selected images from the three databases. The forehead varies between about a fourth and a third of the face, with the mean around 30%. The nose has a wider distribution, with lengths between about 25% and 38%, and a mean closer to one third. The mouth seems to be the longest of the three distances, with lengths between about 32% and 45% of the vertical length of the face, and a mean of about 38%.

One of the confounding factors of these variations is the resolution of the images used in our analysis. Images with lower resolution lead to bigger influence on the misplacement of the landmarks, since 1 or 2 extra pixels could increase or decrease a distance by about 4%, whereas images with higher resolution suffer less from such a misplacement. To evaluate this impact we plotted the density distributions for each dataset separately, as shown in Fig. 3. While there doesn't seem to be significant differences in the lengths of forehead and nose, across the three datasets, the length of the mouth seems to have more variance for images with lower resolution, than for images with higher resolution.

Nonetheless, one thing that is common across these density plots is the fact that these distances are not equal, as stated in the neoclassical canon, but rather that they have a range of values, with longer length for mouth than for nose and forehead. This suggests that this canon is not valid, and therefore should be used with caution.

This analysis would require further evaluation, as many groups were not well represented in these datasets: there were very few children, very few people over the age of 80, and a relatively small proportion of women. In addition, many ethnicities have very minor representation or none at all. When creating a new dataset with a wider representation, we also recommend collecting metadata about the images, which should include the details about each individual, such as age, race, whether they have all teeth or if they have dentures, which is difficult to determine from these images.

3.2   3D Facial Landmarks Annotation

Figure 7 shows the results of the landmark placement for three faces in neutral expressions. Figure 8 shows the results of the landmark placement for three smiling faces. From the results of using the proposed method for landmarking 3D scans, it's clear that the pronasal and endocanthions are placed more accurately than the cheilions. There may be multiple reasons for this discrepancy.

First, the regression models for the cheilions were trained without including any information about the y-coordinates of the points of interest. The absence of y-coordinate information was motivated by the fact that the collapsed mouths of edentulous patients distort the y-coordinate information of points near their mouths, so training with y-coordinate information using a training set of people without collapsed mouths could lead to overfitting.

Second, it was difficult to pinpoint the points of interest for the cheilions. In particular, in order to obtain all points in the region around the corners of the mouth, the criteria for determining points of interest had to be loosened, which caused points too close to the center of the face and points below the lower lip to be included as candidates for the cheilions. For an example of this phenomenon, see Fig. 6b.

Although we were able to correctly identify some of the facial landmarks, i.e., the tip of the nose, the inner corner of the eyes, and the mouth corners, more work is needed to identify other landmarks needed for the automatic placement of the four lines shown in Fig. 1. For example, we still need to identify the top of the forehead, the nose bridge (or the proxy points used instead: the left- and right-temple, and the left- and right-exterior eyebrow), the nose base (or the proxy points used instead: left- and right-base of the nose), and the tip of the chin. This is left for future work.

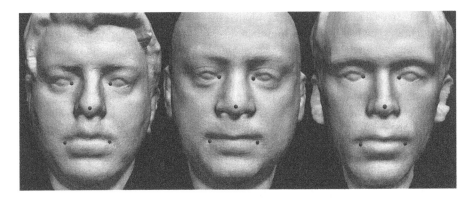

Fig. 7. Face landmarks placement for neutral facial expressions. The pronasal (tip of the nose) and endocanthions (inner eye-corners) are placed more accurately than the cheilions (mouth corners).

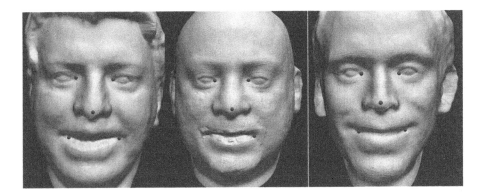

Fig. 8. Face landmarks placement for smiling facial expressions. The tip of the nose and inner eye-corners are not affected by the smile, whereas mouth corners are less accurate than in the neutral face expressions.

4 Related Work

4.1 2D Facial Landmarks Annotation

In [9], Farkas *et al.* first investigated the applicability of the neoclassical facial canons in young North American Caucasian adults. Following this, the canons were also validated on several other population groups including Nigerians, African-Americans, Turkish, Vietnamese, Thai, and Chinese individuals. These studies were performed by adopting the standard anthropometric methods where the measurements were obtained using anthropometric tools like millimetric compass, sliding calipers, etc. Some studies have also used images pre-annotated with the anthropometric landmarks.

In [4], Bozkir *et al.* evaluated the vertical and horizontal neoclassical facial canons in Turkish young adults. They used a millimetric compass to manually measure these distances and found that only one male face had an equally divided facial profile. Thus, the neoclassical canons are not valid for the majority of the population, and vary among races and countries.

In [2], Al-Sebaei evaluated the vertical canon, the orbital canon and the orbito-nasal canon in young adults from the Arabian Peninsula. They measured these distances using a caliper and analyzed them using student's t-test, general linear modeling, and pairwise comparison of means. They found that not only all three canons had variations in measurements, the lower and upper thirds were also longer than the middle thirds, the intercanthal distance was wider than eye fissure length and the nasal width was wider than the intercanthal distance.

In [7], Eboh studied young adults in South-Nigerian ethnic groups, Izon and Urhobo, to determine if there is a variation in length among the upper, middle and lower thirds of the face. They measured these distances using a sliding caliper and analyzed the results using descriptive and inferential statistics. They also found that the three thirds of the face varied in lengths. The mean lengths of the upper and lower thirds were significantly longer in the Izon than the Urhobo, while the mean height of the middle third was significantly longer in the Urhobo than the Izon. The mean height of the male lower third was significantly longer in the Izon than the Urhobo, while Urhobo females had significant longer middle third than the Izon.

In [29], Schmid *et al.* developed a model to predict the attractiveness of the face based on neoclassical canons, symmetry and golden ratios. They used the feature point database that has the locations of points for the faces from the FERET database and the faces of famous people. Their experiment showed that the vertical canon had a significant relationship with attractiveness, and the attractiveness scores decreased significantly as the proportions of the face deviated from the proportions defined by the canons.

In [28], Pavlic *et al.* explored the presence of neoclassical canons of facial beauty among young people in Croatia, and checked for any possible psychosocial repercussions for those with deviations from canons. They analyzed nine neoclassical canons on a sample of 249 people with face and profile photographs taken in natural head position. They found that there were significant deviations from neoclassical facial beauty canons in 55–65% of adolescents and young adults, and gender and age showed no relation to deviations. Most of the deviations from canons that affected the quality of life were the ones related to proportions of facial thirds.

In [20], Le *et al.* evaluated six neoclassical canons among healthy young adult Chinese, Vietnamese and Thais by taking nine projective linear measurements, using standard anthropometric methods, corresponding to six neoclassical facial canons. They found that in neither Asian nor Caucasian subjects the three sections of the facial profile were equal.

In [5], Burusapat and Lekdaeng did a comparative study among sixteen Miss Universe and sixteen Miss Universe Thailand, using neoclassical canons and facial golden ratios to find out the most beautiful facial proportion in the 21st century. They measured the distances and angles from photographs, and found that the three-section proportion was longer in Miss Universe Thailand than in Miss Universe group.

In [3], Amirkhanov *et al.* proposed a solution for integrating aesthetics analytics into the functional workflow of dental technicians. They presented a teeth pose estimation technique that can generate denture previews and visualizations. Dental technicians can use this technique to design the denture by considering the aesthetics and choosing the most aesthetically fitting preset from a library of dentures. The dental technician had to use the facial and dental proportions to identify the correspondence between the denture and the face, which means that it is important to have the facial proportions correct for the denture to fit well on a patient.

4.2 3D Facial Landmarks Annotation

Vezzetti and Marcolin proposed a method for detecting landmarks on 3D face scans that used measurements such as the first, second, and mixed derivatives; the coefficients of the first and second fundamental forms; the maximum and minimum principal curvatures; the Gaussian and mean curvatures; and the Shape and Curvedness Indices [33]. With these descriptors in hand, Vezzetti and Marcolin developed a two-stage process for identifying face landmarks. First, the above descriptors were used to select a subset of the points within a given 3D face scan that were candidates for the target landmark. Then, among these candidate points, one of the features, typically a coefficient of a fundamental form, was maximized or minimized to finalize the location of the target landmark. Nine landmarks located in the vicinity of the nose and eyes were detected; however, in this work they did not specify a process for finding landmarks located near the mouth or brow.

This omission was rectified by another work by Vezzetti and Marcolin [34]. In this paper, they employed a method similar to the method utilized in their previous paper to detect landmarks around the mouth and brow on 3D face scans. Although the core of their technique remained unchanged, one addition they applied to their method was the inclusion of a point's position relative to previously located landmarks when evaluating that point's candidacy for the target landmark.

Liu *et al.* devised a strategy that fully integrated global and local constraints to locate landmarks on 3D face scans [21]. In particular, for a given target landmark, they specified the position of the target relative to previously located landmarks as the global constraints and used thresholds on the same geometric descriptors used in [33] as the local constraints. Their method differed from Vezzetti's and Marcolin's as it relied on a more varied array of descriptors when conducting the optimization necessary for finalizing landmark locations.

Galvanek *et al.* proposed another method for finding 3D face landmarks that combined both global and local constraints [10]. Similar to previously mentioned papers, they based the search for landmarks off of the positions of theses landmarks relative to the pronasal. However, unlike the methods from the previously mentioned papers, they employed only the maximum and minimum principal curvatures as the local constraints and independently calculated these curvatures for each landmark it located. Moreover, landmarks located in the center of the face (e.g., labrum superior, nasion, etc.) were extracted by determining the locations of local minima and maxima along the symmetry profile of the face.

While many of the above methods used the same or very similar geometric descriptors, it is an open question whether there exists more powerful descriptors that have yet to be wielded in the pursuit of locating landmarks on 3D face scans. To provide insight into this question, Marcolin and Vezzetti, investigated the utility of new descriptors generated from the aforementioned base geometric properties (derivatives, coefficients of the fundamental forms, curvatures, etc.) [22]. Specifically, they derived new descriptors from the base properties through the application of a function like mean, median, natural logarithm, sine, cosine, tangent, arcsine, arcosine, or arctangent, and created new descriptors by taking linear combinations, fractions, products, etc. of the base properties. They found that some of the new descriptors were more powerful than the original base properties because these new descriptors either highlighted the dividing line between different regions of the face or varied their behavior across the face in a manner that allowed for the easy identification of different regions of the face.

Outside of methods for landmark detection on 3D face scans that require researcher-inputted criteria, there are also methods that learn the criteria for landmark detection from a set of training data. These methods can be divided into two categories: those that use convolutional neural networks (CNNs) for landmark localization and those that do not. Many 3D face landmarking techniques that rely on CNNs use 2D representations of 3D face scans. This is because a volumetric CNN that could operate on detailed 3D face scans would consume too much memory to be practical [27]. Thus, the methods proposed in [27, 32, 36] all first created 2D representations of the 3D face scans before detecting landmarks.

There are multiple approaches to creating these 2D representations of 3D faces. For example, Pales *et al.* extracted 2D representations of 3D face scans by using a multiple-view approach, where images of a particular face scan were captured from different perspectives [27]. On the other hand, a single-view approach was proposed in [32, 36]. Specifically, Zhang *et al.* [36], first determined the orientation of the 3D face scan before rotating the face into a standard position and projecting the face onto a 2D surface. In all three papers, after 2D representations of the 3D face scans were obtained, landmarking occurred on the 2D representations using CNN. These landmarks were then projected back into 3D. In [32, 36], this projection of the detected 2D landmarks into 3D was a relatively straightforward inversion of the 3D to 2D projection. However, in [27], this inverse projection was complicated by the need to correspond the 3D landmark location for a given landmark with the 2D landmark locations for that landmark from multiple views. To accomplish this task, Paulsen *et al.* converted each 2D landmark detected across the multiple views into a line in 3D. Then, to determine the location of a given 3D landmark, the lines derived from the 2D locations of this landmark were intersected.

Similar to the above CNN-based methods, the Gabor wavelet-based approach described in [17] also used 2D representations of 3D face scans. In that approach, the face was first registered by fitting it to an ellipsoid. Then, a Mercator projection was used to project the 3D face scan onto the ellipsoid, and five different 2D maps were extracted. These maps corresponded to texture, height of the scan above the ellipsoid (relief map), derivatives with respect to the x and y axes, and the Laplacian of Gaussian. After these maps were extracted, an Elastic Bunch Graph Matching (EBGM) algorithm for 2D face landmark detection was employed to detect the locations of the landmarks in 2D. Then, the locations of these 2D landmarks were projected back into 3D using the height above the ellipsoid stored in the relief map. As with the approach described in [17], the three-stage process described in [31] also used 2D representations of face scans during a portion of its landmark localization. They first used curvature to pinpoint the location of the tip of the nose and the inner corners of the eyes. Then, maps describing the x, y, and z components of the normal vectors were generated, and an Active Normal Model was trained to locate the face landmarks. As a final step, local binary features and cascaded regression were combined to tune the landmark locations predicted by the Active Normal Model.

Another approach that makes use of local binary patterns is the approach described in [8]. The authors built a constrained local model (CLM), which used patch experts to determine the probability that all landmarks were placed correctly by analyzing features in the local region that surrounded the predicted location of each landmark. In particular, the patch experts used included three histogram-based descriptors: mesh local binary patterns (mesh-LBP), mesh scale-invariant feature transform (mesh-SIFT), and mesh histogram of gradients (mesh-HOG). Mesh-LBP operated by determining whether a given scalar value (such as curvature) exceeded a designated threshold for a set of facets arranged in a ring around the target landmark. Mesh-SIFT built histograms using the descriptors of shape index and slant angle for a set of circular regions around the target landmark. And mesh-HOG built histograms by measuring the gradient of a scalar function such as curvature in a circular region around the target landmark.

The approach described in [6] is another approach that employed a CLM. However, in this work the authors emphasized the use of features derived from the face scans' normal vectors as patch experts. Specifically, they created a histogram of normal vectors to describe the normal vectors of the cells near each landmark and used local normal binary patterns, which calculated histograms for the landmarks based on how closely the normal vectors for a ring of cells around the landmark aligned with the normal vector at the landmark.

Unlike the previous two approaches, the approaches outlined in [11] and [1] did not build CLMs. Instead, the approach in [11] sampled points from both high and low curvature regions of the face and built a mean face by corresponding these sampled points across its training faces through the minimization of bending energy. Then, to determine the locations of landmarks on a target 3D face scan, the mean face was reshaped through rigid transformations and non-rigid deformations. The final landmark locations were determined by using a nearest-neighbor search from the morphed mean face to the target face.

In a similar vein, the approach outline in [1] generated a template mesh by placing and corresponding 16 anatomical landmarks and 484 randomly and uniformly distributed semi-landmarks on each training face. Then, target faces were landmarked by fitting the template mesh to the target mesh through six iterations of bending energy minimization, which ultimately allowed for the extraction of landmarks.

5   Conclusions and Future Work

The face proportions defined by the neoclassical canons have been recommended in textbooks on orthodontics, prosthodontics, plastic and dental reconstructive surgeries. We tested their hypothesis of the face being vertically divided equally into thirds, on 2D images, using machine learning. Our results indicate that not all faces are equally divided into thirds. Thus, this vertical canon should be used with caution in cosmetic, plastic or dental surgeries or any reconstruction procedures. Also, while placing the landmarks automatically on 2D images, we found that the landmarks were inaccurate due to pose sensitivity. Hence, we recommend to use 3D face scans for improving the design and visualization of dentures.

For future work, there are a couple of avenues that could help remedy the issue of cheilion inaccuracy in 3D facial landmark annotation. For instance, a more selective set of criteria for determining the cheilion points of interest could be developed. Alternatively, feature selection could be applied before the feature vectors for candidate points are fed into the regression model to improve the performance of the regression model.

Outside of correcting the inaccuracy of the cheilions, there exists a plethora of further research that could sprout from this work. With regards to the process used for orienting face scans into the standard position, the current process sometimes requires many iterations to successfully orient the face scan. It would be interesting to explore whether improved objective functions or a more adroit application of numerical optimization could help decrease the time spent orienting the face scan. Alternatively, it may be possible to completely rework the strategy for orienting the face scan. Perhaps the use of a template face mesh and an iterative closest point algorithm could provide an optimal solution.

Another facet of this proposed method that could be examined further is the possibility of reusing a set of points of interest to predict the locations of multiple landmarks. Currently, each set of points of interest is used to predict the location of only one landmark. Accordingly, the detection of a large number of landmarks is prohibitively time-consuming because researchers need to specify a new set of point of interest criteria for each new landmark detected. If the the work in [22] concerning the use of geometric descriptors to locate different regions of the face could be extended and combined with a refinement procedure capable of discerning multiple different landmarks from the same set of points of interest, the procedure outlined within this paper could be used to detect a much larger number of face landmarks without a commensurate increase in time and effort invested by researchers.

Acknowledgements. This work was supported in part by NSF REU grant #2050883.

References

1. Agbolade, O., Nazri, A., Yaakob, R., Ghani, A.A., Kqueen Cheah, Y.: Homologous multi-points warping: an algorithm for automatic 3D facial landmark. In: 2019 IEEE International Conference on Automatic Control and Intelligent Systems (I2CACIS), pp. 79–84 (2019). https://doi.org/10.1109/I2CACIS.2019.8825072
2. Al-Sebaei, M.O.: The validity of three neo-classical facial canons in young adults originating from the Arabian peninsula. Head Face Med. **11**(1), 1–7 (2015)
3. Amirkhanov, A., et al.: Visual analytics in dental aesthetics. In: Computer Graphics Forum, vol. 39, pp. 635–646. Wiley Online Library (2020)
4. Bozkir, M., Karakas, P., Oguz, Ö.: Vertical and horizontal neoclassical facial canons in Turkish young adults. Surg. Radiol. Anat. **26**(3), 212–219 (2004)
5. Burusapat, C., Lekdaeng, P.: What is the most beautiful facial proportion in the 21st century? Comparative study among miss universe, miss universe Thailand, neoclassical canons, and facial golden ratios. Plast. Reconstr. Surg. Glob. Open **7**(2) (2019)
6. Cheng, S., Zafeiriou, S., Asthana, A., Pantic, M.: 3D facial geometric features for constrained local model. In: 2014 IEEE International Conference on Image Processing (ICIP) (2014). https://doi.org/10.1109/icip.2014.7025285
7. Eboh, D.E.O.: Horizontal facial thirds of young adults in two south-south Nigerian ethnic groups. Anat. Biol. Anthropol. **32**(4), 115–119 (2019)
8. El Rai, M.C., Tortorici, C., Al-Muhairi, H., Al Safar, H., Werghi, N.: Landmarks detection on 3D face scans using local histogram descriptors. In: 2016 18th Mediterranean Electrotechnical Conference (MELECON), pp. 1–5 (2016). https://doi.org/10.1109/MELCON.2016.7495382
9. Farkas, L.G., Hreczko, T.A., Kolar, J.C., Munro, I.R.: Vertical and horizontal proportions of the face in young adult north American Caucasians: revision of neoclassical canons. Plast. Reconstr. Surg. **75**(3), 328–338 (1985)
10. Galvánek, M., Furmanová, K., Chalás, I., Sochor, J.: Automated facial landmark detection, comparison and visualization. In: Proceedings of the 31st Spring Conference on Computer Graphics, SCCG 2015, pp. 7–14. Association for Computing Machinery, New York (2015). https://doi.org/10.1145/2788539.2788540
11. Gilani, S.Z., Shafait, F., Mian, A.: Shape-based automatic detection of a large number of 3D facial landmarks. In: 2015 IEEE Conference on Computer Vision and Pattern Recognition (CVPR) (2015). https://doi.org/10.1109/cvpr.2015.7299095
12. Guo, J., Zhu, X., Lei, Z.: 3DDFA (2018). https://github.com/cleardusk/3DDFA
13. Guo, J., Zhu, X., Yang, Y., Yang, F., Lei, Z., Li, S.Z.: Towards fast, accurate and stable 3D dense face alignment. In: Proceedings of the European Conference on Computer Vision (ECCV) (2020)
14. Gupta, S., Castleman, K.R., Markey, M.K., Bovik, A.C.: Texas 3D face recognition database. In: 2010 IEEE Southwest Symposium on Image Analysis & Interpretation (SSIAI), pp. 97–100. IEEE (2010)
15. Gupta, S., Markey, M.K., Bovik, A.C.: Anthropometric 3D face recognition. Int. J. Comput. Vision **90**(3), 331–349 (2010)
16. Huang, G.B., Ramesh, M., Berg, T., Learned-Miller, E.: Labeled faces in the wild: a database for studying face recognition in unconstrained environments. Technical report, 07-49, University of Massachusetts, Amherst (2007)
17. de Jong, M.A., et al.: An automatic 3D facial landmarking algorithm using 2D Gabor wavelets. IEEE Trans. Image Process. **25**(2), 580–588 (2016). https://doi.org/10.1109/TIP.2015.2496183
18. King, D.E.: Dlib-ml: a machine learning toolkit. J. Mach. Learn. Res. **10**, 1755–1758 (2009)

19. Koenderink, J.J., van Doorn, A.J.: Surface shape and curvature scales. Image Vis. Comput. **10**, 557–564 (1992)

20. Le, T.T., Farkas, L.G., Ngim, R.C., Levin, L.S., Forrest, C.R.: Proportionality in Asian and North American Caucasian faces using neoclassical facial canons as criteria. Aesthetic Plast. Surg. **26**(1), 64–69 (2002)

21. Liu, J., Zhang, Q., Tang, C.: Automatic landmark detection for high resolution non-rigid 3D faces based on geometric information. In: 2015 IEEE Advanced Information Technology, Electronic and Automation Control Conference (IAEAC) (2015). https://doi.org/10.1109/iaeac.2015.7428562

22. Marcolin, F., Vezzetti, E.: Novel descriptors for geometrical 3D face analysis. Multimedia Tools Appl. **76**(12), 13805–13834 (2016). https://doi.org/10.1007/s11042-016-3741-3

23. Mehta, A., Abdelaal, M., Sheba, M., Herndon, N.: Automated neoclassical vertical canon validation in human faces with machine learning. In: Proceedings of the 11th International Conference on Data Science, Technology and Applications - Volume 1: DATA, pp. 461–467. INSTICC, SciTePress (2022). https://doi.org/10.5220/0011300200003269

24. Milborrow, S., Morkel, J., Nicolls, F.: The MUCT Landmarked Face Database. Pattern Recognition Association of South Africa (2010). http://www.milbo.org/muct

25. Mutsvangwa, T., et al.: Design, construction, and testing of a stereo-photogrammetric tool for the diagnosis of fetal alcohol syndrome in infants. IEEE Trans. Med. Imaging **28**(9), 1448–1458 (2009). https://doi.org/10.1109/tmi.2009.2017375

26. Patrikalakis, N.M., Maekawa, T.: Shape interrogation for computer aided design and manu-facturing (2010). https://doi.org/10.1007/978-3-642-04074-0

27. Paulsen, R.R., Juhl, K.A., Haspang, T.M., Hansen, T.F., Ganz, M., Einarsson, G.: Multi-view consensus CNN for 3D facial landmark placement. CoRR abs/1910.06007 (2019). http://arxiv.org/abs/1910.06007

28. Pavlic, A., Zrinski, M.T., Katic, V., Spalj, S.: Neoclassical canons of facial beauty: do we see the deviations? J. Cranio-Maxillofac. Surg. **45**(5), 741–747 (2017)

29. Schmid, K., Marx, D., Samal, A.: Computation of a face attractiveness index based on neo-classical canons, symmetry, and golden ratios. Pattern Recogn. **41**(8), 2710–2717 (2008)

30. Sullivan, C.B., Kaszynski, A.: PyVista: 3D plotting and mesh analysis through a streamlined interface for the visualization toolkit (VTK). J. Open Source Softw. **4**(37), 1450 (2019). https://doi.org/10.21105/joss.01450

31. Sun, J., Huang, D., Wang, Y., Chen, L.: Expression robust 3D facial landmarking via pro-gressive coarse-to-fine tuning. ACM Trans. Multimed. Comput. Commun. Appl. **15**(1), 1–23 (2019). https://doi.org/10.1145/3282833

32. Terada, T., Chen, Y.W., Kimura, R.: 3D facial landmark detection using deep convolu-tional neural networks. In: 2018 14th International Conference on Natural Computation, Fuzzy Systems and Knowledge Discovery (ICNC-FSKD) (2018). https://doi.org/10.1109/fskd.2018.8687254

33. Vezzetti, E., Marcolin, F.: Geometry-based 3D face morphology analysis: soft-tissue land-mark formalization. Multimedia Tools Appl. **68**(3), 895–929 (2012). https://doi.org/10.1007/s11042-012-1091-3

34. Vezzetti, E., Marcolin, F.: 3D landmarking in multiexpression face analysis: a preliminary study on eyebrows and mouth. Aesthetic Plast. Surg. **38**(4), 796–811 (2014). https://doi.org/10.1007/s00266-014-0334-2

35. Wang, X., Tang, X.: Face photo-sketch synthesis and recognition. IEEE Trans. Pattern Anal. Mach. Intell. **31**(11), 1955–1967 (2009). https://doi.org/10.1109/TPAMI.2008.222

36. Zhang, J., Gao, K., Zhao, Q., Wang, D.: Pose invariant 3D facial landmark detection via pose normalization and deep regression. In: 2020 2nd International Conference on Image Processing and Machine Vision (2020). https://doi.org/10.1145/3421558.3421570

Combining Image and Text Matching
for Product Classification in Retail*

Sebastian Bast[✉], Christoph Brosch, and Rolf Krieger

Institute for Software Systems, Trier University of Applied Sciences, Birkenfeld, Germany
{s.bast,c.brosch,r.krieger}@umwelt-campus.de

Abstract. The enormous variety of products and their diverse attributes result in a large amount of product data that needs to be managed by retail companies. A single product can have several hundred attributes which are often entered manually. In addition, products have to be classified by hand in many cases by grouping them into categories based on their properties and their relationships to other products. This is a very labor-intensive, time-consuming and error-prone task.

In this paper, we present a hybrid approach for automated product classification, which assigns products automatically to the corresponding product category based on the information on their product images. For this purpose, graphical and textual information is extracted from the product images and matched with already classified data using machine learning methods. Our hybrid approach for automated product classification is based on the Global Product Classification (GPC) standard. Our experiments show that the combination of text-based and image-based classification leads to better results and is a promising approach to reduce the manual effort for product classification in retail.

Keywords: Product classification · Machine learning · Convolutional neural networks · Image matching · Text matching

1 Introduction

High-quality product data is very important for the internal processes of retail companies. Some retailers need to manage several million product records and more than one thousand new product records are created every day. In many cases, incomplete product records must be edited by hand. This process is highly error-prone and can significantly reduce data quality. As a result, retail companies are looking for ways to automate the data entry process. An essential task of this process is the correct assignment of a product to the appropriate category.

In this paper, we investigate the process of automated classification for retail products. We present an approach that can automatically classify products based on the information on product images. For this purpose, we extract image-based and text-based features from the images and compare them with already classified product images to

---

*This scientific work is an extension of the paper "A Hybrid Approach for Product Classification based on Image and Text Matching" by Bast et al. [1].

© The Author(s), under exclusive license to Springer Nature Switzerland AG 2023
A. Cuzzocrea et al. (Eds.): DATA 2021/2022, CCIS 1860, pp. 134–153, 2023.
https://doi.org/10.1007/978-3-031-37890-4_7

derive the correct product classification. In the following, this combination of image-based and text-based classification is denoted as hybrid approach for product classification.

The results in this paper are an extension of our work originally presented in [1], where we introduced a hybrid approach for product classification, which is based on the Global Product Classification (GPC) standard [2]. In this work, we used a larger dataset as the foundation of our experiments to analyze the influence of the size of a dataset on product classification performance. We changed our approach by adding a preprocessing step for standardizing our image data before classification to increase performance. In addition, we conducted an experiment by examining and evaluating the performance of our approach in more detail for each GPC family in the dataset. Furthermore, we describe the implementation of our approach and the performance metrics we used to evaluate our results in more detail. As well, we compare the feature reduction methods Principal Component Analysis (PCA) and Neighborhood Components Analysis (NCA) and analyze their impact on classification performance and runtime.

This paper is structured as follows: First, we give a brief review of the research conducted in the fields of image-based and text-based product classification. In Sect. 3, we describe the underlying product dataset we use in the subsequent sections as the base of our experiments. We describe the architecture of our solution including its components, models, metrics and procedures in Sect. 4. In Sect. 5 we present the results of our experiments. We describe how we tuned the parameters of our models and their impact on classification performance. Furthermore, we describe our hybrid classification approach which combines the image-based and text-based product classification to improve performance. Section 6 concludes with a short summary of our work and a discussion about advantages and disadvantages of our approach. Section 7 is dedicated to ideas for future research.

2 Research Review

Retail companies are looking for ways to increase their level of automation by outsourcing manual activities to information systems. At the same time, they must ensure high data quality. Product classification is a task that is still performed manually in many cases. Products can be classified based on structured data, unstructured data or image data, which contains important product information that can help retail companies to increase their level of automation. Companies use different types of classification systems. Thereby general and company-specific classification systems are distinguished. In this paper we consider the hierarchically structured Global Product Classification (GPC) standard [2] as described in Table 1. This classification system consists of four levels.

Table 1. Structure of the Global Product Classification (GPC) hierarchy.

Hierarchy Level	Frequency	Description	Example
Segment	42	industry sector	Food/Beverage/Tobacco
Family	152	division of a segment	Beverages
Class	922	group of similar categories	Coffee/Coffee Substitutes
Brick	5194	category of similar products	Coffee - Ground Beans

Automated image classification has reached human level performance in certain areas, but there are several problems which need to be solved. A central task of approaches for image-based classification is the extraction of visual features, as these are used to assign an image to a specific class based on pattern recognition. Well-known conventional methods for pattern recognition are algorithms like SIFT, SURF, BRIEF and ORB [3]. These algorithms are based on features that were specified by humans, who set the rules for feature recognition and extraction by hand. However, the manual design of a reliable and robust system for pattern recognition is a very difficult task to solve, since there is an enormous amount of different patterns that all have to be considered. Recent developments in Deep Learning [4] have led to significant improvements in the field of automated image classification by using convolutional neural networks.

In their work on Deep Learning for Retail Product Recognition, Wei et al. identify problem areas that pose significant challenges to researchers [5]. Current challenges are large-scale classification, data limitation, intraclass variation and lack of flexibility.

The first problem is caused by the large number of different product classes which have to be distinguished. The GPC segment Food/Beverage/Tobacco alone consists of 25 GPC families, 137 GPC classes and 884 GPC bricks. In addition to the high product diversity, we also have to deal with dynamic changes, as new products are frequently put on the market and removed from it.

The lack of availability of suitable data, which is also known as data limitation, poses another problem. Convolutional Neural Networks (CNN) require large amounts of already classified image data to classify products with sufficient accuracy. This data has to be generated, annotated and processed, which is a costly and time consuming task.

The third aspect is the differentiation of subcategories. Many classification systems for product data consist of many different categories, which may have several subcategories assigned to them. The degree of difficulty increases from level to level, since the number of classes to be distinguished increases per level, while the visual differences of the products decrease.

The lack of flexibility of artificial neural networks with respect to new products and product categories poses another problem. Changes made to the classification system result in a change of the class assignment. In order to classify product images correctly after the classification system has changed, the CNN used must be trained again with all the data from scratch.

These problems illustrate the need for a flexible approach that can still reliably classify product images despite changes to the classification system or the product assortment. In this work, we classify products based on their images by detecting and matching similar image patterns. The matching is done by comparing their feature vectors [6]. The authors of [7] give a comprehensive overview of handcrafted and trainable image matching techniques. They also describe several image matching-based applications like object recognition, tracking and image retrieval, which is often used in image-based recommender systems and in backward image search engines.

Besides the visual features, product images include texts, which can also be useful for product classification. In [8], the authors compare different machine learning techniques for product classification. The authors of [9] compare the quality of classification models based on short abbreviations text of product names and analyze different strategies for pre-processing. Their text-based model classifies a given product dataset with weighted F1-scores of 0.860 at GPC brick, 0.912 at GPC class and 0.938 at GPC family level. The authors standardized the texts by removing special characters and by transforming uppercase to lowercase letters to increase their classification performance.

In [10] the authors show, that images used in conjunction with the textual product descriptions can improve the precision of the classification task. They achieved a 12% improvement in precision and a 16% improvement in recall compared to methods and approaches that only use textual product descriptions.

3   Dataset

Our experiments are based on 36,624 product data records with corresponding product images provided by a German retailer. The dataset contains 69,256 product images and is denoted as dataset A. This dataset, which was used in [1], was extended by 34,518 images obtained through web crawling. The resulting dataset contains 103.774 product images and is denoted as dataset B.

One goal of the extension was to determine the influence of the image set on the classification result experimentally. The dataset was cleaned before use by removing duplicated and misclassified images manually. In addition, 67.587 texts (dataset A) and 99,494 texts (dataset B) were extracted from our product images. Note that some the images do not contain any text.

The data is labeled based on the Global Product Classification (GPC) standard. Each product image, each text and each product data record is assigned to one specific GPC family, GPC class and GPC brick. The data in our dataset is exclusively assigned to the GPC segment Food/Beverage/Tobacco.

We removed images from the datasets which were assigned to GPC bricks with a total number of less then 10 product images in the corresponding dataset. Table 2 describes the datasets and Fig. 1 illustrates the number of products for each GPC family in dataset B. As shown in Fig. 1 the products are unevenly distributed.

Table 2. Quantity of images, products, texts and labels in dataset A used in [1] and dataset B which we consider in this work additionally.

type	quantity	
	dataset A	dataset B
images	69.256	103.774
texts	67.587	99.494
products	36.624	36.624
GPC bricks	197	216
GPC classes	73	78
GPC families	20	20
GPC segments	1	1

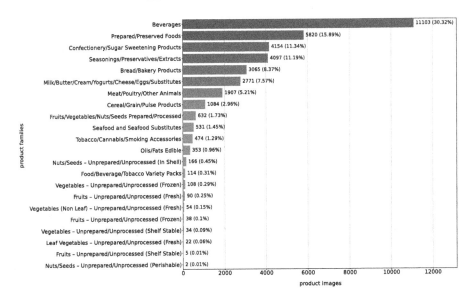

Fig. 1. Number of products per GPC family (dataset B).

Fig. 2. Examples of product images showing a product on a neutral background.

Most of the product images in our datasets show a single product on a white background (Fig. 2). These images are of the types Functional Product Image and Primary Product Image [11]. Also the images in our datasets are unevenly distributed, as shown by the frequency distribution per GPC family for dataset B in Fig. 3.

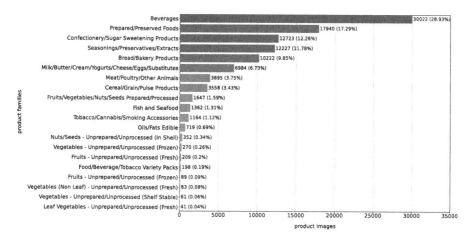

Fig. 3. Distribution of product images per GPC family in dataset B.

4   Methods

In this section, we describe the design of our approach for product classification based on image and text matching.

4.1   Image-Based Product Classification

Figure 4 illustrates the image-based approach, which classifies products according to the Global Product Classification (GPC) standard. The approach is based on the extraction of rich features from product images and the classification of the extracted features based on similarities.

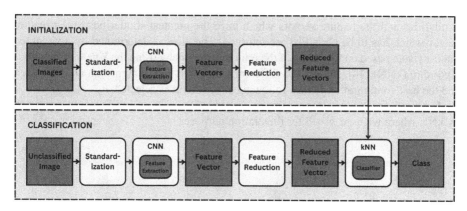

Fig. 4. Overview of our image-based approach.

In the initialization phase we generate feature vectors for every product image in the considered dataset and save them together with the corresponding labels. This data is our search space. It provides the base for all future product classifications. In the classification phase, the visual features are extracted from an unclassified image. Then we compare these features to all the features in our search space, which was created in the initialization step. Afterwards the extracted vectors are matched with the features in our search space.

Standardization. In the first step, the dataset is standardized by removing unnecessary information from the product images. During the standardization task unimportant information is removed by trimming the edges of our images without distorting them. The main idea behind the standardization task is to increase the classification performance by extracting the products from our images. Here we have used the standard operations for image manipulation as described in [12].

Feature Extraction. The process of feature extraction has to be done by a reliable and robust method, which is able to extract all key elements and every important piece of necessary information from our product images. A convolutional neural network [13] is used for feature extraction because of its proven capabilities in this field. In addition, we relied on transfer learning [14] by using weights which were already pre-trained on the ImageNet dataset [15].

Feature Reduction. For each image in the given dataset, a feature vector is calculated and added to the search space. Each of the vectors contains up to 2048 elements. This can slow down the classification runtime when dealing with very large image datasets, as the classification process compares each vector in the search space to the vector of the image that has to be classified. Therefore, we investigated how reducing the elements in the feature vectors affects the performance of our approach in classification. Principal Component Analysis [16] and Neighborhood Components Analysis [17] were used for feature reduction. Their impact on classification performance is described in Sect. 5.2.

Image Classification. The classification of a feature vector is done based on comparisons with the feature vectors in our search space. The search space is screened for similarities and the feature vectors which have the greatest similarities to the feature vector which has to be classified are returned. The class is determined by a weighted majority vote based on the labels of the returned vectors by using the k nearest neighbor algorithm (kNN) [18]. In Sect. 5.1 different parameters of the algorithm are compared and the best configuration for the following experiments is selected.

Figures 5 and 6 illustrate two image classification tasks and their results predicted by kNN where we used $k = 3$ for illustration purposes.

Fig. 5. Unclassified product image (left) and three predicted nearest neighbors with their corresponding brick codes ordered by their distance in ascending order.

| 10000144 | 10000144 | 10000201 | 10000266 |

Fig. 6. Unclassified product image (left) and three predicted nearest neighbors with their corresponding brick codes ordered by their distance in ascending order. Two predicted brick codes do not match with the brick code of the unclassified image.

The images on the left show the unclassified product image and its brick code. The three following images show the predictions sorted by their euclidean distance to the unclassified image in ascending order. In Fig. 5 all predicted brick codes are equal. Therefore the predicted brick code is 10000191 (Dairy Based Drinks - Ready to Drink (Perishable)). In Fig. 6 all predicted bricks are unequal. Here, the second image has the shortest distance to the unclassified image and therefore its brick code 10000144 (Alcoholic Pre-mixed Drinks) is determined as the final class. In both examples our classification method predicts the correct brick code.

4.2 Text-Based Product Classification

Since product images also contain text-based information, the texts from the product images were also extracted. Here, we aimed to increase the performance of the product classification. Optical Character Recognition (OCR) was used for text extraction. Standardization of the extracted texts was performed by removing special characters and by converting uppercase to lowercase letters. Additionally the texts were tokenized to build text-based feature vectors for every image in the dataset as illustrated in Fig. 7. The corresponding labels to each extracted text were also added in the form of GPC brick, class and family codes. In our text classification, an approach similar to image-based classification was used, which is based on commonalities of feature vectors. For the classification of our text vectors, we searched for the vectors with the largest number of common strings in our database and then derived the classification from these.

Fig. 7. Text extraction process based on Optical Character Recognition (OCR) and Standardization of the extracted text.

4.3 Hybrid Approach

The listing 1 illustrates how the final class for a product is calculated based on the results of the image-based and text-based product classification.

Algorithm 1. determination of the final class.

```
 1: begin
 2:     predicted_classes = [imgclass1, imgclass2, txtclass1, txtclass2];
 3:     majority_class = most_common(predicted_classes);
 4:     minority_class = least_common(predicted_classes);
 5:     if majority_class.frequency ≥ 2 and minority_class.frequency == 1 then
 6:         predicted_class = majority_class;
 7:     else
 8:         predicted_class = imgclass1;
 9:     end if
10: end
```

Each of these methods proposes two classes. The one that occurs most frequently in the set of the four proposed classes is chosen as the final class. It is determined by a heuristic which corresponds to a majority vote. If the final class cannot be determined unambiguously by the majority vote, the first class of the image-based method will be chosen as the final class, because the image-based classification method has a better accuracy than the text-based method as the results in Table 10 illustrate.

4.4   Implementation

The Python programming language was used for the implementation of our approach and for scientific calculations and data analysis. Data partitioning, classification tasks and performance measurements were performed by the scikit-learn library [19]. The extraction of visual image features with different artificial neural network architectures and pretrained weights is based on Tensorflow [20]. Optical Character Recognition (OCR) was conducted by the Google Vision API [21].

4.5   Preparation of the Data

The foundation of our experiments is based on the data described in Sect. 3. In the experiments, a 80/20 split of the data was chosen for performance assessment. Here the principle of stratification was applied, where the division of the data is done by preserving the percentage of the data for each class. We used 20% of the data as test data and the remaining 80% of the data for classifying the test data according to the GPC classification system by predicting brick, class and family codes for each image of the testset.

4.6   Performance Metrics

In order to evaluate the performance of our classification approach the metrics precision, recall and F1-score [22] were used for classification performance evaluation, because the images in our dataset are unevenly distributed across the different classes. We calculated the metrics for each class weighted by the number of images per class. The metrics were calculated according to the definition given in [23], where the *sample* can be interpreted as the image of a product or its text and the *label* as its Global Product Classification code (brick code, class code or family code).

$$precision_w = \frac{1}{\sum_{l \in L} |\hat{y}_l|} \sum_{l \in L} |\hat{y}_l| \frac{|y_l \cap \hat{y}_l|}{|y_l|} \tag{1}$$

$$recall_w = \frac{1}{\sum_{l \in L} |\hat{y}_l|} \sum_{l \in L} |\hat{y}_l| \frac{|y_l \cap \hat{y}_l|}{|\hat{y}_l|} \tag{2}$$

$$F1score_w = \frac{1}{\sum_{l \in L} |\hat{y}_l|} \sum_{l \in L} |\hat{y}_l| 2\frac{|y_l \cap \hat{y}_l|}{|y_l| + |\hat{y}_l|} \tag{3}$$

As outlined in [23] y denotes a set of predicted label pairs $(sample, label)$ and $\hat{y}$ a set of true $(sample, label)$ pairs. L denotes a set of labels, y_l is the subset of y with label l and $\hat{y}_l$ is the subset of $\hat{y}$ with the label l.

5   Results

In this section, we present the results of our experiments. In Sect. 5.1, the parameters of the kNN algorithm and their effects on the performance of our approach are investigated. We have determined the optimal configuration of the algorithm for all following experiments by tuning the various parameters and measuring performance results.

In Sect. 5.2, different neural network architectures were used and their impact on classification performance was measured. Afterwards, approaches for reducing the amount of data by reducing the features are considered in Sect. 5.3 and their effects of reduction on classification performance are analyzed. In the corresponding experiments, only dataset B is considered. In Sect. 5.4, stratified k-fold cross validation was used to measure and analyze the classification performance of our approach based on dataset A and B. In Sect. 5.5 our hybrid classification approach is described where we combined our image-based with a text-based approach to increase the classification performance.

5.1   Nearest Neighbor Classification

As described before, we made use of the k nearest neighbor algorithm for classification [24]. The different parameters of the algorithm are tested to determine the optimal configuration for all the following experiments.

Nearest Neighbor Computation. In this experiment, we examine different computational methods for calculating nearest neighbors by comparing the three different calculation methods brute, kd_tree and ball_tree. The brute method calculates the euclidean distance to each element in the search space when determining the nearest neighbors, while kd_tree and ball_tree build an inner tree structure to determine the nearest neighbors. The best calculation method cannot be determined on the basis of the classification results, since all three methods produce the same results, as the values in Table 3 show. Because of the long tree construction time of the methods kd_tree and ball_tree in our experiments the method brute will be used in all subsequent experiments.

Table 3. kNN computation performance comparison at GPC brick level with $k = 2$ and 20% of our data as testset (dataset B).

metric	kd_tree	ball_tree	brute
precision	0.904	0.904	0.904
recall	0.903	0.903	0.903
F1-score	0.903	0.903	0.903

Weighted Vs Unweighted Neighbors. We investigated how the chosen number of nearest neighbors (k) and their weighted and unweighted distances affect the classification accuracy of our image-based approach. We performed the classification at GPC brick level with different values of k and measured the classification performance. Figure 8 illustrates, that an increasing value of k results in a decreasing classification performance of our approach.

Furthermore, the influence of the weighting of the nearest neighbors on the classification are investigated by performing the described experiment with weighted and unweighted nearest neighbors. Better classification results are achieved when the nearest neighbors are determined in a weighted form by calculating the inverse of their distance. The weighted results of $k = 1$ and $k = 2$ are equal. But in the subsequent experiments $k = 2$ was chosen for the following experiments, as this gives the user an additional suggestion in a productive environment.

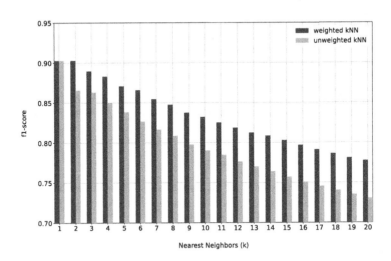

Fig. 8. F1-score for weighted and unweighted kNN with different values of k (dataset B).

Distance Computation Metrics. The implementation of the kNN algorithm provides several different metrics for computing nearest neighbor distances. In this experiment the influence of the metrics euclidean, minkowski and chebychev on the accuracy of the approach during classification is investigated. Table 4 illustrates, that each of the considered metrics performs differently. In our case, the approach achieves the best performance in classification by using the euclidean metric for distance calculation to the nearest neighbors.

Table 4. Comparison of the kNN distance metric performance for product image classification at GPC brick level (dataset B).

algorithm	precision	recall	F1-score
euclidean	0.904	0.903	0.903
minkowski	0,890	0.890	0.890
chebyshev	0.783	0.783	0.782

5.2   Feature Extraction

In this experiment, the influence of different model architectures on classification performance is analyzed. Furthermore the impact of feature reduction on classification performance and on classification runtime is examined.

The influence of different model architectures on the classification performance at GPC brick level is researched by comparing the network architectures ResNet50 [13], InceptionV3 [25] and VGG16 [26]. Each of the architectures is used for feature extraction and classification performance is measured for each feature set. The results in Table 5 illustrate the impact of different model architectures on classification performance. Of the three network architectures considered, ResNet50 is best suited for feature extraction with respect to our dataset.

Table 5. Performance comparison of different model architectures at GPC brick level (dataset B).

model	precision	recall	F1-score
ResNet50	0.904	0.903	0.903
VGG16	0,891	0.891	0.891
InceptionV3	0.846	0.847	0.844

5.3   Feature Reduction

The feature vectors generated with ResNet50 contain 2048 elements per vector. This can lead to a high impact on classification runtime when working with a large number of product images. In order to determine the prediction as quickly as possible, the generated feature vectors were reduced to decrease runtime. Principal Component Analysis (PCA) [16] and Neighborhood Components Analysis (NCA) [17] were used for dimensionality reduction and the classification performance is compared by classifying the differently sized feature vectors at GPC brick level.

Table 6 and 7 indicate that the best classification performance was achieved by using original feature vectors which consist of 2048 elements per vector. We see a correlation between the number of elements per vector and classification performance when PCA is used as the reduction method. A decreasing number of elements per vector results in a decreasing classification performance.

A reduction by 75% with PCA to 512 elements per vector results in a performance decrease of only 0.2% and a runtime increase by a factor of 2.22. By using PCA, the speed of our approach can be doubled if we accept a small loss in accuracy. Analyzing the results for NCA illustrated in Table 7, the best performance can be achieved with a reduction to 128 elements per vector, because this results in a performance decrease of only 0.003% and a runtime increase by a factor of 2.78.

Table 6. Classification performance with PCA-reduced feature vectors at GPC brick level (dataset B).

vector size	precision	recall	F1-score	time [s]	data [MB]
2048	0.904	0.903	0.903	59.16	834.35
1024	0.903	0.902	0.902	35.39	830.19
512	0.902	0.902	0.901	26.69	415.10
256	0.898	0.897	0.897	22.74	207.55
128	0.891	0.891	0.890	20.60	103.78

Table 7. Classification performance with NCA-reduced feature vectors at GPC brick level (dataset B).

vector size	precision	recall	F1-score	time [s]	data [MB]
2048	0.904	0.903	0.903	59.16	834.35
1024	0.780	0.781	0.779	45.30	830.19
512	0.774	0.776	0.773	31.87	415.10
256	0.744	0.746	0.744	23.45	207.55
128	0.903	0.901	0.900	21.31	103.78

5.4   Performance Evaluation

In this experiment, we measured the classification performance of our approach by performing 5-fold stratified cross-validation by dividing our data into 5 subsets, each containing 20% of the data while maintaining the percentage of samples for each class in our dataset. The kNN algorithm was used to classify the data in each subset on brick, class and family level based on the remaining 80% of the data. The metrics precision, recall and F1-score were calculated for each fold as described in Sect. 4.6. In this paper we considered dataset A and dataset B. Figure 9 illustrates the F1-scores which was calculated for each fold for dataset B.

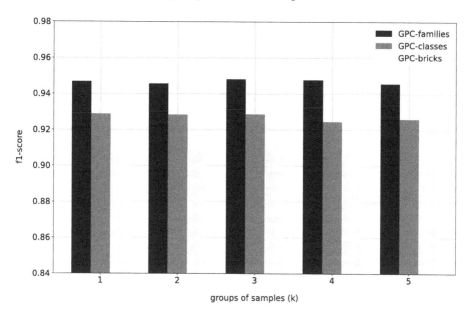

Fig. 9. 5-fold cross validation results (dataset B).

Table 8 illustrates the total performance of our approach, which was measured by calculating the arithmetic mean of the values shown in Fig. 9 for dataset B. The values for dataset A were calculated in the same way. Considering the weighted F1-scores, we achieved different results for each GPC layer for both datasets. This can be explained by the fact that the visual differences of the product images at GPC brick level are smaller than the visual differences at GPC family level. Furthermore, it can be stated that a larger amount of data leads to better results. For instance, the classification results for the larger dataset B are always better than the results for dataset A.

Table 8. Comparison of the classification performance evaluation based on the dataset used in [1] (dataset A) and the dataset used in this work (dataset B).

dataset	GPC Layer	k	classes	precision	recall	F1-score
A	Brick	5	197	0.859	0.857	0.856
	Class	5	73	0.887	0.886	0.886
	Family	5	20	0.911	0.911	0.911
B	Brick	5	216	0.906	0.905	0.904
	Class	5	78	0.924	0.923	0.923
	Family	5	20	0.944	0.943	0.943

In addition, we examined classification performance separately for every GPC family in the dataset. Figure 10 illustrates the different F1-scores for each family in dataset B. Furthermore, we compared the amount of test data for each family. Figure 11 shows the amount of data for each family sorted by the performance of the classification in descending order for dataset B.

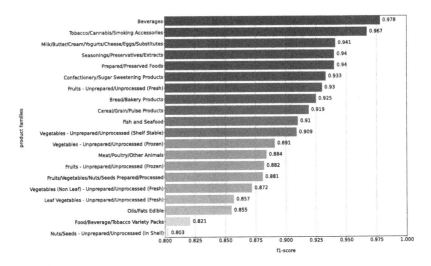

Fig. 10. Family-based classification performance per GPC family (dataset B).

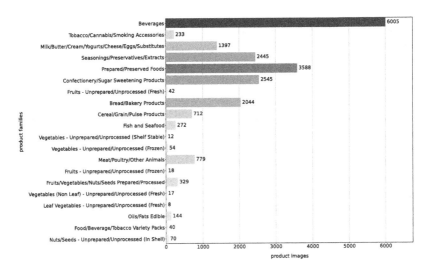

Fig. 11. Test data (product images) per GPC family sorted by classification performance in descending order (dataset B).

The calculation of the pearson correlation coefficient between the amounts of test data and the F1-scores results in an r-value of 0.624 which indicates a significant large positive correlation between the amount of test data and the F1-scores.

In a further experiment, we analyzed the influence of different product images showing the same product on the product classification performance. In doing so we compared the product classification performance for two different datasets which include the same number of products but a different number of product images. First, product classification performance was determined based on the dataset used in [1] which contained 36.624 products and 69.256 product images (dataset A). We made a stratified 80/20 split of the dataset and removed images belonging to products in the 20% testset from the remaining 80% to make sure that images of a product are only present in one of the two subsets. Afterwards the data in our testset was classified and product classification performance was calculated. Then we took the 20% testset and classified it based on the dataset which contains 36.624 products and 103.774 product images (dataset B). Again, product images that show products which were present in the testset have been removed from the search space defined by dataset B.

The results in Table 9 demonstrate that product classification performance increases when a larger amount of images per product is used. The performance increased by 1.2% on brick level, by 0.9% on class-level and by 0.8% on family level.

Table 9. Comparison of the product classification results based on the dataset used in [1] and the dataset used in this work.

dataset	GPC Layer	precision	recall	F1-score	images	products
A	Brick	0.827	0.826	0.825	67.587	36.624
	Class	0.862	0.862	0.861	67.587	36.624
	Family	0.891	0.890	0.891	67.587	36.624
B	Brick	0.839	0.838	0.837	99.494	36.624
	Class	0.871	0.871	0.870	99.494	36.624
	Family	0.899	0.899	0.899	99.494	36.624

5.5 Hybrid Classification Approach

In order to improve the classification performance of our approach, the image-based classification was combined with text-based classification. The predictions were merged as described in Sect. 4.3.

For classification, we took 20% of the image data and the corresponding texts for each image that we classified separately at brick, class and family level. In addition, hybrid classification which combines the image-based and text-based classification was performed. According to the results in Fig. 12 and Table 10 the image-based approach has a better product classification performance on our dataset than the text-based approach, but the combination of the two approaches leads to the best results and a better overall classification performance. We achieved F1-scores of 0.917 on brick level, 0.931 on class level and 0.953 on family level by combining our image-based and text-based approaches.

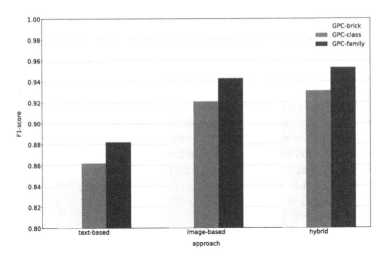

Fig. 12. Performance comparison of the text-based, image-based and hybrid approach on GPC family, class and brick level (dataset B).

Table 10. Product Classification results of the text-based, image-based and hybrid approach at GPC family, class and brick level (dataset B).

GPC level	approach	precision	recall	F1-score
brick	texts only	0.836	0.865	0.848
	images only	0.909	0.906	0.907
	images and texts	0.915	0.920	0.917
class	texts only	0.849	0.881	0.862
	images only	0.922	0.922	0.921
	images and texts	0.928	0.936	0.931
family	texts only	0.870	0.902	0.882
	images only	0.943	0.943	0.943
	images and texts	0.949	0.957	0.953

6   Discussion

In this paper we proposed a hybrid approach for automated product classification. The approach classifies products based on the visual features of product images according to the GPC standard. The classification of a product is determined by combining the image-based and text-based classification approach.

In our experiments, we considered different datasets. One of the datasets contains 103.774 product images and 99.494 texts of 36.624 different products assigned to 216 different GPC families, 78 GPC classes and 20 GPC bricks. We evaluated our approach by calculating the weighted performance metrics precision, recall and F1-score as described in Sect. 4.6. The performance of our image-based and text-based approach was increased by combining the two approaches, as the results in Sect. 5.5 illustrate. On the product classification task, we achieved a classification performance of 91.7% at GPC brick level, 93.1% at GPC class level and 95.3% at GPC family level (see Table 10).

6.1 Advantages

The approach presented here uses a neural network exclusively for feature extraction, while classification is performed by the kNN algorithm. This approach has the advantage that the neural network does not need to be retrained when new classes or new images are added. Furthermore, although our approach is based on the GPC standard, it is possible to switch to another classification standard without retraining the neural network and without recalculating all our feature vectors. Therefore, our approach does not require any computational and time intensive training. Furthermore, due to the nearest neighbor approach, less data per class is required. In addition, our hybrid approach delivers better results when we have a larger amount of data available.

6.2 Limitations

The proposed approach increases the degree of automation in product classification. Our experiments show, the approach achieves a high accuracy in classification, but products can also be classified incorrectly. Therefore, in practice, a system based on our approach should only be used in cooperation with humans to further reduce the error rate. Our approach can only assign the class of a product correctly if there are already product images in the search space that belong to this class. If a class is unknown, the first product of this class must be classified manually by the user.

7 Future Research

In this work, we considered only product images that display a product in front of a neutral background. If product images with non-neutral backgrounds are used, then a decrease in classification performance is expected. By using object detection and image segmentation, it would be possible to detect products in images and to separate them from the background. By removing noisy backgrounds, the use of a wider variety of different image types is made possible.

To further increase the performance of the approach, it should be used in collaboration with users. By calculating probability values for each classification, it would be possible to ask the user to classify products whose class was predicted with a low probability. In this way, the user actively contributes to the labeling of subsequent data. This technique is also known as Active Learning [27]. By using data augmentation to artificially expanding the amount of data, we could further improve the classification performance of the approach. Operations to consider would include slight rotation and vertical flipping of the product images in our dataset. By using product knowledge graphs, the results of our approach can be enriched with further knowledge to increase the explainability of the results by making products and their relationships to each other visible.

Our method is suitable for use in several practical applications. The method can be used in image-based search engines for product images and in image-based recommendation systems for products. An application for planogram compliance checks in conjunction with object detection methods is also conceivable. So far, we have only considered product images as a whole. However, our method can also be used to classify parts of product images, such as brands and symbols on product packaging.

Acknowledgments. This work was funded by the German Federal Ministry of Education and Research as part of the research program KMU-innovativ: IKT (FKZ 01IS20085).

References

1. Bast, S., Brosch, C., Krieger, R.: A hybrid approach for product classification based on image and text matching. In: Proceedings of the 11th International Conference on Data Science, Technology and Applications - DATA, pp. 293–300. SciTePress, Lisbon, Portugal (2022)
2. How Global Product Classification (GPC) works, GS1. https://www.gs1.org/standards/gpc/how-gpc-works. Accessed 20 Oct 2022
3. Karami, E., Prasad, S., Shehata, M.: Image matching using SIFT, SURF, BRIEF and ORB: performance comparison for distorted images. In: Proceedings of the 2015 Newfoundland Electrical and Computer Engineering Conference, St. Johns, Canada (2015)
4. LeCun, Y., Bengio, Y., Hinton, G.: Deep learning. Nature **521**, 436–444 (2015)
5. Wei, Y., Tran, S., Xu, S., Kang, B., Springer, M.: Deep learning for retail product recognition: challenges and techniques. Comput. Intell. Neurosci. **2020**, 1–23 (2020)
6. Szeliski, R.: Computer Vision: Algorithms and Applications. Springer, CJam (2022). https://doi.org/10.1007/978-1-84882-935-0
7. Ma, J., Jiang X., Fan A., Jiang J., Yan J.: Image matching from handcrafted to deep features: a survey. Int. J. Comput. Vis. **129**, 23–79. Springer International Publishing (2021)
8. Chavaltada, C., Pasupa, K., Hardoon, D.R.: A comparative study of machine learning techniques for automatic product categorisation. In: Cong, F., Leung, A., Wei, Q. (eds.) ISNN 2017. LNCS, vol. 10261, pp. 10–17. Springer, Cham (2017). https://doi.org/10.1007/978-3-319-59072-1_2
9. Allweyer, O., Schorr, C., Krieger, R.: Classification of products in retail using partially abbreviated product names only. In: Proceedings of the 9th International Conference on Data Science, Technology and Applications - DATA, pp. 67–77. SciTePress, Paris, France (2010)
10. Kannan, A., Talukdar, P. P., Rasiwasia, N., Ke, Q.: Improving product classification using images. In: IEEE 11th International Conference on Data Mining, pp. 310–319 (2011)
11. GS1 Product Images Application Guideline for the Retail Grocery & Foodservice Industries, GS1, https://www.gs1us.org/content/dam/gs1us/documents/industries-insights/by-industry/food/guideline-toolkit/GS1-US-Product-Images-Application-Guideline-for-the-Retail-Grocery-And-Foodservice-Industries.pdf. Accessed 14 Oct 2022
12. Basic Operations on Images, OpenCV. https://docs.opencv.org/4.x/d3/df2/tutorial_py_basic_ops.html. Accessed 16 Dec 2022
13. He, K., Zhang, X., Ren, S., Sun, J.: Deep residual learning for image recognition. In: IEEE Conference on Computer Vision and Pattern Recognition - CVPR, pp. 770–778. IEEE, Las Vegas, USA (2016)

14. Tan, C., Sun, F., Kong, T., Zhang, W., Yang, C., Liu, C.: A survey on deep transfer learning. In: Kůrková, V., Manolopoulos, Y., Hammer, B., Iliadis, L., Maglogiannis, I. (eds.) ICANN 2018. LNCS, vol. 11141, pp. 270–279. Springer, Cham (2018). https://doi.org/10.1007/978-3-030-01424-7_27

15. Deng, J., Dong, W., Socher, R., Li, L., Kai, L., Fei-Fei, L.: ImageNet: a large-scale hierarchical image database. In: IEEE Conference on Computer Vision and Pattern Recognition - CVPR, pp. 248–255, IEEE, Miami, USA (2009)

16. Lever, J., Krzywinski, M., Altman, N.: Principal component analysis. Nat. Methods **14**, 641–642 (2017)

17. Goldberger, J., Roweis, S., Hinton, G., Salakhutdinov, R.: Neighbourhood components analysis. In: Proceedings of Advances in Neural Information Processing Systems - NIPS, pp. 513–520. NeurIPS Proceedings, Vancouver, Canada (2004)

18. Mitchell, T.: Machine Learning. McGraw-Hill Education Ltd, New York City (1997)

19. Machine Learning in Python, scikit-learn, https://scikit-learn.org. Accessed 14 Oct 2022

20. Tensorflow software library for machine learning and artificial intelligence, Google Brain. https://www.tensorflow.org. Accessed 02 Nov 2022

21. Google Vision API. https://cloud.google.com/vision. Accessed 14 Oct 2022

22. Sokolova, M., Lapalme, G.: A systematic analysis of performance measures for classification tasks. Inf. Process. Manag. **45**, 427–437 (2009)

23. Metrics and scoring: quantifying the quality of predictions, section 3.3.2.9. Precision, recall and F-measures, scikit-learn, https://scikit-learn.org/stable/modules/model_evaluation.html. Accessed 14 Oct 2022

24. Nearest Neighbors, section 1.6.2. Nearest Neighbors Classification, scikit-learn, https://scikit-learn.org/stable/modules/neighbors.html. Accessed 02 Nov 2022

25. Szegedy, C., Vanhoucke, V., Ioffe, S., Shlens, J., Wojna, Z.: Rethinking the inception architecture for computer vision. In: IEEE Conference on Computer Vision and Pattern Recognition - CVPR, pp. 2818–2826. IEEE, Las Vegas, USA (2016)

26. Simonyan, K., Zisserman, A.: Very deep convolutional networks for large-scale image recognition. In: 3rd International Conference on Learning Representations - ICLR, San Diego, USA (2015)

27. Settles, B.: Active learning literature survey. Computer Sciences Technical Report 1648. University of Wisconsin-Madison, Wisconsin, USA (2009)

Automatic Sentiment Labelling of Multimodal Data

Sumana Biswas[✉], Karen Young, and Josephine Griffith[✉]

School of Computer Science, University of Galway, Galway, Ireland
s.biswas2@nuigalway.ie,
{karen.young,josephine.griffith}@universityofgalway.ie

Abstract. This study investigates the challenging problem of automatically providing sentiment labels for training and testing multimodal data containing both image and textual information for supervised machine learning. Because both the image and text components, individually and collectively, convey sentiment, assessing the sentiment of multimodal data typically requires both image and text information. Consequently, the majority of studies classify sentiment by combining image and text features ('Image+Text-features'). In this study, we propose 'Combined-Text-Features' that incorporate the object names and attributes identified in an image, as well as any accompanying superimposed or captioned text of that image, and utilize these text features to classify the sentiment of multimodal data. Inspired by our prior research, we employ the Afinn labelling method to automatically provide sentiment labels to the 'Combined-Text-Features'. We test whether classifier models, using these 'Combined-Text-Features' with the Afinn labelling, can provide comparable results as when using other multimodal features and other labelling (human labelling). CNN, BiLSTM, and BERT models are used for the experiments on two multimodal datasets. The experimental results demonstrate the usefulness of the 'Combined-Text-Features' as a representation for multimodal data for the sentiment classification task. The results also suggest that the Afinn labelling approach can be a feasible alternative to human labelling for providing sentiment labels.

Keywords: Sentiment analysis · NLP · Deep learning · Automatic labelling · Multimodal data

1 Introduction

People frequently share their daily life experiences on social networks and have become accustomed to sharing images with captions of their daily activities to convey their feelings to others. Extraction of sentiment from this type of social media data is complicated and provides researchers with a hard challenge. Sentiment analysis is the classification of emotions into binary (Positive and Negative) or ternary (Positive, Negative, and Neutral) categories. When using supervised learning approaches to analyze sentiment, getting the important ground truths or sentiment labels for multimodal social media data is often an important step. A common simple and inexpensive approach is to acquire the labelled data via online crowdsourcing platforms such as Rent-A-Coder and Amazon Mechanical Turk [38,47]. However, one is frequently unaware of the availability,

© The Author(s), under exclusive license to Springer Nature Switzerland AG 2023
A. Cuzzocrea et al. (Eds.): DATA 2021/2022, CCIS 1860, pp. 154–175, 2023.
https://doi.org/10.1007/978-3-031-37890-4_8

Fig. 1. Sample image with description. Detected objects list: ['necklace', 'woman', 'hair', 'woman', 'woman', 'hair', 'shirt', 'sweater', 'hair', 'picture'] and detected attributes list: ['silver', 'smiling', 'brown', 'smiling', 'smiling', 'blonde', 'blue', 'brown', 'blonde', 'white'].

efficacy, and quality of labellers for a particular field or task. Erroneous and unbalanced labelling can be the result of labelling mistakes made by non-expert labellers and biased labelling because of inefficiency. To assure high-quality labels, the alternative is to directly employ human professionals to perform the labelling, which can be both time-consuming and costly. Another alternative is to utilise existing automatic labelling techniques for providing sentiment to the textual and multimodal data. Due to advances in Natural Language Processing (NLP), a number of tools are available to extract emotions from the text. Examples of these include TextBlob, Vader, and Afinn which are capable of quickly computing the polarity of text to determine the sentiment.

In previous work, we compared the performance of these three automatic labelling techniques to provide sentiment labels for Twitter text data without any human intervention [4]. We used two Twitter datasets from the SemEval13 and SemEval16 contests, which had ground truth. The results of the automatic labelling were compared to the results of the ground truth using three deep learning algorithms (CNN, BiLSTM, CNN-BiLSTM) for sentiment analysis in order to determine which labelling approach, and which model, gave the best performance. Using a BiLSTM deep learning model, Afinn labelling achieved the highest accuracy.

In this paper, we consider another challenging task which is to automatically provide sentiment labels for multimodal data which contains both image and text data. This is a challenging task because each part, the image and the text, individually and collectively, evoke sentiments. Typically, considering only a single modality is insufficient to determine the sentiment of multimodal data - both image and text data are necessary and the relationship between the text and image can also be quite significant [53]. Whereas the human mind can interpret the meaning of an image and its accompanying text, computers still perform poorly on cognitive tasks such as the description of an image and the textual relationship between an image and associated text. Additionally, it is impossible to comprehend the sentiment of an image without a semantic description. For example, in Fig. 1, in the image, the woman is smiling, which human eyes can perceive and recognize, but for a computer to comprehend the image, it requires a textual description of the image. Moreover, an image often incorporates regions or objects that evoke emotions. The identification of these objects' names in textual form can offer a textual description of the image's components [20, 44]. In Fig. 1, for example, a set of objects are detected as ['necklace', 'woman', 'hair', 'woman', 'woman', 'hair', 'shirt', 'sweater', 'hair', 'picture'], and their attributes are detected as ['silver', 'smiling', 'brown', 'smiling', 'smiling', 'blonde', 'blue', 'brown', 'blonde', 'white']; when they are combined as ['necklace silver', 'woman smiling', 'hair brown', 'woman smiling', 'woman smiling', 'hair blonde', 'shirt blue', 'sweater brown', 'hair blonde', 'picture white']; it is clear that the collective meaning is more powerful than the individual meaning. Here, all pairs of objects' names and their attributes collectively describe an image. In addition, this description helps to infer sentiment labels. For example, "woman smiling" conveys a positive sentiment that can help to provide automatic sentiment labels.

In recent years, numerous advancements have been made towards the objective of translating images into words [1, 23], including image description [1, 23], image categorization [15], object detection [1, 7, 23], attribute detection [1, 23], and scene comprehension. The interaction and relationship between objects in images have also been studied for image captioning [56, 61]. In a few previous works, image objects and their spatial information (spatial vectors) were employed to determine emotions. Some researchers have found methods to obtain sentiment by combining both sets of image and text data [52, 53, 62].

In this work, we investigate the viability of using the object-level textual descriptions of an image, combined with the available associated text, for the classification of multimodal sentiment. We refer to this combined textual information as 'Combined-Text-Features' which are obtained from two modalities: image and text. In our previous study, in the comparison of automatic labelling of textual data, the Afinn approach performed best [4]. This is why, here, we also investigate if the Afinn labelling approach can be successfully used to provide sentiment labels for the 'Combined-Text-Features' for two multimodal datasets which also have existing ground truth (as provided by human labellers).

We investigate two hypotheses: first, whether the 'Combined-Text-Features' is a sufficient representation for multimodal data to classify sentiment; and second, whether the Afinn labelling approach can be used to provide sentiment labels for multimodal data automatically. We conducted four experiments on two multimodal datasets: the first and second experiments were undertaken to demonstrate the first hypothesis, and the second, third, and fourth experiments were conducted to establish the second hypothesis. For hypothesis 1, we obtained the 'Image+Text-features' by combining image features extracted using ResNet50 with text features extracted with the BiLSTM or BERT model. In the first experiment, we employed the 'Image+Text-features' in a fusion model. Here, both the training and testing datasets with ground truth are used to cate-gorize the sentiment of multimodal data. For the second hypothesis, we classified the sentiment of multimodal data using 'Combined-Text-Features'. We used three models: the CNN, BiLSTM, and BERT models for the second, third, and fourth experiments. In the second experiment, we used ground-truth-containing training and testing datasets. The third experiment uses training and testing datasets with automated labels, whereas the fourth experiment uses automatic labels for the training dataset and ground truth labels for the testing dataset.

Our contributions are as follows: Firstly, we propose 'Combined-Text-Features' that include the object names of an image and their attributes, combined with any available accompanying superimposed or captioned text of that image, which can be used to clas-sify the sentiment of multimodal data. Secondly, we use the Afinn labelling approach to provide sentiment labels to the 'Combined-Text-Features' in order to demonstrate the benefit of automatically applying sentiment labels to multimodal datasets. We con-ducted extensive experiments and compared the results to demonstrate the advantage of providing automatic labels over obtaining ground truth through human effort.

The remaining sections of the paper are as follows: Sect. 2 outlines relevant work based on the application of automatic labelling approaches on both textual and multi-modal data, as well as the related method and models employed in this paper for both textual and multimodal sentiment analysis; Sect. 3 describes the methodology which is used here for the sentiment classification of the multimodal data, and Sect. 4 describes the experimental results and discussion that establish the considered two hypotheses comparing the results. Section 5 concludes and makes recommendations for future research.

2   Related Work

In this section, we briefly review the existing sentiment labelling techniques used to provide sentiment labels to the textual data automatically. We also review some existing methods for textual and multimodal sentiment analysis.

2.1   Sentiment Labelling for Training and Testing Datasets

Labelling a large quantity of social media data for the task of supervised machine learning is not only time-consuming but also difficult and expensive. Several authors [14,26,42] studied data labelling costs. In contrast, some online crowdsourcing sys-tems like Rent-A-Coder, Amazon Mechanical Turk, etc. [38,47] are available to pro-vide sentiment labels quickly and with low cost, In this case, there is a high probability of labelling errors from non-expert labellers, and skewed labelling due to a lack of effi-ciency might lead to erroneous and unbalanced labelling. Automatic labelling is a time- and cost-effective alternative to manually obtaining sentiment labels. The lexicon-based automatic labelling techniques of TextBlob, Vader, and Afinn use the NLTK (Natural Language Toolkit) of Python libraries to automatically classify the sentiment of text and have been used in many studies [11,37]. Each lexicon-based sentiment labelling app-roach needs a predefined word dictionary to infer the polarity of the sentiment according to their rules. Vader dictionaries are used to find the polarity scores of each word. Deepa et al. (2019) [11] assessed the polarity scores of words to categorize the sentiment for the Twitter dataset related to UL Airlines with human labels using two dictionary-based methods: Vader dictionaries and Sentibank; the Vader dictionaries outperformed Sentibank by 3% in their analysis to detect the polarity scores for the sentiment classification using the Logistic Regression (LR) model. TextBlob and Afinn were used by Chakraborty et al. (2020) [8] to label a large number of tweets (226k) using ternary classes. Saad et al. (2021) [37] used Afinn, TextBlob, and Vader to assign sentiment labels to a drug review dataset, and they obtained 96% accuracy with TextBlob; similarly, Hasan et al. (2018) [18] and Wadera et al. (2020) [43] also got success with TextBlob labelling on Twitter datasets. There is no one automatic labelling technique that does best consistently in the above-mentioned previous work for providing sentiment to the textual data.

Motivated by the above study, we compared the effectiveness of three automatic labelling methods to assign sentiment labels to Twitter text data without human intervention in our previous work [4]. We used three leading automatic labelling approaches: TextBlob, Afinn, and Vader to provide sentiment labels to two text datasets from the SemEval-13 and SemEval-16 contests that contained ground truth. All of those labelling methods were thoroughly described in that paper. The datasets are described in detail in the papers [12,57]. We merged the training, development, and testing parts of the original dataset to generate a single, complete dataset. Then, we used 80% of each dataset for training and 20% for testing for all the experiments. We ran three experiments utilizing the deep learning algorithms CNN, BiSLTM, and CNN-BiSLTM. In the first experiment, the existing SemEval labels (human labels) were used for both training and testing. In the second experiment, the three automatic labelling algorithms (TextBlob, Vader, and Afinn) were applied to both the training and testing datasets in turn. The third experiment used the current SemEval labels (human labels) for testing, while the training data labels were generated using the three automatic labelling techniques in turn (TextBlob, Vader, and Afinn). The results of automatic labelling were compared to the ground truth in order to establish which labelling strategy and model provided the best performance. Afinn labelling obtained the highest accuracy of 80.17% in SemEval-13 and 80.05% in SemEval-16 using a BiLSTM deep learning model. We showed that automatic Afinn labelling could be an option to provide sentiment labels to the textual datasets.

Providing sentiment labels to multimodal data, on the other hand, is a more difficult issue when working with multimodalities. In this situation, it may cost [42] three times as much as if sentiment labels were applied to text data alone.

2.2 Text Sentiment Analysis

Text sentiment categorization methods can be divided into two groups: lexicon-based models and machine-learning models. Using adjectives as priors for positive or negative polarity, Hu and Liu (2004) [19] predicted the semantic orientation of opinion in sentences. Taboada et al. (2011) [39] introduced a lexicon-based method called Semantic Orientation Calculator (SO-CAL), which uses words dictionaries annotated with semantic orientation and incorporates intensification and negation for text sentiment analysis. Pang et al. (2002) [22] were the first to apply machine learning to the categorization of text sentiment using Naive Bayes, support vector machines and maximum entropy classification methods. Maas et al. (2011) [28] extracted semantic and emotional information from words and developed a probabilistic model of unsupervised documents to learn semantic similarity and a supervised model to predict sentiment. Barbosa et al. (2010) [3] developed a two-step strategy for classifying the sentiment of tweets using internet labels as training data.

Kim et al. (2014) [22] initially used CNN for text sentiment classification inspired by the excellent performance of deep learning models for natural language processing (NLP). Tang et al. (2019) [40] utilized CNN and LSTM to obtain sentence representations and then a gated recurrent neural network to encode phrase semantics and their inherent relationships. The authors made an attention-based LSTM network to improve aspect-level sentiment categorization in [46]. They did this because the concerning aspect is closely related to the polarity of a sentence's sentiment. Recent research has employed embedding from language models (ELMo), generative pre-trained transformers (GPT), bidirectional encoder representations from transformers (BERT) [13], and global vectors for word representation (GloVe) [33] models to produce the word or sentence embedding. Multiple studies have employed the pre-trained BERT model for text sentiment analysis [9,24,62].

2.3 Multimodal Sentiment Analysis

Multimodal sentiment analysis utilizes characteristics from multiple modalities to predict the total sentiment. Text and images are combined and represented by a cross-media bag-of-words model (CBM) as a single bag of words by Wang et al. (2014) [45] for microblog sentiment classification; they experimented on Weibo tweet dataset and obtained 66% accuracy. Cross-modality consistent regression (CCR) is a method presented by You et al. (2016) [59] that employs image and text information for joint sentiment prediction. They crawled Getty Images and Twitter images, which were labelled using both the Vader labelling approach and manually, and obtained almost the same 80% accuracy for both datasets. Xu et al. (2017) [50] proposed MultiSentiNet, a deep network that uses scene and object properties of a picture to highlight relevant sentence words based on attention. They obtained accuracies of 69.84% for MVSA-single and 68.86% for MVSA-multiple datasets. Xu et al. (2018) [51] built a co-memory network to classify multimodal sentiment that models the mutual impacts between image and text. They also experimented on MVSA-single and MVSA-multiple datasets and obtained accuracies of 70.50% and 69.92% respectively. Using linguistic features, social features, low- and mid-level visual features, and image-text similarities, Zhao et al. (2019) [60] developed an image-text consistency-driven technique. Poria et al. (2017) [34] presented an LSTM-based method for the relationships between utterances for multimodal sentiment prediction. Yang et al. (2020) [54] proposed a memory network model to iteratively retrieve semantic image-text features based on the multi-view attention network to classify multimodal sentiment and obtained 72.98% and 72.36% accuracies for MVSA-single and MVSA-multiple datasets, respectively. Tong et al. (2022) [62] investigated the alignment between image regions and text words and proposed a cross-modal interaction between both visual and textual context information to classify overall sentiment and obtained approx. 75% and 73% accuracies for

MVSA-single and MVSA-multiple datasets, respectively. They considered only a maximum of two image regions for visual information, which reduced the sample size of the datasets. As a result, images with no effective region that evokes sentiment words in text or images with more than two effective region datasets were lost. Similarly, Xiaojun et al. (2022) [52] proposed a Multi-Level Attention Map Network (MAMN), which includes a cost-free proposal (a larger object with other small objects) present in the image, and obtained approx. 76% and 78% accuracies for MVSA-single and MVSA-multiple datasets, respectively. In the same way, Yang et al. (2018) [53] used local visual information of one large object and the global visual information of the entire image. However, they neglected the smaller objects and the names of the most significant objects.

Multimodal fusion also plays an important role in multimodal sentiment analysis, a number of studies focusing on the creation of fusion techniques between different modalities have been offered. Most of them used the spatial features information of the whole image and combined them with the associated text features through early fusion [16,17] or late fusion [31,53,55]. Poria et al. (2016) [35] employed a deep convolution neural network to extract visual and textual data and fuse them early to form a single feature vector. Huang et al. (2016) [20] presented an image-text sentiment analysis method called Deep Multimodal Attentive Fusion (DMAF), which combines the unimodal characteristics and the internal cross-modal correlation [10,58]. Liu (2012) [27] and Cambria et al. (2015) [5] introduced low-rank multimodal fusion, an approach utilizing low-rank tensors for multimodal fusion, and demonstrated its efficacy for sentiment analysis. However, there is still a significant gap when analyzing sentiment based solely on the semantic description of an image, without taking into account the spatial features of an image by incorporating all the objects' names on the images, and their attributes. Even though there has been a lot of progress in multimodal sentiment tasks across the different modalities, little attention has been paid to enhancing textual information with image descriptions for image-text sentiment analysis.

Most existing methods just combine information from different sources or try to figure out how images and text relate to each other. We use picture descriptors to describe an image and combine them with the accompanying text to represent multimodal data. We specifically capture image descriptions, including object class names and their attributes of image regions, and combine them with available text phrases to investigate the significance of the semantic descriptions of the image to represent multimodal information.

3   Methodology

In this section, we describe the entire methodology of this study, including the datasets, 'Combined-Text-Features' preparation, Afinn labelling and tokenization, 'Image+Text-features' preparation, model discussion, and experimental details. We denote an image-text pair, as (I, T), where I represents a single image and T represents the available superimposed or caption text associated with that image. An image can have multiple objects and each object can have multiple attributes; P is the pair of each object's name and its attribute names. We denote 'Combined-Text-Features' as S=T+P, and 'Image+Text-features' (T+I) where P is the pair of each object's name and its attribute names, and T is the superimposed or caption text.

The dataset subsection describes the two datasets utilized in greater detail. In the preparation for 'Combined-Text-Features' we discuss the extraction of the image description, the extraction of the superimposed text, and their combination. The Afinn labelling approach used to assign sentiment labels to 'Combine-Text-Features' is described next, followed by tokenization strategies. We also exploited image spatial features; we describe image spatial feature extraction and concatenation with the features extracted from superimposed or caption text (T) to prepare 'Image+Text-features'. Then we describe the models utilized for the experiments. We conclude with a description of the experimental methods used to produce the results.

3.1 Datasets

We have used two multimodal datasets which have existing ground truth (sentiment labels). One dataset is SIMPSoN, in which textual data is superimposed on the image but it does not contain any other text. The other dataset is MVSA [50] which includes text with each image as well as text that is superimposed on the image. We describe both datasets in greater depth in this section.

The SIMPSoN dataset was created by Felicetti et al. (2019) [16] to analyse the visual, textual, and overall sentiment of social media images using Deep Convolution Neural Networks (DCNNs). In the data set, daily news-related images were collected from Instagram, and the sentiment of 9247 images were manually labelled. Every image was labelled for sentiment regarding its visual (Image_labels), its textual (Text_labels), and image and text (Joint_labels). One of three sentiments: "positive", "negative", and "neutral" were assigned in each of the cases. Images displaying solidarity, friendliness, and, in general, all positive facts were assigned a "positive" sentiment; images depicting violence, racism, and overly vulgar comments were assigned a "negative" sentiment; otherwise, the sentiment assigned was "neutral". For our work, since some of the images did not have superimposed text, we removed them for our experiments. Additionally, some of the images had non-English superimposed texts and we also removed these images resulting in 2830 images remaining.

The second multimodal dataset used is MVSA Single where originally 5129 image-text pairs were collected from Twitter [30]. Each pair was given a sentiment – positive, neutral, or negative – for the text (Text_labels) and for the image (Image_labels) by one annotator. Since this dataset had no overall sentiment labels for the joint text and image, we automatically created a new joint label for the multimodal sentiment of text and image according to the approach described in [50,62]. First, we removed images where the image labels and text labels were inconsistent; for example, we removed images where the Text_labels were positive while the Image_labels were negative, and vice versa. Then, the Joint_label was derived from the pairings of equal sentiment labels for both text and image labels; for example, when they both have the same label, the image label and text label both have positive, negative, or neutral sentiments. If one label is negative or positive and the other is neutral, we utilize the negative or positive label as the Joint_label. After this, we had 4347 images with new Joint_labels for the MVSA-Single data set.

Table 1 contains the statistics of the datasets. In this paper, we used only the Joint_labels from this Table as ground truth for all the experiments.

3.2   Combined-Text-Features Preparation

Extraction of Image Descriptions. We retrieved object descriptions from the images in our datasets using the object feature detection method "detectron2", [48] which was used to generate sentences by paying attention to object regions using the objects' names, the names of their attributes, and the relationship between the object names and the attribute names in an image. The authors used Visual Genome (VG) datasets [23] in their work which was extracted from the YFCC100M [41] and COCO datasets [25] before being meticulously annotated by crowdsourced human annotators. According to that paper [23], one image should contain, on average, 35 object-bounding boxes, 26 attributes, and 21 relationships (e.g. jumping, over, above etc.). Thus, the Visual Genome Dataset was ideally suited to the job of scene graph creation, in which all objects, attributes, and relationships are combined from each region description [23]. In our work, we extracted object-bounding boxes, their object's class names with their object scores, and attribute names with their attribute scores; here, scores represent the probability (%) that an object or attribute satisfies the class or attribute names of the object. For example, in Fig. 1, we extracted a set of bounding box coordinates, a set of object names and their scores, and a set of attribute names and scores for a given image.

We used all the objects' names without considering the percentage of their probability scores and their attributes without considering their probability scores because 'woman 72% Smiling 30%', here 'woman' and 'smiling' are important text features, not the percentage of their probability scores. For example, in Fig. 1, we got a set of detected objects class names as ['necklace', 'woman', 'hair', 'woman', 'woman', 'hair', 'shirt', 'sweater', 'hair', 'picture'] and their attributes as ['silver', 'smiling', 'brown', 'smiling', 'smiling', 'blonde', 'blue', 'brown', 'blonde', 'white']. Then we combined objects' class names and their attribute names as ['necklace silver', 'woman smiling', 'hair brown', 'woman smiling', 'woman smiling', 'hair blonde', 'shirt blue', 'sweater brown', 'hair blonde', 'picture white'] because the combined meanings are more powerful than the individual meaning. Then these combined objects' class names and their attribute names are used later with the available caption or superimposed text in the image. In this work, we took the class names and attribute names of an average of 20 objects to describe as many objects as possible in the image. We then remove the redundant objects' class names and attribute pairs (P), that is, those pairs that repeat. For example, in Fig. 1, we removed the redundant pairs, 'hair blonde' and 'woman smiling'.

Extraction of Associated Text with Images. We have used Python-tesseract, which is an optical character recognition (OCR) tool for Python, to extract the superimposed text of an image. It was unnecessary to use an OCR program for the caption text because it was available with the image. Then, we removed usernames and special symbols such as, #, $, and RT from the text data. Because the number of words in each superimposed text varies among images in the SIMPSoN datasets, we limited the text extracted to 20 words, truncating lengthy text and padding shorter phrases with zero values according to the work [16]. We took all words from the caption text for the MVSA dataset because captions had a maximum word length of 29.

Concatenation of Image Description and Text. After extracting the text data, we concatenated the object-attribute pairs (P) with the extracted superimposed English text or caption text (T) available in the images. This is referred to as 'Combined-Text-Features' (S), in which one portion of the text consists of the image's text data and the other contains the image description as represented by the objects' class names and attributes. Then we cleaned the data removing commas and apostrophes.

3.3 Afinn Labelling and Tokenization

We use the Afinn labelling approach to label the 'Combined-Text-Features' as Positive, Negative, or Neutral utilizing the Natural Language Toolkit (NLTK) package from Python, because the Afinn labelling, among the three tested labelling approaches, performed best in our previous work [4]. Here we give a brief description of the Afinn labelling approach.

Afinn Labelling: Finn Arup Nielsen [29] created this popular and condensed lexicon. According to the author's official GitHub repository, the most recent version of the lexicon, Afinn-en-165.txt, comprises almost 3,300 terms with associated polarity ratings. Afinn assigns a score between [-5 and 5] for a particular word. A 'Positive' label is assigned when the score is more than zero, a 'Negative' label is assigned when the score is less than zero, and a 'Neutral' label is assigned otherwise. Table 2 shows a few samples of multimodal data with ground truth and the Afinn labelling.

Tokenization is performed on the cleaned datasets. We have used 300-dimensional GloVe for embedding words. GloVe is an unsupervised learning technique that generates vector representations of words. Large amounts of text are used for training, and an embedding technique is used to generate low-dimensional and dense word structures unsupervised [33]. We have used GloVe embedding for the CNN and BiLSTM models. We also used a pre-trained BERT-Base [13] model to embed each word into a 768-dimensional embedding vector for the BERT model.

Table 1. The summary statistics of two multimodal datasets with the ground truth joint_labels, and the assigned Afinn_labels.

Datasets	SIMPSoN				MVSA-Single			
Sentiment labels	Pos	Neg	Neut	Total	Pos	Neg	Neut	Total
Joint_labels	1016	798	1016	2830	2593	1308	446	4347
Afinn_labels	1020	847	963	2830	1874	1652	821	4347

3.4 Image+Text-Features Preparation

We used ResNet50 [16,62] to extract image features from a multimodal dataset image. Here, spatial features of an image are mostly regarded while extracting image features. The image was initially scaled to 224*224 pixels before being fed into a ResNet50 model that had been pre-trained on the ImageNet2K dataset [36]. Without training this model, we eliminated the final layer of classification and added a dense layer with 1024 hidden units and a Relu activation function to extract 1024 image features. We

Table 2. Few samples of multimodal data and their ground truth (joint_labels) and the Afinn labels.

Sample images	Text and Image description pairs	Ground Truth	Afinn Labels
		Positive	Positive
	– Text: cake is finished proud of it tbh so hey ho – Pairs:[wall white', cake chocolate', grill metal', ground black', pavement black']		
		Positive	Positive
	– Text: a fabulous evening with the kingsolver thanks to hollard for making a very special evening possible elated – Pairs:[necklace silver', woman smiling', hair brown' shirt blue', sweater brown', hair blonde', picture white']		
		Positive	Positive
	– Text: Two brothers returns after the explosion of the fuego volcano in Guatemala – Pairs:[hair black', sign white', sidewalk gray', head black',boy young', jeans blue']		
		Positive	Negative
	– Text: when a girl texts you first and then ignores your reply – Pairs:[face black', eyes blue', sky dark', ground purple', face purple']		
		Neutral	Negative
	– Text: looking forward to disgraced by ayad akhtar monday and tuesday are already sold out – Pairs:[man white', suit gray', sign white', hair short', man black', suit black', sky white']		

used BiLSTM and BERT models to extract text features. We used GloVE embedding vectors of superimposed or caption text (T) into the BiLSTM model and extract 1024 text features from a dense layer with 1024 hidden units and a Relu activation function. We used BERT-base embedding vectors of superimposed or caption text (T) into the BERT model and extract 1024 text features from a dense layer with 1024 hidden units and a relu activation function (Table 3). Then, we combined the image features and text features after flattening the image and text features to make multimodal features called 'Image+Text-features'. For the first experiment, we used two 'Image+Text-features', the combinations were considered as follows:

- 'RN50+BiLSTM'– Concatenated image features of ResNet50 with text features from the BiLSTM model for multimodal data.
- 'RN50+BERT'– Concatenated image features of ResNet50 with text features from the BERT model for multimodal data.

3.5 Model Discussion

We have used four models: CNN, BiLSTM, BERT, and Fusion model for classifying the sentiments of the multimodal data. The structure of the models and their configurations are shown in Table 3 for each of the datasets.

CNN. A CNN is a feed-forward neural network with an input layer, hidden layer, and output layer that can capture all local features. Typically, CNN consists of many blocks. The convolutional layer, non-linear activation function, pooling layer, and fully connected layer are the several layers or blocks of CNN. ConvNet requires less preprocessing than other classification techniques. It computes the most significant features from the CNN output using a Rectified Linear Unit (ReLU) activation and Global max pooling layer. A SpatialDropout1D layer is used on top of the CNN layer which accepts a sentence's word embedding matrix as input. It prevents pixels from co-adapting with their neighbours across feature maps, which helps to promote the independence of feature maps. CNN networks are great for extracting local features from the text [2,21]. Using pre-trained word vectors, text data can be fed into CNN networks in order to classify texts using CNN networks. To do this, each word (w) of the text (S) is treated as a separate word vector. Convolution layers are utilized to extract implicit features from the inputs or intermediate features map. The length of each filter is determined by the constant K, while its height is determined by the hyperparameter h. Given a filter $F \in R^{h*k}$, a feature C_i is generated from the window of words $[V^i : V^{i+h-1})]$, which refers to the sequence $[w^i \oplus w^{i+1} \oplus w^{i+2} \oplus \ldots \oplus w^{i+h-1}]$ as shown in Eq. (1).

$$C_i = g(F.[V^i : V^{i+h-1}] + b) \tag{1}$$

In this Equation, $b \in R$ is a bias term and g is a non-linear function. ReLu is used in this paper as the non-linear function for the convolution layer. The filter F is applied to each possible window of words in the sequence $[v^{1:h}, v^{2:h+1}, \ldots, v^{n-h+1}]$. The result of applying this filter is the feature map represented as $c = [c^1, c^2, \ldots, c^{n-h+1}]$, in which, $c \in R^{n-h+1}$. In this paper, CNN model is used to extract high-level features and classify texts.

BiLSTM. Long Short-Term Memory (LSTM) is a Recurrent Neural Network (RNN) with three gates: input gate, output gate, and forgot gate [49]. It has both a forward and a reverse layer. BiLSTM is capable of remembering and processing future and past information from input sequences in both directions. BiLSTM model, considering each of the 'Combined-Text-Features' initialized word vectors $S = (w_1, w_2, w_3, ..., w_m)$ in one S as the input of the BiLSTM networks, the output of the BiLSTM hidden layer contain every context's forward output and backward output ($\overleftarrow{c}_i$), concatenating forward ($\vec{h}_i$) and backward output ($\overleftarrow{h}_i$) the context is expressed as follows:

$$\overleftarrow{c}_i = \left[\overleftarrow{h}_i; \vec{h}_i \right], i = 1, \ldots, m \tag{2}$$

$$\overleftarrow{h}_i = \text{LSTM}_l \left(\overleftarrow{h}_{i-1}, \overleftarrow{w}_i \right),$$
$$\vec{h}_i = \text{LSTM}_r \left(\vec{h}_{i+1}, \overleftarrow{w}_i \right). \tag{3}$$

BERT. Google created Bidirectional Encoder Representations from Transformers (BERT), a transformer-based machine learning technique for natural language processing (NLP) pre-training. BERT was developed and released in 2018 by Google's Jacob Devlin and his coworkers [13]. In 2019, there are two versions of the original English-language BERT: (1) the BERT-base is comprised of 12 encoders with 12 bidirectional self-attention heads, and (2) the BERT-large is comprised of 24 encoders with 16 bidirectional self-attention heads. Both models are pre-trained using unlabeled data derived from the BooksCorpus [63] corpus of 800 million words and the English Wikipedia corpus of 2.5 billion words. The BERT-base model is utilized in this work, for the extraction of text features. The input phase requires the position encoding of the input words to the input word encoding. Each layer using positional encoding to describe the sequence's order enables the determination of each word's position, which aids in determining the distance between words. Each layer, inside the encoder, a Multi-Head Attention layer and Feedforward Neural Network predominate (FFNN), and then sends it to the next encoder.

Fusion Classifier Model for Multimodal Features. The Fusion model consists of one fully connected layer with 256 hidden units, one dropout layer, and finally, a Softmax activation function with three sentiment classifications. We used the learning rate 1e-4, and dropout 0.2 to determine all multimodal sentiments. The ground truth, joint_labels, as shown in Table 1, was used to train and test for the multimodal features for the two multimodal datasets.

Table 3. Configuration of the models used for the experiments.

Model's Name	Layers	Configuration
CNN	SpatialDropout1D	0.2
	Conv1D	64, 5, Relu
	GlobalMaxPool1D	
	Dropout	0.5
	Fully connected, activation, kernel_regularizer	3, Softmax, 0.01
BiLSTM	SpatialDropout1D	0.1
	BiLSTM, dropout, recurrent_dropout	32, 0.2,0.2
	Fully connected, activation	1024, ReLu
	Fully connected, activation	32, Relu
	Dropout	0.5
	Fully connected, kernel_regularizer	Softmax, 0.01
BERT	BERT	
	Fully connected, activation	1024, ReLu
	Fully connected, activation	32, ReLu
	Dropout	0.2
	Fully connected, activation	3, Sotmax
ResNet50	ResNet	
	Fully connected, activation	1024, ReLu
	Flatten	
Fusion	Concatenate	
	Fully connected, activation	256, ReLu
	Dropout	0.2
	Fully connected, activation	3, Sotmax

Table 4. Hyper-parameters used in experiments for two multimodal datasets.

Model's Name	Hyper-parameters	Values	
		SIMPSoN	MVSA
CNN	Batch size	32	32
	Epochs	70	70
	Learning Rate	0.0005	0.0001
	Word sequence length	45	55
	Word embedding, dimension	GloVe,300	GloVe,300
BiLSTM	Batch size	32	32
	Epochs	30	30
	Learning Rate	0.0002	0.0001
	Word sequence length	45	55
	Word embedding, dimension	GloVe,300	GloVe,300
BERT	Batch size	32	32
	Epochs	30	30
	Learning Rate	3e-06	1e-06
	epsilon	1e-05	1e-05
	decay	0.01	0.01
	clipnorm	1.0	1.0
	Word sequence length	45	55
	Word embedding, dimension	BERT-Base,768	BERT-Base,768
Fusion Model	Batch size	32	32
	Epochs	30	30
	Learning Rate	1e-4	1e-4

3.6   Experiment Details

We investigated two hypotheses: firstly, the significance of the 'Combined-Text-Features' to represent multimodal data; and secondly, the advantages of the automatic Afinn labelling approach to provide sentiment labels to the multimodal data. We conducted four experiments on two multimodal datasets. The first and second experiments were conducted to test the first hypothesis, and the second, third and fourth experiments were conducted to test the second hypothesis.

For all four experiments, 80% of the datasets are used for training and 20% for testing according to [16]. We have considered 10% of the training data (from 80%) for validation according to [62]. Two deep learning models: CNN and BiLSTM, one transformer-based BERT model, and a Fusion model are applied to the clean and preprocessed training data for each experiment, separately, and the models are evaluated using the test data. All the layers used in the models are displayed in Table 3. All the considered hyperparameters settings are described in Table 4 for all the models used in the experiments. We explain all the experiments in detail below.

One hot encoding is a popular technique for categorical data that generates a binary column for each category and, depending on the sparse parameter, either a sparse matrix or dense array. The sentiments of multimodal data were classified into three categories using the one-hot encoding method. Three new columns labelled 'Positive,' 'Negative,' and 'Neutral' are created and populated with zeros (representing False) and ones (representing True) for this purpose (meaning True).

In the first experiment, we employed existing ground truth labels (Joint_labels) for training and testing using the 'Image+Text-features' representation for classifying the sentiment of multimodal data. The main purpose of the experiment is to compare the results with those of the second experiment, which uses the proposed 'Combined-Text-Features'. In addition, this experiment was designed to demonstrate that although an image has a great deal of information, the majority of it is irrelevant, and the majority of its pixels may be too noisy to accurately represent image information.

In the second experiment, we employed the existing ground truths (Joint_labels) for both training and testing using the proposed 'Combined-Text-Features' representation for classifying the sentiment of multimodal data. Instead of using noisy pixel values, 'Combined-Text-Features' incorporated image descriptions with any accompanying text. We accomplish this by considering the significant semantic relationship and link between the two modalities and treating them as multimodal data. By comparing the results of the first and second experiments, we aim to determine whether 'Combined-Text-Features' alone is sufficient for multimodal sentiment classification.

In the third experiment, we used the Afinn approach to label both the training and testing portions of the datasets using the identical models as in the second experiment for classifying the sentiment of multimodal data. The results of these experiments provided the opportunity to evaluate the effectiveness of Afinn labelling.

In the fourth experiment, the existing ground truth labels were used for testing while the training data was labelled using the Afinn approach using the identical models as in the second and third experiments. This shows the effect of a hard test where the training data was labelled by the Afinn automatic labelling approach but tested with the ground truth.

Table 5. Experiment 1: Sentiment classification results of the 'Image+Text-features' using the Fusion model with the ground truth labels.

Model	Multimodal Features	SIMPSoN (%)				MVSA-Single (%)			
		Acc	Pre	Rec	F1	Acc	Pre	Rec	F1
Fusion Model	RN50+BiLSTM	**54**	**54**	**53**	**54**	**65**	**60**	**50**	**52**
	RN50+BERT	52	52	51	51	61	53	50	50

Table 6. Experiment 2: Results of the 'Combined-Text-Features' with the ground truth labels using a CNN, BiLSTM, and BERT models.

Model	SIMPSoN (%)				MVSA-Single (%)			
	Acc	Pre	Rec	F1	Acc	Pre	Rec	F1
CNN	55	56	54	54	70	63	50	52
BiLSTM	65	67	65	65	70	63	54	56
BERT	**69**	**70**	**69**	**68**	**73**	**64**	**62**	**62**

Table 7. Experiment 3: Results of the 'Combined-Text-Features' with Afinn labels using a CNN, BiLSTM, and BERT models.

Model	SIMPSoN (%)				MVSA-Single (%)			
	Acc	Pre	Rec	F1	Acc	Pre	Rec	F1
CNN	75	76	75	75	76	72	71	72
BiLSTM	77	79	77	77	79	74	73	73
BERT	**78**	**79**	**78**	**78**	**80**	**80**	**79**	**78**

Table 8. Experiment 4: Results of the 'Combined-Text-Features' with Afinn labelling for the training dataset and ground truth labelling for the test using CNN, BiLSTM, and BERT models.

Model	SIMPSoN (%)				MVSA-Single (%)			
	Acc	Pre	Rec	F1	Acc	Pre	Rec	F1
CNN	53	50	51	50	60	50	51	50
BiLSTM	55	54	53	52	61	54	50	52
BERT	**59**	**55**	**55**	**54**	**61**	**55**	**53**	**52**

4   Experimental Results and Discussion

In this section, we present the results of the four experiments. The results are reported using accuracy, precision, recall and F1 scores. The best results are highlighted in bold font. The results of the first experiment, in which we used the ground truth for both the training and testing using 'Image+Text-features' are shown in Table 5.

Table 6 depicts the results of the second experiment, which used three models with ground truth joint_labelling for the two multimodal datasets for sentiment classification.

The performance of the CNN and BiLSTM model gave a slightly poorer result when GloVe extracted the features of multimodal data ('Combined-Text-Features'). The pre-trained language model BERT helped to improve the performance of multimodal sentiment classification. Table 6 shows that the BERT model obtains the best result in this experiment for classifying sentiment for both datasets.

The results of the second experiment are superior to those of the first experiment. By comparing the results of the first and second experiments with the ground truth, it is demonstrated that 'Combined-Text-Features' obtained the best result for multimodal data sentiment classification. This suggests that 'Combined-Text-Features' alone are adequate for multimodal sentiment classification.

We can see that all results reported from the third experiment are better than those reported in the second experiment. The results are shown in Table 7 showing higher accuracy, precision, recall, and F1-scores for the two datasets with the Afinn labelling than the ground truth. Additionally, Afinn labelling obtains the highest accuracy using the BERT model for the two datasets compared to the other models. BiLSTM also obtains the next best result. Since the CNN is a feed-forward neural network, it can capture all local neighbour features and could not learn all the dependencies of whole sentences due to the limitation of filter lengths [6]. This limitation of the CNN model is handled using the BiLSTM model. As a result, BiLSTM models learn all the features from both directions and also can remember past information, which helps to make relations between words in sentences to obtain the sentiment classification. The BERT model has the ability to use positional encoding to describe the sequence's order of the word in the sentence, which helps to determine each word's position and the distance between them. Thus BERT is able to make relations using position embedding and segment embedding, the BERT model can establish context by understanding the relationship between neighbouring text. Here, associated texts develop a relation with objects' class name and their attributes, which learns and checks the relatedness between the most important objects-attributes pair and the context in the BERT model for identifying the sentiment of the provided information.

Table 8 displays the results of the fourth experiment, which aims to create a hard test to assess if the model can perform well when the dataset is tested with ground truth labelling after being trained with the Afinn labelling. The accuracy, precision, F1-score, and recall values for the BERT model were the best for the two multimodal datasets, but the results were poor compared to the previous results of the second and third experiments.

Figure 2, represents the percentage of sentiment labels that are the same across the ground truth and Afinn labelling approaches. The Afinn automatic labelling approach obtains an average of 41% and 59% of equal sentiment labels with the ground truth for SIMPSoN and MVSA Single datasets respectively. We can also see in Fig. 2 there is an inconsistency between the labels given by the automatic labelling techniques and the ground truth. This explains why the performance results in experiment four are often poorer than those reported in the second and third experiments. When the labels for the training data are based on Afinn and the labels for the test data are based on ground truth, the learning process becomes significantly more difficult.

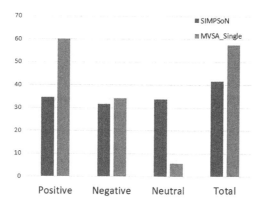

Fig. 2. Percentages of multimodal data that are labelled with the same sentiment labels by the ground truth and the automatic Afinn labelling.

By comparing the outcomes of the second, third, and fourth experiments, it can be seen that the outcomes of the third experiment were superior to those of the second and fourth experiments across all models. Thus, we confirmed our second prediction that the Afinn labelling method can also be used as an alternate option to automatically provide sentiment labels to multimodal data.

From these results, we observe that the proposed 'Combined-Text-Features' approach achieved the best results for the two multimodal datasets. Additionally, because the sizes of the identified objects varied, identified small-sized objects lost their important information due to expanding to the same size as large-sized objects when deep learning algorithms use uniform data sizes during the training and testing phase. Thus, using just the text descriptions of the objects did not cause the same issues as using the textual data of the image in this case. Finally, based on the result and discussion we argue that "Combined-Text-Features", is sufficient to classify the sentiment of multimodal data. Thus, based on the result, we also argue that the Afinn labelling approach is an alternative option to provide sentiment labels automatically to the massive volume of multimodal data.

5   Conclusion

It is difficult, time-consuming, and costly to manually assign sentiment labels to a vast amount of textual and multimodal social media data for the task of supervised machine learning. We propose 'Combined-Text-Features' which incorporate semantic information from two modalities: image and text. For sentiment analysis of multimodal data, specifically, we use image descriptions and combine them with any accompanying text that represents multimodal data, taking into account the significant semantic relationship and link between the two modalities. We conducted four experiments to demonstrate two hypotheses: whether the 'Combined-Text-Features' is a sufficient representation for multimodal data to classify sentiment; and whether the Afinn labelling approach can be used to automatically provide sentiment labels for multimodal data.

The results based on the evaluation of the first and second experiments demonstrate that 'Combined-Text-Features' alone is adequate to represent an alternative form of multimodal data for classifying sentiments of multimodal data. The experimental results also show that the Afinn labelling obtained the best result for classifying multimodal sentiment. In addition, the BERT model achieved the best accuracy, which implies that this model could learn these 'Combined-Text-Features' in the best way among the three models used with Afinn labelling and ground truth.

The limitations of this work are that we evaluated all the experiments using small datasets and we did not utilize the positional attributes (e.g., distant, close, etc.) of the recognized objects in the image. To improve the quality of multimodal feature information in textual form, it is necessary to incorporate additional semantic information related to spatial or positional features and relationship information (e.g., jumping, over, above, is, are, etc.) of the significant sentiment regions of the image, which can also contain the image's description for a larger dataset for future research. We suggest, the semantics of image descriptions and the accompanying text can represent multimodal data and helps to classify their sentiments based on all experimental outcomes. We expect that this research will help to provide multimodal sentiment labels to massive datasets when we want to save time and money by not manually generating ground truth.

Acknowledgements. This work was supported by the College of Engineering, University of Galway, Ireland.

References

1. Anderson, P., et al.: Bottom-up and top-down attention for image captioning and visual question answering. In: CVPR (2018)
2. Balntas, V., Riba, E., Ponsa, D., Mikolajczyk, K.: Learning local feature descriptors with triplets and shallow convolutional neural networks. In: BMVC, vol. 1, p. 3 (2016)
3. Barbosa, L., Feng, J.: Robust sentiment detection on twitter from biased and noisy data. In: Coling 2010: Posters, pp. 36–44 (2010)
4. Biswas, S., Young, K., Griffith, J.: A comparison of automatic labelling approaches for sentiment analysis. In: Proceedings of the 11th International Conference on Data Science, Technology and Applications, DATA, Portugal, pp. 312–319 (2022)
5. Cambria, E., Poria, S., Bisio, F., Bajpai, R., Chaturvedi, I.: The CLSA model: a novel framework for concept-level sentiment analysis. In: Gelbukh, A. (ed.) CICLing 2015. LNCS, vol. 9042, pp. 3–22. Springer, Cham (2015). https://doi.org/10.1007/978-3-319-18117-2_1
6. Camgözlü, Y., Kutlu, Y.: Analysis of filter size effect in deep learning. arXiv preprint arXiv:2101.01115 (2020)
7. Carion, N., Massa, F., Synnaeve, G., Usunier, N., Kirillov, A., Zagoruyko, S.: End-to-end object detection with transformers. In: Vedaldi, A., Bischof, H., Brox, T., Frahm, J.-M. (eds.) ECCV 2020. LNCS, vol. 12346, pp. 213–229. Springer, Cham (2020). https://doi.org/10.1007/978-3-030-58452-8_13
8. Chakraborty, K., Bhatia, S., Bhattacharyya, S., Platos, J., Bag, R., Hassanien, A.E.: Sentiment analysis of COVID-19 tweets by deep learning classifiers-a study to show how popularity is affecting accuracy in social media. Appl. Soft Comput. **97**, 106754 (2020)
9. Chen, F., Ji, R., Su, J., Cao, D., Gao, Y.: Predicting microblog sentiments via weakly supervised multimodal deep learning. IEEE Trans. Multimedia **20**(4), 997–1007 (2017)

10. Chen, M., Wang, S., Liang, P.P., Baltrušaitis, T., Zadeh, A., Morency, L.P.: Multimodal sentiment analysis with word-level fusion and reinforcement learning. In: Proceedings of the 19th ACM International Conference on Multimodal Interaction, pp. 163–171 (2017)

11. Deepa, D., Tamilarasi, A., et al.: Sentiment analysis using feature extraction and dictionary-based approaches. In: 2019 Third International conference on I-SMAC (IoT in Social, Mobile, Analytics and Cloud) (I-SMAC), pp. 786–790. IEEE (2019)

12. Deriu, J.M., Gonzenbach, M., Uzdilli, F., Lucchi, A., De Luca, V., Jaggi, M.: SwissCheese at SemEval-2016 task 4: sentiment classification using an ensemble of convolutional neural networks with distant supervision. In: Proceedings of the 10th International Workshop on Semantic Evaluation (SemEval-2016), pp. 1124–1128 (2016)

13. Devlin, J., Chang, M.W., Lee, K., Toutanova, K.: Bert: pre-training of deep bidirectional transformers for language understanding. arXiv preprint arXiv:1810.04805 (2018)

14. Dimitrakakis, C., Savu-Krohn, C.: Cost-minimising strategies for data labelling: optimal stopping and active learning. In: Hartmann, S., Kern-Isberner, G. (eds.) FoIKS 2008. LNCS, vol. 4932, pp. 96–111. Springer, Heidelberg (2008). https://doi.org/10.1007/978-3-540-77684-0_9

15. Druzhkov, P., Kustikova, V.: A survey of deep learning methods and software tools for image classification and object detection. Pattern Recognit Image Anal. **26**(1), 9–15 (2016)

16. Felicetti, A., Martini, M., Paolanti, M., Pierdicca, R., Frontoni, E., Zingaretti, P.: Visual and textual sentiment analysis of daily news social media images by deep learning. In: Ricci, E., Rota Bulò, S., Snoek, C., Lanz, O., Messelodi, S., Sebe, N. (eds.) ICIAP 2019. LNCS, vol. 11751, pp. 477–487. Springer, Cham (2019). https://doi.org/10.1007/978-3-030-30642-7_43

17. Ghorbanali, A., Sohrabi, M.K., Yaghmaee, F.: Ensemble transfer learning-based multimodal sentiment analysis using weighted convolutional neural networks. Inf. Process. Manag. **59**(3), 102929 (2022)

18. Hasan, A., Moin, S., Karim, A., Shamshirband, S.: Machine learning-based sentiment analysis for twitter accounts. Math. Comput. Appl. **23**(1), 11 (2018)

19. Hu, M., Liu, B.: Mining and summarizing customer reviews. In: Proceedings of the Tenth ACM SIGKDD International Conference on Knowledge Discovery and Data Mining, pp. 168–177 (2004)

20. Huang, P.Y., Liu, F., Shiang, S.R., Oh, J., Dyer, C.: Attention-based multimodal neural machine translation. In: Proceedings of the First Conference on Machine Translation: Volume 2, Shared Task Papers, pp. 639–645 (2016)

21. Huang, Q., Chen, R., Zheng, X., Dong, Z.: Deep sentiment representation based on CNN and LSTM. In: 2017 International Conference on Green Informatics (ICGI), pp. 30–33. IEEE (2017)

22. Kim, Y., et al.: Convolutional neural networks for sentence classification. arXiv preprint arXiv:1408.5882 (2014)

23. Krishna, R., et al.: Visual genome: Connecting language and vision using crowdsourced dense image annotations. Int. J. Comput. Vision **123**(1), 32–73 (2017)

24. Li, X., Chen, M.: Multimodal sentiment analysis with multi-perspective fusion network focusing on sense attentive language. In: Sun, M., Li, S., Zhang, Y., Liu, Y., He, S., Rao, G. (eds.) CCL 2020. LNCS (LNAI), vol. 12522, pp. 359–373. Springer, Cham (2020). https://doi.org/10.1007/978-3-030-63031-7_26

25. Lin, T.-Y., et al.: Microsoft COCO: common objects in context. In: Fleet, D., Pajdla, T., Schiele, B., Tuytelaars, T. (eds.) ECCV 2014. LNCS, vol. 8693, pp. 740–755. Springer, Cham (2014). https://doi.org/10.1007/978-3-319-10602-1_48

26. Lindstrom, P., Delany, S.J., Mac Namee, B.: Handling concept drift in a text data stream constrained by high labelling cost. In: Twenty-Third International FLAIRS Conference (2010)

27. Liu, B.: Sentiment analysis and opinion mining. Synth. Lect. Hum. Lang. Technol. **5**(1), 1–167 (2012)

28. Maas, A., Daly, R.E., Pham, P.T., Huang, D., Ng, A.Y., Potts, C.: Learning word vectors for sentiment analysis. In: Proceedings of the 49th Annual Meeting of the Association for Computational Linguistics: Human Language Technologies, pp. 142–150 (2011)

29. Nielsen, F.Å.: A new anew: evaluation of a word list for sentiment analysis in microblogs. arXiv preprint arXiv:1103.2903 (2011)

30. Niu T., Zhu, S., Pang, L., Saddik, A.El: Sentiment analysis on multi-view social data. In: MultiMedia Modeling: 22nd International Conference, MMM 2016, Miami, FL, USA, January 4-6, 2016, Proceedings, Part II 22, PP. 15–27 (2016) Springer

31. Ortis, A., Farinella, G.M., Torrisi, G., Battiato, S.: Exploiting objective text description of images for visual sentiment analysis. Multimedia Tools Appl. **80**(15), 22323–22346 (2021)

32. Pang, B., Lee, L., Vaithyanathan, S.: Thumbs up? Sentiment classification using machine learning techniques. arXiv preprint CS/0205070 (2002)

33. Pennington, J., Socher, R., Manning, C.D.: Glove: global vectors for word representation. In: Proceedings of the 2014 Conference on Empirical Methods in Natural Language Processing (EMNLP), pp. 1532–1543 (2014)

34. Poria, S., Cambria, E., Hazarika, D., Majumder, N., Zadeh, A., Morency, L.P.: Context-dependent sentiment analysis in user-generated videos. In: Proceedings of the 55th Annual Meeting of the Association for Computational Linguistics (Volume 1: Long Papers), pp. 873–883 (2017)

35. Poria, S., Chaturvedi, I., Cambria, E., Hussain, A.: Convolutional MKL based multimodal emotion recognition and sentiment analysis. In: 2016 IEEE 16th International Conference on Data Mining (ICDM), pp. 439–448. IEEE (2016)

36. Ridnik, T., Ben-Baruch, E., Noy, A., Zelnik-Manor, L.: Imagenet-21k pretraining for the masses. arXiv preprint arXiv:2104.10972 (2021)

37. Saad, E., et al.: Determining the efficiency of drugs under special conditions from users' reviews on healthcare web forums. IEEE Access **9**, 85721–85737 (2021)

38. Snow, R., O'Connor, B., Jurafsky, D., Ng, A.Y.: Cheap and fast-but is it good? Evaluating non-expert annotations for natural language tasks. In: Proceedings of the 2008 Conference on Empirical Methods in Natural Language Processing, pp. 254–263 (2008)

39. Taboada, M., Brooke, J., Tofiloski, M., Voll, K., Stede, M.: Lexicon-based methods for sentiment analysis. Comput. Linguist. **37**(2), 267–307 (2011)

40. Tan, H., Bansal, M.: Lxmert: learning cross-modality encoder representations from transformers. In: Proceedings of the 2019 Conference on Empirical Methods in Natural Language Processing (2019)

41. Thomee, B., et al.: YFCC100M: the new data in multimedia research. Commun. ACM **59**(2), 64–73 (2016)

42. Turney, P.D.: Cost-sensitive classification: empirical evaluation of a hybrid genetic decision tree induction algorithm. J. Artif. Intell. Res. **2**, 369–409 (1994)

43. Wadera, M., Mathur, M., Vishwakarma, D.K.: Sentiment analysis of tweets-a comparison of classifiers on live stream of twitter. In: 2020 4th International Conference on Intelligent Computing and Control Systems (ICICCS), pp. 968–972. IEEE (2020)

44. Wang, D., Xiong, D.: Efficient object-level visual context modeling for multimodal machine translation: masking irrelevant objects helps grounding. In: AAAI, pp. 2720–2728 (2021)

45. Wang, M., Cao, D., Li, L., Li, S., Ji, R.: Microblog sentiment analysis based on cross-media bag-of-words model. In: Proceedings of International Conference on Internet Multimedia Computing and Service, pp. 76–80 (2014)

46. Wang, Y., Huang, M., Zhu, X., Zhao, L.: Attention-based LSTM for aspect-level sentiment classification. In: Proceedings of the 2016 Conference on Empirical Methods in Natural Language Processing, pp. 606–615 (2016)

47. Whitehill, J., Wu, T.F., Bergsma, J., Movellan, J., Ruvolo, P.: Whose vote should count more: optimal integration of labels from labelers of unknown expertise. In: Advances in Neural Information Processing Systems, vol. 22 (2009)

48. Wu, Y., Kirillov, A., Massa, F., Lo, W.Y., Girshick, R.: Detectron2 (2019). https://github.com/facebookresearch/detectron2

49. Xu, G., Meng, Y., Qiu, X., Yu, Z., Wu, X.: Sentiment analysis of comment texts based on BiLSTM. IEEE Access **7**, 51522–51532 (2019)

50. Xu, N., Mao, W.: Multisentinet: a deep semantic network for multimodal sentiment analysis. In: Proceedings of the 2017 ACM on Conference on Information and Knowledge Management, pp. 2399–2402 (2017)

51. Xu, N., Mao, W., Chen, G.: A co-memory network for multimodal sentiment analysis. In: The 41st International ACM SIGIR Conference on Research & Development in Information Retrieval, pp. 929–932 (2018)

52. Xue, X., Zhang, C., Niu, Z., Wu, X.: Multi-level attention map network for multimodal sentiment analysis. IEEE Trans. Knowl. Data Eng. (2022)

53. Yang, J., She, D., Sun, M., Cheng, M.M., Rosin, P.L., Wang, L.: Visual sentiment prediction based on automatic discovery of affective regions. IEEE Trans. Multimedia **20**(9), 2513–2525 (2018)

54. Yang, X., Feng, S., Wang, D., Zhang, Y.: Image-text multimodal emotion classification via multi-view attentional network. IEEE Trans. Multimedia **23**, 4014–4026 (2020)

55. Yang, Z., Yang, D., Dyer, C., He, X., Smola, A., Hovy, E.: Hierarchical attention networks for document classification. In: Proceedings of the 2016 Conference of the North American Chapter of the Association for Computational Linguistics: Human Language Technologies, pp. 1480–1489 (2016)

56. Yao, T., Pan, Y., Li, Y., Mei, T.: Exploring visual relationship for image captioning. In: Proceedings of the European Conference on Computer Vision (ECCV), pp. 684–699 (2018)

57. Yoon, J., Kim, H.: Multi-channel lexicon integrated CNN-BiLSTM models for sentiment analysis. In: Proceedings of the 29th Conference on Computational Linguistics and Speech Processing (ROCLING 2017), pp. 244–253 (2017)

58. You, Q., Cao, L., Jin, H., Luo, J.: Robust visual-textual sentiment analysis: when attention meets tree-structured recursive neural networks. In: Proceedings of the 24th ACM International Conference on Multimedia, pp. 1008–1017 (2016)

59. You, Q., Luo, J., Jin, H., Yang, J.: Cross-modality consistent regression for joint visual-textual sentiment analysis of social multimedia. In: Proceedings of the Ninth ACM International Conference on Web Search and Data Mining, pp. 13–22 (2016)

60. Zhao, Z., et al.: An image-text consistency driven multimodal sentiment analysis approach for social media. Inf. Process. Manag. **56**(6), 102097 (2019)

61. Zhou, L., Palangi, H., Zhang, L., Hu, H., Corso, J., Gao, J.: Unified vision-language pre-training for image captioning and VQA. In: Proceedings of the AAAI Conference on Artificial Intelligence, vol. 34, pp. 13041–13049 (2020)

62. Zhu, T., Li, L., Yang, J., Zhao, S., Liu, H., Qian, J.: Multimodal sentiment analysis with image-text interaction network. IEEE Trans. Multimedia (2022)

63. Zhu, Y., et al.: Aligning books and movies: towards story-like visual explanations by watching movies and reading books. In: Proceedings of the IEEE International Conference on Computer Vision, pp. 19–27 (2015)

From Cracked Accounts to Fake IDs: User Profiling on German Telegram Black Market Channels

André Büsgen[1(✉)], Lars Klöser[1(✉)], Philipp Kohl[1(✉)], Oliver Schmidts[1(✉)], Bodo Kraft[1(✉)], and Albert Zündorf[2(✉)]

[1] Aachen University of Applied Sciences, 52066 Aachen, Germany
{buesgen,kloeser,p.kohl,schmidts,kraft}@fh-aachen.de
[2] University of Kassel, 34109 Kassel, Germany
zuendorf@uni-kassel.de

Abstract. Messenger apps like WhatsApp and Telegram are frequently used for everyday communication, but they can also be utilized as a platform for illegal activity. Telegram allows public groups with up to 200.000 participants. Criminals use these public groups for trading illegal commodities and services, which becomes a concern for law enforcement agencies, who manually monitor suspicious activity in these chat rooms. This research demonstrates how natural language processing (NLP) can assist in analyzing these chat rooms, providing an explorative overview of the domain and facilitating purposeful analyses of user behavior. We provide a publicly available corpus of annotated text messages with entities and relations from four self-proclaimed black market chat rooms. Our pipeline approach aggregates the extracted product attributes from user messages to profiles and uses these with their sold products as features for clustering. The extracted structured information is the foundation for further data exploration, such as identifying the top vendors or fine-granular price analyses. Our evaluation shows that pretrained word vectors perform better for unsupervised clustering than state-of-the-art transformer models, while the latter is still superior for sequence labeling.

Keywords: Clustering · Natural language processing · Information extraction · Profile extraction · Text mining

1 Introduction

Nine of ten germans use messenger apps daily [8]. While accessible communication facilitates many everyday challenges for millions of people, it also brings criminals broad reach. Private or public chat groups offer easy availability and a configurable amount of privacy. Law-enforcement agencies need to analyze chat histories manually to detect criminal behavior. An effective reduction of efforts may lead to a more effective criminal prosecution. This research investigates how *natural language processing* (NLP) can assist in analyzing chat groups and

A. Cuzzocrea et al. (Eds.): DATA 2021/2022, CCIS 1860, pp. 176–202, 2023.
https://doi.org/10.1007/978-3-031-37890-4_9

detecting criminal behaviors. We concentrate on public Telegram chat groups that focus on trading illegal goods.

Our research answers questions like, what is the range of offered goods? Or, can we extract features of offerings, such as prices or quantities, that allow conclusions about market characteristics? At the same time, we have law enforcement's workload and resource limitations in mind, resulting in the loose condition to answer those questions with as little manual effort as possible. This research proposes a pipeline approach (Fig. 1) to answer such questions under low human resource constraints. Our training corpus contains 2541 annotated documents. The trained model can analyze arbitrary numbers of documents without additional human effort. We analyze the resulting extracted structures and combine them with techniques from unsupervised learning to get a domain overview.

In more detail, we first apply *information extraction* (IE) techniques to extract entities and relations. For example, the sentence *Nike Air for 25 €* contains information about a product and its price. The entities *Nike Air* of type *PROD* and *25* of type *MONEY* form a *PROD_PRICE* relation. Our annotation scheme defines six entity types and two relation types. These entities and relations create instances of *product offerings* and are our primary target data structure. We train deep learning NLP *entity recognition* (ER) and *relation extraction* (RE) models to extract product offerings from the text. For each, we define rule-based baselines and compare their performance against state-of-the-art transformer models. We associate all products with the sender of a chat message to form a profile. We use pretrained word vectors, like FastText, to get product representations and apply a pooling operation to receive a representation for each profile. A *t-sne* plot [31] visualizes user clusters. Finally, we introduce an evaluation strategy for profile clusterings. Our evaluation shows that combining IE and word vectors leads to meaningful representation for custom-extracted structures. The resulting data exploration strongly indicates illegal activities in the analyzed chat data. We see offerings of accounts for online services, like media streaming, clothing, or fake documents. The extracted information about product offerings allows a more profound analysis of market structures. We provide a case study that reveals insights into streaming account prices' characteristics.

The proposed methodology is more comprehensive than the use case under consideration. Vast amounts of textual data are present in many domains. Approaches like [16] analyze text based on pure textual features. Our approach allows an analysis on the level of domain-specific structures. While we focus on products and prices, our methodology allows the definition, extraction, and analysis of custom structures. We provide an entry point for practitioners and researchers of various domains to gain insights from existing textual data. Both our data and source code are available via GitHub[1]. We discuss design decisions in detail for each pipeline step and provide evaluation strategies to adopt alternative solutions.

This paper is an extension of [10]. We significantly extended the schema of product offerings. Instead of grouping prices and products via a nearest-neighbor

---

[1] https://github.com/Abuesgen/From-Cracked-Accounts-to-Fake-IDs.git.

approach, trained a RE model. Additionally, we defined the concept of *price criteria*. The concept includes price-related information, such as quantities or subscription periods. We applied FastText vectors optimized for german twitter text [11] and compared them to the previously used static general-purpose embeddings. Further, we added a more detailed analysis of our dataset, annotations, and the resulting product information in the crawled corpus. In summary, the following are this research's main contributions.

1. We crawled different german Telegram chat rooms and annotated entities and relations among them. The corpus is freely available.
2. We defined a domain-specific IE pipeline and discussed various design decisions with particular attention to the required workload.
3. We show that word vectors are a suitable representation of user profiles and create an explorative clustering.

In the following, Sect. 2 introduces the domain-specific goals and how we derive NLP tasks from those, and Sect. 3 investigates the annotations and corpus statistics. Section 4.4 introduces the pipeline to extract and vectorize user profiles before discussing the application on the crawled chat data in Sect. 5 exemplary for streaming accounts. Finally, we present related works in Sect. 6 and conclude, list future works, and discuss limitations in Sect. 7.

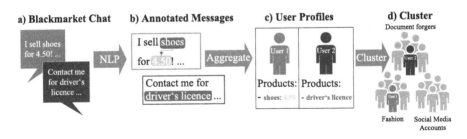

Fig. 1. Profile clustering pipeline visualization based on [10]. After crawling the messages using the Telegram API, we perform entity recognition to extract all relevant message attributes for chat user clustering and profile creation. We extended the pipeline based on the extracted entities by applying a relation extraction model on all PROD-MONEY and MONEY-CRIT pairs to extract prices and tariffs for product offerings. Together with the message's metadata, we aggregate all extracted entities and offerings to user profiles on which we perform the clustering operation in the last pipeline step.

2 Domain Discovery

Telegram messenger offers an encrypted and secure online messaging service. In addition to bilateral and private group chats, Telegram facilitates public groups with up to 200.000 members. A vast amount of websites emerge on the internet, providing a search engine for Telegram groups[2]. Besides groups for music, studies,

---

[2] Google request for the keyphrase "telegram groups" gives many results for search engines.

and TV shows, users provide groups for selling partially illegal commodities and services in so-called black market groups. The sellers (called vendors in the following) advertise, for instance, brand-name clothing and cigarettes, but also illegal things such as hacked accounts, counterfeit documents, and prescription drugs.

Vendors do not want to communicate publicly in groups with their customers. They prefer to switch to private bilateral chats with interested parties. Probably due to marketing methods, avoiding overloading the group and exposing all interactions, which could allow conclusions on the vendor's identity.

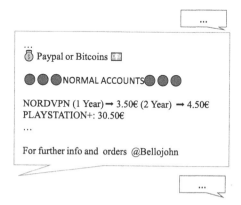

Fig. 2. The conversation shows a translated excerpt of a vendor message offering accounts with prices and partially additional price criteria (tariffs) information for the different subscription periods. The message shows highlighting emojis and a Telegram user mention.

Law enforcement agencies wish to gain insights into market structures and user behavior of the Telegram black market chat rooms. They want to avoid manually driven approaches to reduce the error-prone, monotonous, and laborious task of reading, marking relevant messages, and keeping track of recurring conspicuous users. Our research equips law enforcement agencies with a framework for analyzing german black market chat rooms by our top-down approach.

Figure 2 shows an excerpt of a typical vendor message with three product offerings. *Product offerings* contain information about a product with an optional price and product characteristic (e.g., quantities or like in Fig. 2 subscription periods). *NordVPN* and *PLAYSTATION+* represent such product offerings. Additional to the offerings, the vendor states two different accepted payment methods (*Paypal* and *Bitcoins*) and himself as the contact person (*@Bellojohn*) via the Telegram mention function[3] (see Fig. 3 for schema details). Telegram mentions (user names prefixed with an @) create hyperlinks to the user's profile to start private bilateral conversations quickly. Vendors prefer to post their offerings in the group chat and communicate with the customers via private chats.

---

[3] https://core.telegram.org/api/mentions.

In contrast to [10], we introduce a new entity *criteria (CRIT)* for normalizing product prices. Otherwise, we cannot compare the market prices of specific products directly. The price ranges would be large because not considering different product characteristics: e.g., *Netflix for 2 Years 35€* and *Netflix for 5 Years 50€* would result in a price range of 35–50€ without criteria; with the criteria, we can compute an annual price of 10–17.50€.

For the extraction of product offerings, we split the task into two NLP tasks: First, finding the products and their attributes (product, prices, and criteria) and, afterward, aggregating them to product offerings.

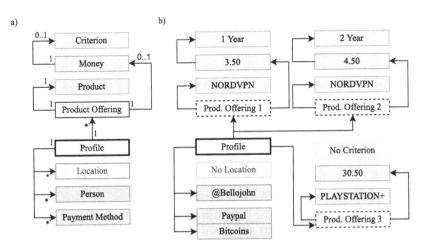

Fig. 3. a) shows the target data schema. We want to extract the natural language information into this schema. The profile represents the central entity. A profile links to any number of locations, persons, and payment methods. We define a new high-level concept *product offering* to aggregate different product-related attributes. We link a product to an optional price (money) and want to distinguish and normalize different tariffs. Thus, we introduce a price-changing criterion (e.g., quantities or subscription periods). The criterion links to money instead of the product offering. Because it shall directly influence the price by our definition. Thus linking criteria to money entities was chosen over linking them to the product entities. Product offerings cannot belong to a criterion without a corresponding price. **b)** represents an instance of the schema based on the example from Fig. 2. Note that the message does not provide information about locations or criteria for the *PLAYSTATION+* product.

2.1   Black Market Entities

We focus on the following concepts to map the previously mentioned information to a fixed schema (Fig. 3) for profile creation. These definitions describe the label set:

- **PROD (Product):** Describes offered commodities and services (e.g., Nord-VPN, Pullover, Spotify, ...).

– **MONEY (Money):** Represents the currency amount without the unit. This depends on the stated payment method. E.g., **10€**, **5** BTC (bold characters belong to the money label). The unit creates its own label type (see payment method below).
– **CRIT (Criteria):** Criteria represent product characteristics impacting the product prices. This label addresses a prior limitation of [10], which now allows us to differentiate between various periods and tariffs. E.g., 1 year, 2 years, 100 Views, 1k Views, ...
– **PAYM (Payment Method):** Vendors restrict their accepted payment methods to their preferred ones (cash, PayPal, BTC, ...).
– **PER (Person):** Mentions of person names functioning as a contact person: prefixed with @ as Telegram Mention or the plain name. Telegram Mention is preferred over a plain user name (e.g., @bellojohn).
– **LOC (Location):** Vendors use geographical information restricting their shipping country or region (Germany, Cologne).

Extracting this offering information from the unstructured natural language text is challenging: We face typical NLP social media challenges [40], such as heavy usage of emojis, non-continuous text, slang, and spelling mistakes. Furthermore, we face additional challenges: Vendors pitch their products with different names for the same product (*Disney* and *Disney+*, *Netflix UHD* and *Netflix Subscription*, ...). Additionally, we face highly correlated products which belong to different product categories: e.g., the offering *Spotify account* or *Spotify subscription* belongs to the category account credentials, while *Spotify views* count as social media service. It induces a challenge for the sequence labeling and the clustering approach. Subsection 4.4 discusses this challenge.

We use *entity recognition* (ER) to label text spans as one of the given labels (PROD, MONEY, ...). Thus, we can achieve an unlinked collection of sales attributes but cannot combine this information into product offerings (Fig. 3). Subsection 4.1 addresses the model architecture and training procedure. The following section addresses the preparation for training a relation extraction model to link the collection of sales attributes.

2.2   Black Market Relations

The black market chat messages often show a very high information density. Vendors state their offerings compressedly, such as enumerations (outlined in Fig. 2) and mention of product attributes. We restrict the label set to the ones stated in Subsect. 2.1. These entities represent mutual relations. The entities near each other likely build a product offering, but the evaluation will show that this heuristic does not hold for a significant amount of relations (Subsect. 4.2). The vendors use, e.g., indentation to show hierarchy and generic attributes regarding all indented elements. Thus, we use relation extraction to conclude the semantical connection between different entities and aggregate them into product offerings. We define two types of relation labels between the stated entities:

- **PROD_PRICE:** connects a money entity (*MONEY*) to a product (*PROD*). Not every product has a price.
- **PRICE_CRIT:** enriches a price - and therefore transitive the product - with a price-changing product characteristic.

Subsection 4.2 deals with extracting the product offerings with a deep learning approach. Addressing the defined tasks needs labeled data for training and evaluation. Therefore, in the next section, we describe the data collection, annotation approach, and the resulting corpus.

3   Corpus Composition

We crawled the textual group content of four black market groups from 6th July 2020–22nd October 2020 (107 days) via the Telegram API[4]. In this manner, we acquired a corpus with 28,312 messages. We randomly sampled 2,563 messages for further processing: annotating the concepts for the entity recognition and relation extraction task. We calculated an inter-annotator agreement on the triple-labeled test set to assess the annotation guidelines and our consensus with them on labeling entities. In [10] we calculated Krippendorff's alpha [28] for *PROD, MONEY, LOC, PER, PAYM*. We achieved a score of 0.61. Landis and Koch [30] rank this score as *substantial*[5]. After an annotation approval process, we labeled the new entity *CRIT* on a common base of the already annotated labels. Krippendorff's alpha reports 0.82 for the *CRIT* annotations, which [30] classify as *almost perfect*.

Table 1. The relative and absolute amount of data points in train development and test datasets with the corresponding number of tokens and annotations. Some multi-character emojis lead to indexing errors. Thus, we filtered out 22 data points.

Split	Ratio	# Samples	# Tokens	# Entities	# Relations
Train	0.70	1,779	38,271	5,792	2,143
Dev.	0.15	381	7,644	1,136	403
Test	0.15	381	8,882	1,416	542
Full	1.00	2,541	57,360	8,344	3,088

To our best knowledge, assessing the agreement on relations is challenging and less common than for entities. Differences in labeled entities will transitively impact the argument possibilities for the relations. In our case, the main challenge is achieving a high agreement for the entities. If we agree on them, the relations are pretty straightforward: Which price belongs to which product and criteria? The comparably high F1 score of .88 for RE with gold entity labels supports this intuition (Table 4). Thus, we mainly focus on the entity agreement.

---

[4] https://core.telegram.org/.
[5] The lower boundary of the second-best score.

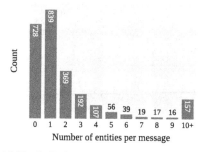
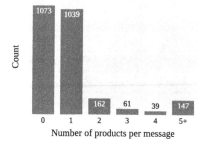

(a) The distribution shows that the corpus' dominant part contains no or up to 4 entities per message. We aggregated all counts for more than nine entities in a single class due to the low frequencies across the broad range. The maximum number in one message reaches 88 entities.

(b) The products represent the central concept in this corpus. Most messages mention no or a single product. We aggregated the counts for more than four products in a single class (5+). Few vendors offer up to 38 products in one message.

Fig. 4. Entity Statistics.

For the training of our deep learning models, we divided the 2,541 messages randomly into training, development, and test set. See Table 1 for details. The corpus provides information about entities and relations. One message contains on average 3.3 (1.0 for median) entities. Most messages have less than ten entities (see Fig. 4a). Focusing on the product annotations reveals that the messages mostly contain less than two products (see Fig. 4b). Messages with no product annotations address the previous posts and represent questions regarding prices, sizes, or general questions and information to the users.

Users prefer to offer or ask for a single specific product in a message. The question mark is an indicator for product requests. 1,039 messages contain only a single product mention. 17% of these messages are identified as requests.

The label distribution (Fig. 5a) supports the latter due to the messages' ratio of products and money occurrences. Requests or questions about a product do not need a linked price. Furthermore, vendors sometimes mention the same product several times in a message, but not every mention has a corresponding price tag. Payment method, person, and location are the less frequent concepts. Vendors state multiple payment methods once per message but only one contact person or often no one at all (see mention definition in Sect. 2). Locations are very rare due to the wish to stay anonymous. Vendors use locations to restrict the shipping region or country. Few vendors offer SMS verification services for several countries. Thus, we face outliers with up to 17 locations in a single message.

We use relations between the stated entities to aggregate product information to product offerings. 2,005 messages do not contain any relations. 412 messages contain one to five relations, and 671 messages contain up to 48 relations. Figure 5b compares the number of offerings with additional criteria and products with solely price information. The difference between these two relation types indicates that about 40% of the product offerings with prices show additional criteria. In [10] the extracted prices are inaccurate for these offerings. This accords with the criteria's entity label distribution.

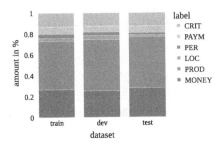 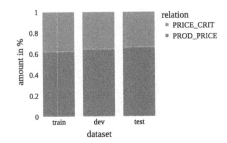

(a) The relative entity label frequencies comparison across all data sets. *PROD* represents the dominant label. Not every product links to a *MONEY* entity. Less frequent labels are *PAYM*, *PER*, and *LOC*. The label distribution across the data sets is nearly identical.

(b) The relative relation label frequencies are similar across the data sets. PROD_PRICE and PRICE_CRIT are limited by the corresponding entities. See a) and Table 1 for details.

Fig. 5. Entity and relation frequencies across data sets.

Entities and relations show nearly the same distribution across our training, development, and test dataset. This indicates a common data distribution and reflects a consistent training and evaluation setting.

The *PROD_PRICE* relation between the entities facilitates evaluating our heuristical nearest-neighbor approach (see Subsect. 4.2). It also reveals a new opportunity to train a machine learning model to improve the information extraction of product offerings (see Subsect. 4.2). The following chapters will address each pipeline step, including the architectures and training details for the ER and RE task using the corpus at hand.

4   Profile Clustering Pipeline

In this section, we will discuss the complete profile clustering pipeline. We will explain each pipeline step in a dedicated subsection. Figure 1 shows the extended profile clustering pipeline based on [10]. The main extension of the pipeline is incorporating a sophisticated relation extraction (RE) model. Further, in addition to *product-price* (PROD_PRICE) relations, we added the new relation type *price-criteria* (PRICE_CRIT), allowing us to recognize different tariffs. As shown in Fig. 1, the profile clustering pipeline consists of the following steps:

a) In this pipeline step, we used the dedicated Telegram API to crawl chat messages from self-proclaimed german black market chat groups. We then saved all crawled messages in JSON format for further processing. Section 3 describes the crawled dataset in detail.

b) In step b), we apply the black market entity recognition and relation extraction models to every chat message. This step yields chat messages containing PROD, MONEY, PAYM, LOC, CRIT, and PER annotations together with the earlier described relations PROD_PRICE and PRICE_CRIT. Subsection 4.1 and Subsect. 4.2 describe the training of black market entity recognition and relation extraction models.

c) Based on the annotated chat messages, we create user profiles by aggregating the annotations for each user's chat messages. Together with the metadata of the chat messages, this step allows us to gain deep insights into the products, prices, tariffs each user offers, and usage behavior. Further, the aggregation of the annotations allows us to create vector representations for clustering. Subsection 4.3 describes the aggregation of annotated chat messages into user profiles.

d) The last pipeline step uses the aggregated profiles to cluster users into groups using the product catalog of each user. This step allows us to group users who sell similar products together. This step is essential to enable law enforcement agencies to analyze such groups quickly and efficiently. It allows them to focus on relevant user groups (e.g., users selling products from specific product categories) instead of checking each user individually. Section 4.4 describes the creation and evaluation of different vector representations for product entities, and Subsect. 4.4 describes how these representations enable the clustering of black market chat users.

We conducted our experiments using a private infrastructure with a carbon efficiency of 0.488 kgCO$_2$eq/kWh. Our experiments took 40 h of computation on Nvidia hardware of type RTX 8000 (TDP of 260W). Total emissions are estimated to be 5.08 kgCO$_2$eq. For our estimations, we used the MachineLearning Impact calculator[6] presented in [29].

4.1 Black Market Entity Recognition Model Training

Analyzing the content of chat messages poses a complex task because they are usually short and use social media language excessively, as described in Sect. 3. Further, the extraction of sales attributes such as product offerings and different product tariffs differ from traditional natural language benchmarks as they usually use other data sources such as newspaper articles. We divided the black market entity recognition and relation extraction into two separate NLP tasks for our processing pipeline. This division allows us to use the entity recognition model architecture described in [10].

In addition to the original model architectures, we added the new concept *CRIT* to the entity recognition task. We re-iterated all 565 documents containing both PROD and MONEY entities for this extension and added annotations for the concept *CRIT*. Subsection 2.1 describes the new concept in detail.

We used the same baseline (BASE) approach described in [10] for evaluation. This approach labels all consecutive characters and tokens representing numbers as MONEY entities. For non-MONEY entities, the baseline approach uses a dictionary that contains the lowercase representation of every entity annotated in the train set. For this reason, the baseline approach can not generalize to unknown terms. The classic model (CLASSIC) shown in Fig. 6 achieved the same overall F1-Score of 0.79 (see [10]), although the model now has to predict the additional label CRIT.

---

[6] https://mlco2.github.io/impact#compute.

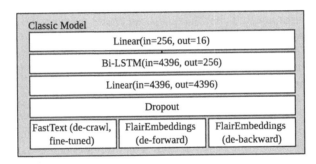

Fig. 6. Block diagram of the Classic Model (CLASSIC) architecture used in [10]. The architecture uses german FastText embeddings in conjunction with contextual string embeddings [4] (de-forward and de-backward). A linear layer with a BI-LSTM-CRF [24] produces the label for each token. In contrast to the original model in [10], the model has two additional outputs for the labels B-CRIT and I-CRIT.

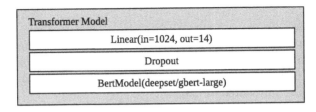

Fig. 7. Block diagram of the Transformer Model (BERT) architecture used in [10]. The architecture uses the german BERT model from deepset (*deepset/gbert-large*) [12] in conjunction with a dropout and a linear layer for classification. In contrast to the original model in [10] the model has two additional outputs for the labels B-CRIT and I-CRIT.

The transformer model (BERT) shown in Fig. 7 achieves the highest overall micro F1-score of 0.82. Except for the label *CRIT* the BERT model achieves the highest F1 scores (the baseline model achieves an F1-score of 0.8 on the CRIT label, but the BERT model only achieves a performance of 0.7). However, the overall F1-score of 0.82 stayed the same. This difference may indicate that the BERT model could improve further with more annotated examples containing CRIT labels.

In addition to re-evaluating the sequence tagger models described in [10], we trained two new models using 100-dimensional FastText embeddings trained on german Twitter posts [11]. The first model uses the mentioned Twitter FastText embeddings (TWITTER) as is. Therefore the architecture is almost identical to the Classic model (CLASSIC) shown in Fig. 6. The only difference is that the used FastText model differs and that the tokens were lowercased before the embedding step because the original FastText vectors are optimized for lowercased texts [11]. The second model uses fine-tuned Twitter FastText embeddings (FTWITTER). We fine-tuned the model for five epochs on all raw text chat messages in the black market dataset. While the fine-tuned twitter model achieved a higher F1-Score (0.80) than the classic model, the transformer model stayed the best model we tested. However, we found that Twitter embeddings yield better results for user clustering than BERT (see Sect. 4.4). Table 2 shows a detailed comparison of the achieved F1 scores per label.

Table 2. F1 score for each label and model. MICRO shows the micro-averaged F1 score for each model. In contrast to [10], this table includes the F1 scores for the new label CRIT as well as the data of the new Twitter models TWITTER and FTWITTER. However, the best model is still the transformer model (BERT).

	BASE	CLASSIC	BERT	TWITTER	FTWITTER
CRIT	**.80**	.68	.70	.67	.71
LOC	.67	.81	**.89**	.81	.83
MONEY	.77	.98	**.98**	.98	.97
PAYM	.77	.94	**.98**	.94	.93
PER	.63	.82	**.87**	.75	.81
PROD	.69	.69	**.74**	.67	.69
MICRO	.73	.79	**.82**	.78	.80

4.2   Black Market Relation Extraction Model Training

Subsequently, to the black market entity recognition, we perform a relation extraction (RE) on all recognized PROD-MONEY and MONEY-CRIT span pairs. These relations allow us to gain deep insights into the product offerings and tariffs in the black market chat groups. Further, this new relation extraction yields more sophisticated results and allows a better evaluation of the nearest-neighbor approach discussed in [10]. The current section describes the training process and results for the relation extraction model.

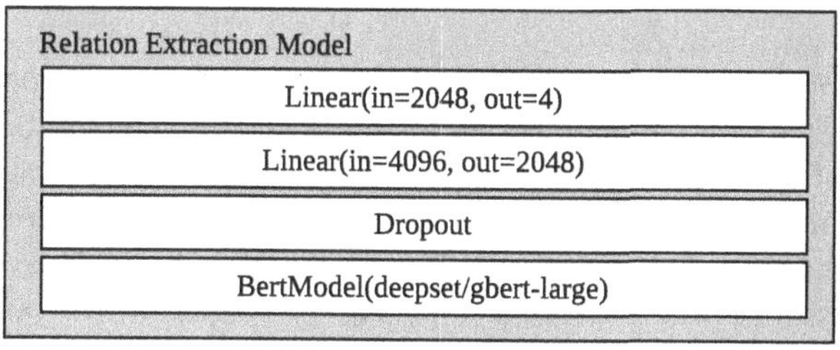

Fig. 8. Block diagram of the relation extraction model. The model consists of a BERT model, which encodes all relation candidates. The BERT encodings are passed through different dropouts and into two stacked linear layers for classification. For each entity pair, the model yields one of the four classes PROD_PRICE, PRICE_CRIT, no relation, and a technical *unknown* class created by flair.

We decided to use flairs' *RelationExtractor* model [3] for extracting PROD_PRICE and PRICE_CRIT relations. The relation extraction model classifies all possible PROD-MONEY and MONEY-CRIT pairs as either PROD_PRICE, PRICE_CRIT, or no relation. The model embeds the textual information for every pair using the german BERT model *deepset/gbert-large* in conjunction with a linear classification layer. Figure 8 shows the corresponding block diagram of the RelationExtractor.

To reduce the training-production gap, we trained our RE model on the predicted entities of the BERT black market entity recognition model instead of using the gold entity annotations. We evaluated the resulting model against the baseline nearest-neighbor approach presented in [10] on the test set. The original paper only considered one price per product. As shown in Fig. 3, multiple prices can be associated with one product. This is common for different subscription periods or quantities. We consider all prices present for each product. Additionally, we performed a hyperparameter search using Optuna [5]. We trained 100 models for 100 epochs each and took the model configuration with the best micro F1-score for our final training. Table 3 shows each parameter we considered in our hyperparameter search.

Table 3. Resulting parameters of the hyperparameter search for the relation extraction model performed with Optuna [5]. We performed a total of 90 trials in which we trained the model for 100 epochs. For our final training, we used the values from the column *best value*.

parameter	search space	best value
optimizer	ADAM, SGD	ADAM
learning rate	1e−7–1e−4	3.17e−5
transformer model	gbert-large, twhin-bert-large	gbert-large
word dropout	0–0.2	0.1431
locked dropout	0–0.2	0.0713
dropout	0–0.2	0.0253

Our model achieves an overall micro F1-score of 0.88 on the gold entity labels. The product-price relation achieves an F1-score of 0.88, which is 0.22 higher than the F1-score of our baseline model (nearest-neighbor) for this relation (0.66). In [10], the gold annotations relate products only to the nearest prices. The resulting F1 score (0.74) is comparably high. We extend this definition and annotate all product price relations. The nearest-neighbor (NN) approach misses many relations following the novel definition. Therefore the performance drops to 0.66.

A comparison for the price-criteria relation was not performed because the baseline model does not predict this relation. However, the relation extraction model achieves a performance of 0.90 for the price-criteria relation. We also evaluated our model on the predicted entity labels to assess the model performance in a more realistic setting. This *chained* approach yields an overall performance of 0.62, while the product-price relation achieves a performance of 0.64, which is almost on par with the performance of the NN relation extraction with gold entity labels. Table 4 shows the scores for the relation extraction for comparison.

Table 4. F1 scores for the gold annotations from [10] (NN [10]), baseline nearest-neighbor approach (NN (baseline)), and our relation extraction model (RE) on the gold entities as well as the F1 scores for the RE model on the predictions of the best black market entity recognition model.

	NN [10]	NN (baseline, gold)	RE (gold)	RE (chained)
PROD-PRICE	.74	.66	.88	.64
PRICE-CRIT	–	–	.90	.58
MICRO	.74	.66	.88	.62

4.3 Profile Creation

We use the entity recognition and relation extraction components' results to extract the product offerings and store the information in a structured schema (Fig. 3). They allow the algorithmic analysis of the initial unstructured natural language. We iterate over all messages, run the NLP components, and aggregate the extracted information by each user (see Fig. 1 step b) to c)). Thus, we gain a collection of different information types per user: user id, names, messages with structured product data, and metadata such as post times per day or daytime. See Fig. 13 in the appendix and the case study in [10] for an example visualization. The profiles help law enforcement agencies to gain insights into the user's behavior. Based on the structured data, they can perform their own analysis. More in Sect. 5.

4.4 Profile Clustering

The generated structured user profiles allow us to perform complex analyses, such as grouping users by the product categories they sell. The following section explains how we create and evaluate vector representations for user profiles. We evaluated four additional embedding mechanisms in our extension to [10]. Of which some yielded significantly better results for the user profile clustering task. In the current section, we will evaluate and compare these product embeddings and create user clusters based on the product catalog of each user.

Product Embeddings Comparision. To create meaningful user clustering, one must choose an appropriate vectorization and distance measure for the objects to cluster. Choosing the right vectorization and distance measure is essential to create clusters fit for the targeted use case. We will explain the product vectorization evaluation method developed in [10]. Afterward, we evaluate

Table 5. Table of annotated product categories and the number of contained products from [10]. The authors divided 1,040 products into ten product categories. They argue that a *good* product vector representation should yield high similarity scores within each group and low similarity between groups. We used the same dataset for the evaluation of additional vector representations.

Name	Size
Accounts	259
Cigarettes	20
Documents	30
Drugs and Medication	21
Electronics	42
Fashion	334
Social Media Services	77
Software	67
Watches	75
Other	115
Sum	1,040

new vectorization methods and choose a method that achieves higher separation scores than the ones reported in the original paper. In [10], the authors developed a benchmarking procedure to compare different vectorizations for products by dividing a sample of 1,040 product names into ten defined product categories (Table 5). The authors argue that products from the same category should yield a high similarity score and products from different categories should yield a low similarity score. This procedure enabled the authors to compare these embeddings to the human understanding of product categories and choose an appropriate embedding to generate meaningful user profile clusters. We use the same dataset as in the original paper for our evaluation. Table 5 shows the number of products per category in the evaluation dataset. To create the evaluation dataset, the authors normalized the product names by lowercasing, removing non-word characters, and condensing whitespaces. After normalization, three annotators divided a sample of 1,040 products into ten categories. The authors achieved an inter-annotator agreement of 0.84[7] [10, p. 6]. Based on these annotations, they use the concept of affinity to motivate affinity difference matrices $D \in \mathbb{R}^{n \times n}$ for n product categories to compare different product vectorizations. The entries $d_{i,j}, 1 \leq i, j \leq n$ of the affinity difference matrix are computed as shown in Eq. 1 (see [10]).

$$d_{i,j} = \begin{cases} a_{i,j} - a_{i,i} & j \geq i \\ a_{i,j} - a_{j,j} & \text{otherwise} \end{cases} \quad (1)$$

---

[7] Following Krippendorff's alpha.

$a_{i,j}, 1 \leq i, j \leq n$ are the entries of the affinity matrix A, which describes the mean cosine affinity between the product categories i and j. Equation 2 shows the equation to compute the entries for the affinity matrice (adapted from [10]).

$$a_{i,j} = \begin{cases} \frac{2}{n(n-1)} \sum_{i=0}^{n-1} \sum_{j=i+1}^{n} \frac{<s_i,s_j>}{||s_i||\cdot||s_j||} & i = j \\ \frac{1}{nm} \sum_{i=0}^{n} \sum_{j=0}^{m} \frac{<s_i,t_j>}{||s_i||\cdot||t_j||} & \text{otherwise} \end{cases} \tag{2}$$

In addition to the CLASSIC, BERT, and GBERT embeddings which the authors evaluated in [10], this extension evaluates four additional vector representations:

1. the raw Twitter FastText embeddings [11],
2. the fine-tuned Twitter FastText embeddings ([11], but fine-tuned on our data for five epochs),
3. T-Systems Roberta sentence transformer model (*T-Systems-onsite/cross-en-de-roberta-sentence-transformer*) [2],
4. and a multilingual BERT model trained on tweets (*Twitter/twhin-bert-large*) [42]

We observed that the fine-tuned FastText Twitter embeddings yield the best separation score of -0.17, which is by 0.08 better than the previously best separation score of -0.09 (see Table 6). Therefore we conclude that the fine-tuned FastText Twitter embeddings yield better vector representations for the clustering task than the previously used CLASSIC embeddings. The full matrix can be found in the Appendix (Fig. 12).

Table 6. Overview of the mean separation score and variance for the tested product vectorizations. Lower scores indicate better separation of the different product categories. We observed that the fine-tuned FastText embeddings performed as well as the default Twitter embeddings; however, the fine-tuned embeddings yielded a lower variance.

Vectorization	Separation Score
CLASSIC (baseline) [10]	$-.09 \pm .0002$
Twitter	$-.17 \pm .0052$
Twitter (fine-tuned)	$\mathbf{-.17 \pm .0048}$
T-Systems	$-.12 \pm .0042$
TWHIN	$-.09 \pm .0031$

User Clustering and Naming. In the previous section, we compared four additional token vectorization methods and chose one vectorization method which yielded better token vector representations for product similarity and dissimilarity. In [10], the authors used these vector representations to create *user profile* vector representations p_f by averaging all product vectorizations (p_{r_i}) for one profile. Equation 3 shows this averaging process.

$$p_f = \frac{1}{n} \sum_{i=1}^{n} p_{r_i} \tag{3}$$

Based on these vectorizations, the authors applied clustering algorithms to find clusters of users having a similar product portfolio. They used scikit-learn's agglomerative clustering [1,35] algorithm. They argued that the agglomerative clustering algorithm is useful for this application because it allows the data analyst to choose a custom distance threshold, allowing flexibility while exploring chat groups. Further, this clustering algorithm does not require the user to input the desired cluster count, which is usually unknown.

The authors applied the same averaging to the profile vectors within each cluster to create cluster vectors c_{vec} (see Eq. 4). These cluster vectors could then be compared to each product using the same cosine distance. The product with the lowest distance to the cluster vector became the representative product p_{rep} for the cluster and, therefore, the name for the given cluster (see Eq. 5). This method allows law enforcement agencies to only focus on clusters of interest at the start of their investigation. Figure 9 shows a clustering result we conducted using fine-tuned Twitter embeddings.

$$c_{\text{vec}}(C) = \frac{1}{|C|} \sum_{p_f \in C} p_f \tag{4}$$

$$p_{\text{rep}}(C, P) = \underset{p \in P}{\operatorname{argmin}}(1 - \frac{<p, c_{\text{vec}}(C)>}{||p|| \cdot ||c_{\text{vec}}(C)||}) \tag{5}$$

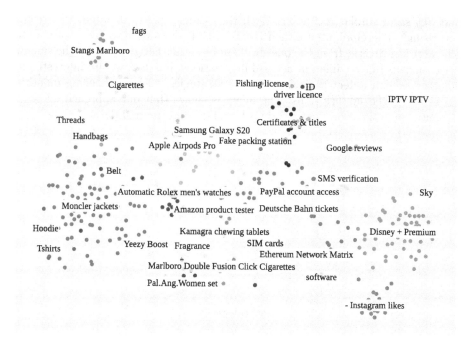

Fig. 9. t-sne plot of the clustering results using the fine-tuned Twitter FastText embeddings. Each point represents one user profile. Besides fashion items and cracked streaming accounts, one can find the clusters *Fishing license, ID, and driver licence*, which contain users selling counterfeit documents.

5   Case Study

The profile clustering visualization in Fig. 9 gives a high-level overview of the range of goods in the crawled chat groups. [41] explains how the *t-sne* plot may wrongly represent some features of the clustering, like distance or size of clusters. Nevertheless, the cluster titles indicate a wide variety of offered products.

[10] includes a detailed analysis of the messages' metadata, entity annotations, and the nearest-neighbor product price relation. This chapter aims to point out the benefits of our extensions. Especial, we focus on the learned relation extraction and the price criteria. Besides the effects on this data analysis, Sect. 4 discusses how the extensions positively affect the various performance measures—the improved performance results in a more accurate analysis. This section aims to provide an intuition about the insights made possible by our analysis framework. For an exemplary analysis, we focus on the product category of *cracked streaming accounts*. Figure 9 represents this cluster by the tag *Disney+ Premium*. In a similar fashion, law enforcement may focus on other areas, such as *fake ids* or *fake branded clothes*.

We aim to investigate the price structure of illegal streaming access. Regarding the PROD_PRICE relations, the unnormalized price ranges for *NordVPN* and *Sky* seem similar in Fig. 11. With their official prices in mind, this seems surprising[8]. Therefore, we use the PRICE_CRIT annotation to investigate if the official prices diverge from the ones in these black market groups or if the similar price range is due to different accessibility periods. Further, we are interested in whether we can detect typical marketing strategies, such as reducing monthly prices on longer subscriptions. The analysis shows that our approach allows a semantic analysis of product offerings based on pure textual data.

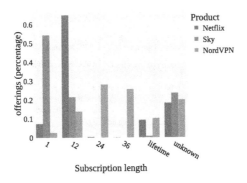

Fig. 10. Histogram showing the most frequent subscription periods for streaming offerings. While Netflix is mostly offered as a yearly subscription, Sky is offered as a monthly subscription. The numerical values on the x-axis represent months.

Subsection 2.2 describes the PRICE_CRIT annotation. We assume we have three major categories for the analysis: monthly, yearly, and lifetime constraints. String matching differentiates the three categories. Users may specify time ranges for the first two, as *12 months* or *2 years*. We apply regular expressions to identify such numeric patterns. If we detect *month* or *year* as keywords without a numeric value, we assume that one month or year is the specified period. If we detect neither *month*, *year*, nor *lifetime*, we specify it as an unknown criterion. Figure 10 shows the relative quantities of time-related price criteria for different product categories. Vendors tend towards long-time offers for NordVPN and one or 12-month accessibility for Sky. We cannot investigate the causalities, but the observation indicates that our framework extracts semantical and non-random structures.

As a next step, we investigate the prices per month. Figure 11a shows the impact of accessibility periods on the overall price. While *Netflix* has the highest overall price, its monthly price is substantially below Sky. Similarly, the package prices for NordVPN and Sky are similar, but the monthly prices for NordVPN are substantially lower. The figure shows various outliers, overall prices for Nord-VPN, for example. These may be due to model prediction errors. A distinction

---

[8] At the time of writing this paper, the monthly premium package prices are 5.29 € for NordVPN and 30,00 € for the first year, and 66,90 € afterward for Sky in Germany.

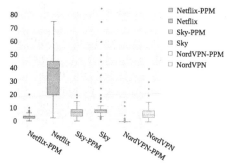
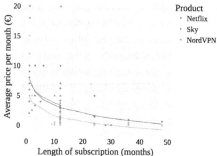

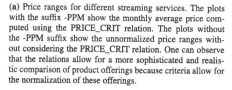

(a) Price ranges for different streaming services. The plots with the suffix -PPM show the monthly average price computed using the PRICE_CRIT relation. The plots without the -PPM suffix show the unnormalized price ranges without considering the PRICE_CRIT relation. One can observe that the relations allow for a more sophisticated and realistic comparison of product offerings because criteria allow for the normalization of these offerings.

(b) Scatterplot of the length of subscription periods compared to their average monthly price. We fitted a log-linear model (least square method with logarithmic x values) to illustrate the pricing trend better. As intuition suggests, the average monthly price decreases for longer subscription periods. The plot also suggests that Sky subscriptions are only possible monthly and yearly, as no other subscription periods were found in the dataset.

Fig. 11. Price analysis for streaming services.

from arguably high prices, yearly access to a Sky account requires a manual error inspection. Finally, we want to show that our results indicate standard marketing properties in the offerings. Figure 11b shows the correlation between monthly price and accessibility period. Even though this seems intuitive, this result hints at a supposedly correct content trend of the extracted product offerings and the extracted user profiles.

6 Related Work

Social media is omnipresent in many parts of modern societies. The vast amount of publicly available data makes it an attention-grabbing research subject. [15,39] analyze social media to gain insight into social moods regarding the COVID-19 pandemic, or [13] investigates how social media analysis helps to predict the outcome of elections. These researchers apply sentiment analysis and opinion mining to draw topic-related conclusions about large groups of individuals. We must note that we characterize users by product offerings, which are extracted semantic structures from text. Therefore, a more sophisticated NLP Pipeline is needed. It is common to focus on large groups of individuals when analyzing social networks. [34] introduced the field of community detection. The network graph consists of arcs, which are network-dependent relations among users, for example, *following* or *friendship*. Current methods combine graph theoretical concepts with deep learning methods [25,37]. Communities consist of users sharing certain sets of attributes. For example, they are like-minded relative to specific topics. The goal is related to ours, but the underlying data is different. We do not use any underlying network information but the meaning of product names to group users. [20] combines textual features extracted via NLP with community detection to identify fake Twitter users.

Many social media platforms do not focus on direct user-to-user relationships. Users send each other direct messages or broadcast messages to groups or channels. Instant messaging (IM) has become part of everyday communication and an essential part of social media usage. It is the subject of various research directions. For example, [26] investigates the influence on language learners, or [33] explores how IM services spread news. Companies offer chat-based customer service. [32,38] analyze business-to-customer communication. Their major focus is the user's intent and the resulting conversation history. [20] create user profiles from text entities. Both publications aim to increase customer satisfaction by analyzing moods in messages rather than extracting structured information.

Telegram started in 2013 and became a popular communication medium during the COVID-19 pandemic. [16] analyze the contents and social phenomena of the Telegram messenger service. They focus on Telegram's combination of private and public communication. Mainly how viral messages spread across groups and channels. As a part, they determine messages' sentiment and category with supervised NLP techniques. Similar to our findings, using word embeddings as text features improves system performance. The results in [23] are exemplary for domain-specific topic analysis of Telegram data. They identify topics related to the QAnon conspiracy theory and analyze the evolvement of the toxic language across languages in this domain. [9] also focuses on Telegram as a market for illegal psychoactive substances. They explore how the COVID-19 pandemic and related events affected market behaviors. In contrast to our deep learning NLP-based methodology, messages are drug-related based on keywords.

[6,14] investigate black markets available via the TOR network. [21] creates user profiles from crawled data. These investigations use structured data and develop more focused insights compared to [9,23], which focuses on overall text features. The application of NLP and IE enables us to create insights comparable to the previously mentioned dark web studies without the need for structured data.

Our analysis focuses on users and related product offerings. These product offerings are information structures extracted from text. Common relation extraction methodology focuses on binary relations [19,43]. Event extraction removes semantic structures with multiple attributes. It defines event-central *trigger* annotations, and each attribute is in a binary relation with such trigger annotation [18]. [27] investigates the influence of these trigger annotations on the extraction of event structures. For the german language, [22] introduced a corpus with traffic events. Other IE sources focus on entity recognition [7,36].

We apply pretrained transformer models [17]. These build the foundation of state-of-the-art NLP and IE models for various languages. [4] introduces flair, a state-of-the-art NLP library. We apply this library to our IE models.

7   Conclusion and Future Work

In this extension study of [10], we refined the method for extracting vendor profiles from anonymous chat messages with a new entity, relation extraction, and additional word representations for the clustering technique. We provide reproducible research, thus, making the corpus and the code publicly available. The corpus allows the utilization of product attributes and mutual relations between these for analyzing social media user behavior in the black markets.

We applied natural language processing (NLP) techniques to extract relevant information from the corpus and cluster the profiles based on their selling behavior. Our evaluation found that transformer models were effective for entity recognition, but a fine-tuned Twitter FastText model performed better for clustering. As demonstrated in our case study (Sect. 5), besides analysis of metadata and sold products, the new entity CRIT facilitates the normalization of product prices. It allows a less biased automatic comparison of products with different properties (e.g., subscription periods and quantities). The case study shows the information gain related to marketing strategies for different products and their offered subscription periods. The structured data facilitates various custom analyses of the black market chat data. Our framework makes textual analyses easier and more accessible for a broad user range.

Explorative approaches can be challenging to evaluate due to their inherent nature of seeking to uncover new and unknown information. To address this issue, we developed a method for assessing the relative quality of different approaches. We discovered through this process that fine-tuned FastText embeddings allow better product separation (by a relative performance gain of 47%) than the best approach in [10]. Our findings suggest that we can find the semantic classes reasonably by having a better separation score. This yields a better-performing explorative analysis and meaningful insights.

In future work, we aim to explore alternative approaches for generating profile vectors and finding cluster names. Currently, we use an averaging strategy for aggregating the vectors of individual products. However, other aggregating strategies may provide more accurate or valuable representations of profiles. In addition, we want to investigate methods for allowing a single profile belonging to multiple clusters. In this study, each profile can only be part of a single cluster, but there may be cases where a profile belongs to multiple clusters simultaneously. One potential approach for addressing this issue is to use topic modeling techniques, which allow the assignment of multiple topics to a single document. Further research is needed to determine the feasibility and effectiveness of these methods for our purposes.

Appendix

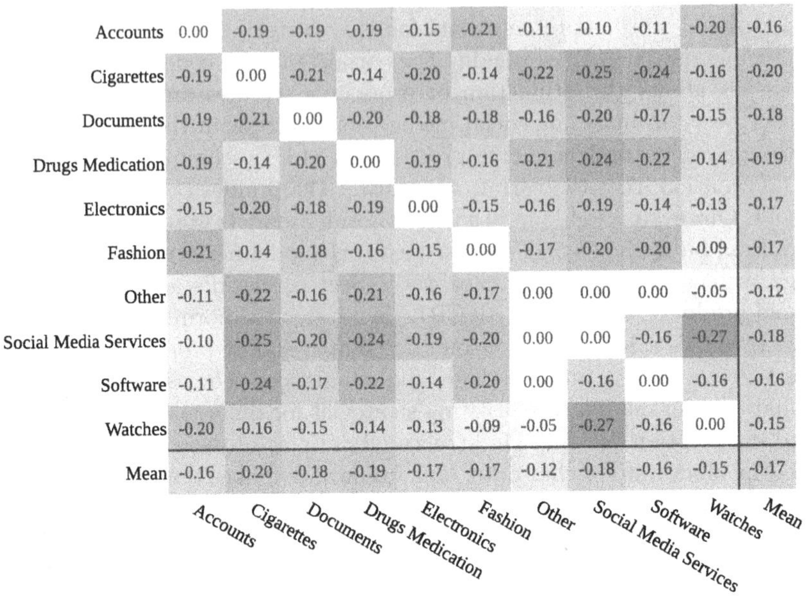

	Accounts	Cigarettes	Documents	Drugs Medication	Electronics	Fashion	Other	Social Media Services	Software	Watches	Mean
Accounts	0.00	-0.19	-0.19	-0.19	-0.15	-0.21	-0.11	-0.10	-0.11	-0.20	-0.16
Cigarettes	-0.19	0.00	-0.21	-0.14	-0.20	-0.14	-0.22	-0.25	-0.24	-0.16	-0.20
Documents	-0.19	-0.21	0.00	-0.20	-0.18	-0.18	-0.16	-0.20	-0.17	-0.15	-0.18
Drugs Medication	-0.19	-0.14	-0.20	0.00	-0.19	-0.16	-0.21	-0.24	-0.22	-0.14	-0.19
Electronics	-0.15	-0.20	-0.18	-0.19	0.00	-0.15	-0.16	-0.19	-0.14	-0.13	-0.17
Fashion	-0.21	-0.14	-0.18	-0.16	-0.15	0.00	-0.17	-0.20	-0.20	-0.09	-0.17
Other	-0.11	-0.22	-0.16	-0.21	-0.16	-0.17	0.00	0.00	0.00	-0.05	-0.12
Social Media Services	-0.10	-0.25	-0.20	-0.24	-0.19	-0.20	0.00	0.00	-0.16	-0.27	-0.18
Software	-0.11	-0.24	-0.17	-0.22	-0.14	-0.20	0.00	-0.16	0.00	-0.16	-0.16
Watches	-0.20	-0.16	-0.15	-0.14	-0.13	-0.09	-0.05	-0.27	-0.16	0.00	-0.15
Mean	-0.16	-0.20	-0.18	-0.19	-0.17	-0.17	-0.12	-0.18	-0.16	-0.15	-0.17

Fig. 12. Affinity difference matrix between all product categories using the fine-tuned FastText embeddings. Equation 1 describes the computation yielding this matrix.

Profile for User 'SchikkasLuxuxlaedchen (482381205)'

User

ID	482381205
Username	SchikkasLuxuxlaedchen
First name	Danny
Last Name	Die Patin⚡
Telephone	

Payment Methods

Method	Message count
Paypal	1
Remittance	2
PayPal	1
PP	3

Persons

Person	Message count
@admin	2

Locations

Location	Message count
De	2

Products

Product	Prices	Criteria	Message count
Purses			1

Show Messages

Message IDs	Message
• 36365	What exactly are you looking for I have bags **PROD** and purses **PROD**

Fig. 13. We generate an HTML site for the aggregated message information. The translated excerpt shows general information about the user and an example product with prices and counts. If vendors offer the same product in several messages, we aggregate all these messages by the product. The interested viewer can inspect each message from which the NLP approach extracted information. We changed the visualization slightly for the compressed presentation.

References

1. Sklearn.cluster.AgglomerativeClustering.   https://scikit-learn.org/stable/modules/generated/sklearn.cluster.AgglomerativeClustering.html.   Accessed 01 Mar 2022
2. T-Systems-onsite/cross-en-de-roberta-sentence-transformer · Hugging Face. https://huggingface.co/T-Systems-onsite/cross-en-de-roberta-sentence-transformer. Accessed 14 Dec 2022
3. Akbik, A., Bergmann, T., Blythe, D., Rasul, K., Schweter, S., Vollgraf, R.: FLAIR: an easy-to-use framework for state-of-the-art NLP. In: Proceedings of the 2019 Conference of the North American Chapter of the Association for Computational Linguistics (Demonstrations), pp. 54–59. Association for Computational Linguistics, Minneapolis, June 2019. https://doi.org/10.18653/v1/N19-4010. https://aclanthology.org/N19-4010
4. Akbik, A., Blythe, D., Vollgraf, R.: Contextual string embeddings for sequence labeling. In: Proceedings of the 27th International Conference on Computational

Linguistics, pp. 1638–1649. Association for Computational Linguistics, Santa Fe, August 2018. https://aclanthology.org/C18-1139

5. Akiba, T., Sano, S., Yanase, T., Ohta, T., Koyama, M.: Optuna: a next-generation hyperparameter optimization framework. In: Proceedings of the 25th ACM SIGKDD International Conference on Knowledge Discovery & Data Mining, KDD 2019, pp. 2623–2631. Association for Computing Machinery, New York, July 2019. https://doi.org/10.1145/3292500.3330701

6. Baravalle, A., Lopez, M.S., Lee, S.W.: Mining the dark web: drugs and fake ids. In: 2016 IEEE 16th International Conference on Data Mining Workshops (ICDMW), pp. 350–356, December 2016. https://doi.org/10.1109/ICDMW.2016.0056

7. Benikova, D., Biemann, C., Reznicek, M.: NoSta-D named entity annotation for German: guidelines and dataset. In: Proceedings of the Ninth International Conference on Language Resources and Evaluation (LREC 2014), pp. 2524–2531. European Language Resources Association (ELRA), Reykjavik, May 2014. http://www.lrec-conf.org/proceedings/lrec2014/pdf/276_Paper.pdf

8. Bitkom: Neun von zehn Internetnutzern verwenden Messenger | Bitkom Main (2018). http://www.bitkom.org/Presse/Presseinformation/Neun-von-zehn-Internetnutzern-verwenden-Messenger.html. Accessed 18 Feb 2022

9. Blankers, M., van der Gouwe, D., Stegemann, L., Smit-Rigter, L.: Changes in online psychoactive substance trade via telegram during the COVID-19 pandemic. Eur. Addict. Res. **27**(6), 469–474 (2021). https://doi.org/10.1159/000516853. https://www.karger.com/Article/FullText/516853

10. Büsgen, A., Klöser, L., Kohl, P., Schmidts, O., Kraft, B., Zündorf, A.: Exploratory analysis of chat-based black market profiles with natural language processing. In: Proceedings of the 11th International Conference on Data Science, Technology and Applications, pp. 83–94. SCITEPRESS - Science and Technology Publications, Lisbon (2022). https://doi.org/10.5220/0011271400003269. https://www.scitepress.org/DigitalLibrary/Link.aspx?doi=10.5220/0011271400003269

11. Camacho-Collados, J., Doval, Y., Martínez-Cámara, E., Espinosa-Anke, L., Barbieri, F., Schockaert, S.: Learning cross-lingual embeddings from Twitter via distant supervision, March 2020. http://arxiv.org/abs/1905.07358

12. Chan, B., Schweter, S., Möller, T.: German's next language model. arXiv:2010.10906 [cs], December 2020

13. Chauhan, P., Sharma, N., Sikka, G.: The emergence of social media data and sentiment analysis in election prediction. J. Ambient Intell. Human. Comput. **12**(2), 2601–2627 (2021). https://doi.org/10.1007/s12652-020-02423-y

14. Christin, N.: Traveling the silk road: a measurement analysis of a large anonymous online marketplace. In: Proceedings of the 22nd International Conference on World Wide Web (2013). https://doi.org/10.1145/2488388.2488408

15. Dangi, D., Dixit, D.K., Bhagat, A.: Sentiment analysis of COVID-19 social media data through machine learning. Multimedia Tools Appl. **81**(29), 42261–42283 (2022). https://doi.org/10.1007/s11042-022-13492-w

16. Dargahi Nobari, A., Sarraf, M., Neshati, M., Daneshvar, F.: Characteristics of viral messages on Telegram; the world's largest hybrid public and private messenger. Expert Syst. Appl. **168**, 114303 (2020). https://doi.org/10.1016/j.eswa.2020.114303

17. Devlin, J., Chang, M.W., Lee, K., Toutanova, K.: BERT: pre-training of deep bidirectional transformers for language understanding. arXiv:1810.04805 [cs], May 2019

18. Doddington, G., Mitchell, A., Przybocki, M.A., Ramshaw, L., Strassel, S., Weischedel, R.: The automatic content extraction (ACE) program - tasks, data, and evaluation. In: International Conference on Language Resources and Evaluation (2004). https://www.semanticscholar.org/paper/The-Automatic-Content-Extraction-(ACE)-Program-and-Doddington-Mitchell/0617dd6924df7a3491c299772b70e90507b195dc

19. Eberts, M., Ulges, A.: Span-based joint entity and relation extraction with transformer pre-training, June 2021. https://doi.org/10.3233/FAIA200321. http://arxiv.org/abs/1909.07755

20. Gomathi, C.: Social tagging system for community detecting using NLP technique. Int. J. Res. Appl. Sci. Eng. Technol. **6**, 1665–1671 (2018). https://doi.org/10.22214/ijraset.2018.4279

21. Griffith, V., Xu, Y., Ratti, C.: Graph theoretic properties of the darkweb. arXiv:1704.07525 [cs] (2017)

22. Hennig, L., Truong, P.T., Gabryszak, A.: MobIE: a German dataset for named entity recognition, entity linking and relation extraction in the mobility domain. In: Proceedings of the 17th Conference on Natural Language Processing (KONVENS 2021), pp. 223–227. KONVENS 2021 Organizers, Düsseldorf (2021). https://aclanthology.org/2021.konvens-1.22

23. Hoseini, M., Melo, P., Benevenuto, F., Feldmann, A., Zannettou, S.: On the globalization of the QAnon conspiracy theory through Telegram. ArXiv, May 2021. https://www.semanticscholar.org/paper/On-the-Globalization-of-the-QAnon-Conspiracy-Theory-Hoseini-Melo/1b0f3a6da334b898ddb070657c980349d31be4e2

24. Huang, Z., Xu, W., Yu, K.: Bidirectional LSTM-CRF models for sequence tagging. arXiv:1508.01991 [cs], August 2015

25. Jin, D., et al.: A survey of community detection approaches: from statistical modeling to deep learning. IEEE Trans. Knowl. Data Eng. **35**(2), 1149–1170 (2021). https://doi.org/10.1109/TKDE.2021.3104155. https://ieeexplore.ieee.org/document/9511798/

26. Kartal, G.: What's up with WhatsApp? a critical analysis of mobile instant messaging research in language learning. Int. J. Contemp. Educ. Res. **6**(2), 352–365 (2019). https://doi.org/10.33200/ijcer.599138. https://dergipark.org.tr/en/doi/10.33200/ijcer.599138

27. Klöser, L., Kohl, P., Kraft, B., Zündorf, A.: Multi-attribute relation extraction (MARE) - simplifying the application of relation extraction. In: Proceedings of the 2nd International Conference on Deep Learning Theory and Applications, pp. 148–156 (2021). https://doi.org/10.5220/0010559201480156. http://arxiv.org/abs/2111.09035

28. Krippendorff, K.: Reliability. In: Content Analysis: An Introduction to Its Methodology, Revised edition. Sage Publications Inc., Los Angeles, April 2012

29. Lacoste, A., Luccioni, A., Schmidt, V., Dandres, T.: Quantifying the carbon emissions of machine learning. arXiv:1910.09700 [cs], November 2019

30. Landis, J.R., Koch, G.G.: The measurement of observer agreement for categorical data. Biometrics **33**(1), 159 (1977). https://doi.org/10.2307/2529310. https://www.jstor.org/stable/2529310?origin=crossref

31. van der Maaten, L., Hinton, G.: Visualizing data using t-SNE. J. Mach. Learn. Res. **9**(86), 2579–2605 (2008). http://jmlr.org/papers/v9/vandermaaten08a.html

32. McLean, G., Osei-Frimpong, K.: Examining satisfaction with the experience during a live chat service encounter-implications for website providers. Comput. Hum. Behav. **76**, 494–508 (2017). https://doi.org/10.1016/j.chb.2017.08.005. https://linkinghub.elsevier.com/retrieve/pii/S0747563217304727

33. Naseri, M., Zamani, H.: Analyzing and predicting news popularity in an instant messaging service. In: Proceedings of the 42nd International ACM SIGIR Conference on Research and Development in Information Retrieval, pp. 1053–1056, July 2019. https://doi.org/10.1145/3331184.3331301

34. Newman, M.E.J.: Finding community structure in networks using the eigenvectors of matrices. Phys. Rev. E **74**(3), 036104 (2006). https://doi.org/10.1103/PhysRevE.74.036104. http://arxiv.org/abs/physics/0605087

35. Pedregosa, F., et al.: Scikit-learn: machine learning in Python. J. Mach. Learn. Res. **12**(85), 2825–2830 (2011). http://jmlr.org/papers/v12/pedregosa11a.html

36. Sang, E.F.T.K., De Meulder, F.: Introduction to the CoNLL-2003 shared task: language-independent named entity recognition. arXiv:cs/0306050, Jun 2003

37. Su, X., et al.: A comprehensive survey on community detection with deep learning. IEEE Trans. Neural Netw. Learn. Syst. 1–21 (2022). https://doi.org/10.1109/TNNLS.2021.3137396. https://ieeexplore.ieee.org/document/9732192/

38. Subhashini, L.D.C.S., Li, Y., Zhang, J., Atukorale, A.S., Wu, Y.: Mining and classifying customer reviews: a survey. Artif. Intell. Rev. **54**(8), 6343–6389 (2021). https://doi.org/10.1007/s10462-021-09955-5

39. Tsao, S.F., Chen, H., Tisseverasinghe, T., Yang, Y., Li, L., Butt, Z.A.: What social media told us in the time of COVID-19: a scoping review. Lancet Digit. Health **3**(3), e175–e194 (2021). https://doi.org/10.1016/S2589-7500(20)30315-0. https://linkinghub.elsevier.com/retrieve/pii/S2589750020303150

40. Vajjala, S., Majumder, B., Gupta, A., Surana, H.: Social media. In: Practical Natural Language Processing. O'Reilly Media, Inc., June 2020. https://www.oreilly.com/library/view/practical-natural-language/9781492054047/

41. Wattenberg, M., Viégas, F., Johnson, I.: How to use t-SNE effectively. Distill **1**(10), e2 (2016). https://doi.org/10.23915/distill.00002. http://distill.pub/2016/misread-tsne

42. Zhang, X., et al.: TwHIN-BERT: a socially-enriched pre-trained language model for multilingual tweet representations, September 2022. https://doi.org/10.48550/arXiv.2209.07562. http://arxiv.org/abs/2209.07562

43. Zhong, Z., Chen, D.: A frustratingly easy approach for entity and relation extraction. In: Proceedings of the 2021 Conference of the North American Chapter of the Association for Computational Linguistics: Human Language Technologies, pp. 50–61 (2021). https://doi.org/10.18653/v1/2021.naacl-main.5. https://aclanthology.org/2021.naacl-main.5

Data Mining and Machine Learning to Predict the Sulphur Content in the Hot Metal of a Coke-Fired Blast Furnace

Wandercleiton Cardoso$^{(\boxtimes)}$ ⓘ and Renzo Di Felice ⓘ

Università degli Studi di Genova, Dipartimento di Ingegneria Civile, Chimica e Ambientale, Via All'Opera Pia, 15, 16145 Genova (GE), Italy
wandercleiton.cardoso@ieee.org

Abstract. In order to combat climate change, the European Parliament adopted the European Climate Law, making the goal of climate neutrality by 2050 legally binding, in this sense, there has been increased interest in data mining and machine learning in the steel industry. Reducing energy consumption and neutralizing greenhouse gas emissions have become challenges for the steel industry. Nowadays, it is normal to use artificial intelligence to integrate Industry 4.0 technologies to improve and monitor production conditions in the steel industry. In the current scenario of the global economy, strict control of all stages of the production process is of utmost importance to increase productivity and reduce costs, decrease atmospheric emissions and reduce energy consumption. In steel production, the temperature of the hot metal is one of the most important parameters to evaluate, as a lack of control can negatively affect the final quality of the product and increase energy consumption. In this sense, data mining, machine learning and the use of artificial neural networks are competitive alternatives to contribute to solving the new challenges of the steel industry. The database used for the numerical simulation corresponds to 11 years of operation of a blast furnace. For this research, a Big Data with 301,125 pieces of information divided into 75 variables was used. The neural network input consists of 74 input variables and 1 output variable. The conclusion is that data mining and neural networks can be used in practice as a tool to predict and control impurities in the production of pig iron in a blast furnace, to reduce energy consumption, and to reduce the emission of gasses into the atmosphere.

Keywords: Big Data · Machine Learning · Blast Furnace · Sulphur · Industry 4.0

1 Introduction

This scientific paper is an extended version of the paper "Prediction of Sulfur in the Hot Metal based on Data Mining and Artificial Neural Networks" presented at the "11th International Conference on Data Science, Technology and Applications" in Lisbon, Portugal, held between July 11–13, 2022. New in this extended version is information on the cost of steel production and detailed information on the use of data mining and applications of Big Data in the steel production industry.

A. Cuzzocrea et al. (Eds.): DATA 2021/2022, CCIS 1860, pp. 203–218, 2023.
https://doi.org/10.1007/978-3-031-37890-4_10

The blast furnace is a chemical metallurgical reactor used to produce molten iron. This product is formed by the reduction of metal oxides that react chemically with reducing elements such as carbon monoxide and hydrogen gas. Blast furnaces are chemical metallurgical reactors used to produce hot metal and blast furnace slag. Hot metal is obtained in liquid state and consists of iron (92 to 95%), carbon (3 to 4.5%), and impurities such as sulphur, phosphorus, and silica [1–3]. The raw materials (metallic feedstock) used are sinter, granulated ore and pellets. The main fuel is metallurgical coke. All these materials are loaded into the upper part of the reactor and hot air is injected into the lower part. The injected hot air gasifies the coke and produces CO reducing gas and a large amount of heat that rises in countercurrent to the sinking of the charge and provides heating, reduction, and melting of the metallic charge. Pulverized coal is used as an additional fuel, which is blown in along with hot air [2, 4–6].

The preheated air with a temperature of about 1200 °C is blown through the blast tuyeres of the blast furnace and comes into contact with the coke in the runway area. The contact of the oxygen in the air with the carbon of the coke heated to 1500 °C initially leads to a reaction that produces carbon dioxide. This highly exothermic reaction generates a large amount of heat for the process. The carbon dioxide immediately reacts with the carbon in the coke to form carbon monoxide (CO) following the loss-of-solution or Boudouard reaction ($C + CO_2 \rightarrow 2CO$), which is highly endothermic. The moisture contained in the injected air reacts with the carbon in the coke to produce the reducing gasses CO and H_2. Although these reactions are endothermic, i.e., proceed under heat absorption, the exit of the reducing gasses from the duct effectively results in a high heat input to the process, producing flame temperatures in excess of 2000 °C [2, 3, 6–9]. The rest of the way through the furnace, the rising gas releases heat to the descending metal layers and leaves the furnace with temperatures approximately 100 to 150 °C. Due to the different heat requirements for a number of chemical reactions taking place at different levels in the furnace, the temperature profile takes a characteristic shape: an upper preheating zone (0-800°C) separated from a lower melting zone (900-1500°C) and a vertical thermal reserve zone whose temperature is in the range of 800-1000°C. The thermal reserve zone, where there is little heat exchange between gas and solids, occupies 40–50% of the total height of the furnace [2, 6, 10–12].

The nature of the countercurrent process allows a highly reducing gas (high content of CO) to come into contact with the metallic mineral wustite, which has the lowest oxygen potential of the iron oxides, and then reduce hematite and magnetite in the upper zone by a gas with a lower reduction potential. Since CO_2 is the product of carbon combustion, the more oxygen removed, the more fully the thermal and chemical energy of carbon is utilized. These reactions are called indirect reduction, and the overall reaction is slightly exothermic. If some of the wustite remains unreduced, it is further reduced by direct reduction in the region where temperatures exceed. The high-temperature ramp gas generated in the combustion zone (the tuyeres region) causes heating of the charge, decomposition reactions, and reduction of oxides during its ascent in the blast furnace. As a result, the temperature of the gas gradually decreases while its chemical composition changes [2, 3, 6, 9, 12–15]. Initially, the charge evaporates moisture near the level and is preheated. When the charge decreases, the reduction of iron oxides takes place. In the softening and melting zone, near the bottom vat and belly, softening and melting of the charge begins, which evolves toward the crucible. The pig iron (hot metal) and slag that are in the crucible are removed at controlled intervals through the drum holes. In this area, the coke gradually decreases in size as it burns. Together with the melting of the materials making up the charge, this causes the level in the blast furnace to drop, so that a new charge has to be transported up [9, 12, 16–18]. Coke is considered the permeabilizer of the blast furnace charge. No other fuel can play this role because coke is the only material that can maintain bed permeability for both the ascending gas and the descending liquid slag and hot metal. Coke remains solid under the high-temperature conditions prevailing in the furnace and resists the various stresses to which it is subjected in the furnace. This allows it to maintain a suitable size and size distribution for good permeability, without which the production of hot metal in a blast furnace would be impossible [3, 12, 15, 19–21]. However, the thermal and chemical role can be played by other liquid fuels (fuel oil and coal tar), gaseous fuels with high calorific value (reduction gas, natural gas and coke oven gas) or solid fuels (mainly hard coal) injected through the tuyeres of the furnace. Thus, these auxiliary fuels also serve as heat and reduction gas sources for the process. Figure 1 illustrates the operating principle of a blast furnace [6, 22, 23].

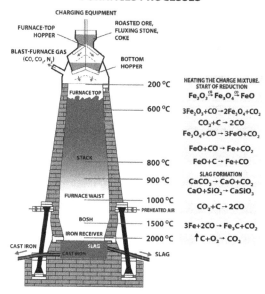

Fig. 1. Blast furnace working principle [2].

Monitoring the blast furnace is paramount to producing a quality product. Sulphur in steel is an undesirable residue that negatively affects properties such as ductility, toughness, weldability and corrosion resistance [2, 6, 12, 15, 21, 24–26]. In recent years, the demand for steels with higher toughness and ductility has increased, and low sulphur content is important to achieve these properties. In addition, sulphur can play an important role in some corrosion processes in steel. Therefore, controlling sulphur content is critical in the production of steel for the pipe and automotive industries. The production of low-sulphur steel is of utmost importance for shipbuilding and pipelines for the oil industry. This requires high production control in the blast furnace and an efficient desulphurization process at the lowest possible cost [27].

The operating costs of the various steel mills are subject to wide fluctuations depending on raw material and energy prices. Despite the fluctuations in raw material prices, end prices have been declining for a long time. However, the momentum of falling steel production costs worldwide in this century is greater than it could be due to cheaper raw materials (Fig. 2). The profitability of the steel market has declined due to the increase in raw material costs. Although the steel market experienced years of prosperity in 2000–2008 and 2010–2014 due to the increase in orders from China (Fig. 3), it is noted that the cost of raw materials (iron ore and metallurgical coke) is increasing over the years, which makes it interesting to invest in operating techniques that reduce operating costs [6, 21, 27–31].

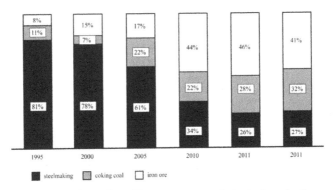

Fig. 2. The share of specific cost components in steel production.

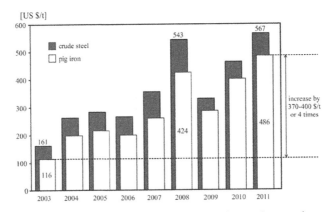

Fig. 3. Increased cost of producing blast furnace hot metal.

In the area of technology and modeling, in addition to predicting the effects of changes in production parameters, several blast furnace simulation models have been developed to improve production conditions. These include two- and three-dimensional models that allow progress and detailed information on fluid flow and mass and heat balances within the blast furnace. When it comes to data mining, people often talk about Big Data. These are larger and more complex data sets that come mainly from new data sources. These data sets are so large that conventional data processing software cannot handle them. But these huge data sets can be used to solve business problems that you could not solve before. While the concept of Big Data itself is relatively new, the origins of big data sets date back to the 1960s and 1970s, when the world of data was just beginning with the first data centers and the development of the relational database [2, 3, 6, 9, 12, 15, 18, 26, 32–34].

Big Data has come a long way, but its usefulness is just beginning. Cloud computing has added to the capabilities of Big Data. The cloud offers truly elastic scalability, where developers can easily create ad hoc clusters to test a subset of data. And graphical databases are becoming increasingly important thanks to their ability to visualize large amounts of data in a way that enables rapid and comprehensive analysis. Big Data allows you to get more complete answers because you have more information. More complete answers mean more confidence in the data, which in turn requires a completely different approach to solving problems. Machine learning is a hotly debated topic right now, especially Big Data, is one of the reasons why. Now we are able to teach machines instead of programming them. The availability of Big Data to train machine learning models makes this possible [15, 18, 35–37].

Operational efficiency is not always a hot topic, but it is an area where Big Data is having the biggest impact. With Big Data, you can analyze and measure production, customer feedback, returns and other factors to reduce disruption and anticipate future demand. Big Data can also be used to improve decision making according to current market demand. Big Data can help society innovate by exploring the connections between people, institutions, businesses, and processes, and then finding new ways to use those insights. Figure 4 shows the possibilities of Big Data applications [38–40].

Considering the existing difficulties in the field of simulation of complex processes, the use of solutions based on neural networks has gained space due to its diversity of applications and increasing the reliability of responses, since the neural network receives new data in the operating process/training without necessarily making inferences about values or types of interaction between raw materials for the use of neural models. In computer science and related fields, artificial neural networks are computational models inspired by the central nervous system of an animal, especially the brain, that can perform both machine learning and pattern recognition. Artificial neural networks are generally represented as systems of "interconnected neurons that can compute input values" that simulate the behavior of biological neural networks [2, 3, 6, 18, 21, 39, 41–43]. Figure **5** illustrates the synaptic connections of a neuron, while Fig. 6 illustrates an artificial neural network.

The objective of this work is to mine a database and numerically simulate an artificial neural network with 30 neurons in the hidden layer.

Fig. 4. Big Data Applications.

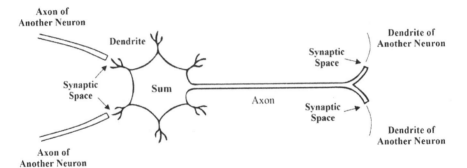

Fig. 5. Synaptic connections of a neuron.

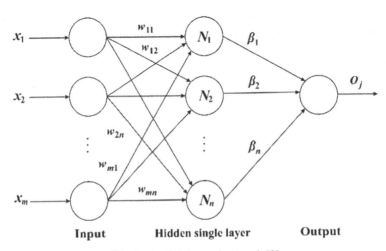

Fig. 6. Artificial neural network [2].

2   Research Method

The database used for numerical simulation corresponds to 11 years of reactor operation. Big Data contains 301,125 pieces of information divided into 75 variables. The neural network input consists of 74 input variables and 1 output variable. The artificial neural network has a similar structure to Fig. 7 with a simple layer and 30 neurons in the hidden layer, using the Levenberg-Marquardt training algorithm and a sigmoid activation function.

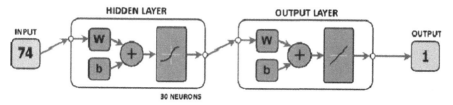

Fig. 7. Artificial neural network architecture [2].

According to the literature, 85% of the database should be used for training and validation of the neural network, while the remaining 15% is used to check the predictive ability of the model during the testing step [12, 33, 36, 44–46]. Table 1 illustrates the distribution of the database. Tables 1, 2, 3, 4, 5, 6, 7 and 8 illustrate the input variables and Table 9 the output variables.

Table 1. Big Data Division [2].

Step	Samples
Training	210.789
Validation	45.168
Testing	45.168

Table 2. Blast Furnace Gas composition [2].

Variable	Unit	Mean	Standard deviation
CO	%	23.8	0.74
CO_2	%	24.3	0.66
N_2	%	47.2	1.39
H_2	%	4.50	0.43
$CO + CO_2$	%	47.9	0.6
CO efficiency	%	49.5	0.85
H_2 efficiency	%	40.7	3.25

Table 3. Hot metal [2].

Variable	Unit	Mean	Standard deviation
Estim. Production	ton	7789.5	314.5
Real production	ton	7787.2	324.5
Carbon	%	4.635	0.169
Chrome	%	0.025	0.002
Copper	%	0.007	0.001
Manganese	%	0.29	0.03
Manganese ratio	–	0.13	0.22

Table 4. Fuel [2].

Variable	Unit	Mean	Standard deviation
Injection PCI	kg/ton	58.99	6.16
Gas rate	kg/ton	–	–
Coal/O_2 tax	–	755.27	75.57
Coal/air tax	–	170.03	74.12
PCI rate	–	175.98	15.61
Direct reduction	%	23.38	12.41
PCI tax	kg/ton	1078.3	540.9
Coke total	kg/ton	1932.2	911.7
Small coke	kg/ton	294.63	134.86
Coke (type 1)	kg/ton	210.7	259.8
Coke (type 2)	kg/ton	742	716
Coke (type 3)	kg/ton	946	956
Coke (type 4)	kg/ton	1878	143
Coke (type 5)	kg/ton	1327.5	847.6
Moisture	kg/ton	6.4	1.41
Coke/load	kg/ton	11.89	9.56
Small coke total	kg/ton	4.28	0.03
PCI/load	kg/ton	174.74	14.32
Fuel rate/load	kg/ton	484.08	18.14
Coke total/load	kg/ton	24.52	0.89
PCI/day	–	1214.4	44.9
Coke rate	kg/ton	319.68	25.98

The method used to assess the quality of the neural network model was the root mean square error (RMSE). Small values close to zero indicate a better predictive ability of the model. Pearson's mathematical correlation coefficient (R) was also used to validate the mathematical models. Figure 8 shows the mathematical equation for the RMSE and Pearson's mathematical correlation coefficient [2].

Table 5. Blast Furnace Slag [2].

Variable	Unit	Mean	Standard deviation
Slag rate	kg/ton	246.99	13.74
B2 basicity	–	1.2	0.04
B4 basicity	–	1.07	0.04
Al_2O_3	%	10.71	0.62
CaO	%	43.06	1.55
Sulphur	%	1.15	0.14
FeO	%	0.42	0.04
MgO	%	6.83	0.86
MnO	%	0.31	0.1
SIO_2	%	36.05	1.36
TIO_2	%	0.58	0.05
Production	ton	1980.6	190.8
Mn ratio	–	0.87	0.22

Table 6. Thermal control [2].

Variable	Unit	Mean	Standard deviation
Hot metal	°C	1508.3	12.2
Blowing air	°C	1243.3	13.9
Top gas	°C	121,35	10,34
Flame temperature	°C	2177.6	2108
Slag temperature	°C	1508.3	12.2
Thermal index	-	504.7	54.03

Table 7. Air blowing [2].

Variable	Unit	Mean	Standard deviation
Volume	Nm^3/min	4852.9	148.6
Pressure	kgf/cm^2	3.87	0.1
Moisture	kg/m^3	19.81	3.73
O_2 enrichment	%	5.27	0.95
Steam	%	1.51	1.01
Consumption	Nm^3/min	7030.3	213.6

Table 8. Minerals [2].

Variable	Unit	Mean	Standard deviation
Ore/Coke	–	5.1	0.31
Sinter (type 1)	ton	4536.3	884.2
Sinter (type 2)	ton	1697.2	1326.2
Pellet (type 1)	ton	5132	1898.3
Pellet (type 2)	ton	4813.7	2183.1
Total metal load	ton	12312	670
Raw material rate	%	1578.8	15.1
Ore	%	8.9	4.5
Sinter	%	39.6	2.8
Pellet	%	51.5	5.1
Ore (day)	ton	12747	703

Table 9. Descriptive statistics of sulphur (output) in percentage (%) [2].

Mean	Std deviation	Minimum	Median	Maximum	Skewness	Kurtosis
0.023	0.008	0.008	0.021	0.083	1.5	4.8

$$RMSE = \sqrt{\dfrac{\sum_{i=1}^{N}(Predicted_i - Actual_i)^2}{N}} \qquad r = \dfrac{\sum_{i=1}^{n}(x_i - \bar{x})(y_i - \bar{y})}{\sqrt{\sum_{i=1}^{n}(x_i - \bar{x})^2}\sqrt{\sum_{i=1}^{n}(y_i - \bar{y})^2}}$$

Fig. 8. RMSE equation on the left and Pearson equation on the right [2].

3   Results and Discussions

The sulphur prediction model showed greater difficulty in prediction, but even then, the result was excellent compared to the literature. There was no evidence of overfitting or underfitting of the sulphur prediction model for hot metal. There was no discrepancy between the RMSE values in the training, validation, and testing phases. The artificial neural network required a maximum of 687 epochs to converge the model, indicating higher complexity to stabilize the error values. The mathematical correlation (R) and RMSE of the artificial neural network are shown in Table 10 and Table 11, confirming an excellent correlation value. Figure 9 illustrates the scatter between the values calculated by the neural network and the values from Big Data [2].

In addition to computational analysis, it is necessary to carry out a metallurgical analysis, because it is known that most of the sulphur diluted in the hot metal (about 80%) comes from the raw material introduced into the reactor. The metallurgical coke contains ferrous sulphide (FeS) and calcium sulphide (CaS), which are normally contained in the fuel ash. The rest of the dissolved sulphur depends on the metal load, the gas flows and the operating temperature of the reactor. In this type of metallurgical reactor, about 75%

Table 10. RMSE values [2].

Step	Value
Overall	0.0027
Training	0.0031
Validation	0.0030
Testing	0.0031

Table 11. Pearson values [2].

Step	Value
Overall	0.9632
Training	0.9682
Validation	0.9660
Testing	0.9373

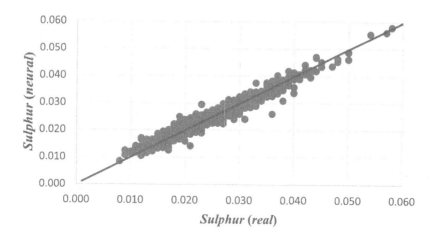

Fig. 9. Scatterplot sulphur [2].

to 85% of the sulphur is diluted in the blast furnace bore, up to 15% is removed from the reactor when diluted in the blast furnace gas, while the originally mentioned 80% when diluted in the pig iron corresponds to 2% and 5% of the total. In this sense, the mechanism of sulphur reactions is known to be very similar to that of silicon [21, 26, 33, 47–49].

Molten iron is removed from the reactor, a small amount of sulphur is absorbed from the hot metal by the slag. Sulphur forms various compounds, such as sulphur dioxide (SO_2) and carbon disulphide (CS), which are transported through the gas stream and undergo chemical reactions [21, 42, 44, 47, 50, 51]. However, among the sulphur gases, silicon sulphide (SiS) is the most common compound and usually reacts with calcium (Ca), silicon (Si) and iron (Fe) according to Eq. 1, Eq. 2 and Eq. 3. A chemical reaction to remove the sulphur is shown by Eq. 4.

$$CaS_{(ash\ coke)} + SiO_{(g)} \rightarrow SiS_{(g)} + CaO \tag{1}$$

$$FeS + SiO + C \rightarrow SiS + CO + Fe \tag{2}$$

$$SiS_{(g)} \rightarrow [Si] + [S] \tag{3}$$

$$S + (CaO) + C \rightarrow (CaS) + CO_{(g)} \tag{4}$$

Desulphurization in gaseous form takes place in the drip zone of the reactor. In the softening and melting zone, the silicon dissolves in the hot metal and makes it difficult for the sulphur to pass from the pig iron into the slag, especially if silicon and sulphur penetrate through the slag and no manganese oxide (MnO) is present. However, in the presence of manganese oxide, the silicon in the shell is diluted, the manganese is diluted in hot metal and the sulphur moves more easily into the slag. The literature states that gases such as SiO and sis are formed in the treatment zone, while silicon and sulphur migrate into the pig iron in the combustion zone [21, 44, 47, 51].

Silicon is reduced by FeO and MnO and dissolved in the slag, while the hot metal droplets penetrate the slag layer. It should be mentioned that CaO has a much greater desulphurization potential than MgO, about 100 times stronger. It should also be noted that for proper desulphurization, the oxygen content of the metal must be very low. This is possible due to the reaction of oxygen dissolved in the hot metal with strong oxide forming elements [15, 52–56]. So, look at the oxide-forming elements, it can write the following reactions given in Eq. 5, Eq. 6, and Eq. 7.

$$(CaO) + [S] + [C] \rightarrow (CaS) + CO(g) \tag{5}$$

$$(CaO) + [S] + [Mn] \rightarrow (CaS) + (MnO) \tag{6}$$

$$(CaO) + [S] + 0, 5[Si] \rightarrow (CaS) + 0.5(SiO_2) \tag{7}$$

CaO activity and favors desulphurization. Low FeO concentrations in the slag favor the incorporation of sulphur into the hot metal. Carbon and silicon dissolved in the hot metal favor desulphurization by increasing the thermodynamic activity of sulphur in the slag. Considering all this information and the fact that sulphur is an extremely harmful chemical element for steel, the use of a ANN to predict sulphur in metal production is justified.

4   Conclusions

Regarding simulation methods to predict process variables, the increasing development of computing capacity, leading to cheaper and more powerful equipment, is driving the development of more complex algorithms with better results, such as neural networks. Thus, the progress in computing capacity allowed the development of different types of simulation models. This is one of the factors that enabled the use of the ANN model in this study, as well as the identification of the main variables that affect the model. The processing of the data to be used for the development of the model is highlighted as an important part of the process, which is sometimes a slow process, since the information must be evaluated to find the best way to identify outliers for the development of models.

However, it is important to emphasize that the model itself can predict good results for each of the target variables. It should be noted that the use of the above modeling technique has enabled the construction of higher accuracy models that can be used as tools for decision making and operational planning related to fuel consumption, operational stability, and delivery of a steelmaking product, and help improve process monitoring. In short, neural networks can be used in practice because the model is both a predictive tool and a guide for operations due to the excellent correlations between the real values and the values calculated by the neural network.

References

1. Ducic, N., Jovicic, A., Manasijevic, S., Radisa, R., Cojbasic, Z., Savković, B.: Application of machine learning in the control of metal melting production process. Appl. Sci. **10**(17), 6048–6063 (2020)
2. Cardoso, W., di Felice, R.: Prediction of sulfur in the hot metal based on data mining and artificial neural networks. In: Proceedings of the 11th International Conference on Data Science, Technology and Applications, pp. 400–407 (2022)
3. Cardoso, W., Barros, D., Baptista, R., di Felice R.: Mathematical modelling to control the chemical composition of blast furnace slag using artificial neural networks and empirical correlation. In: IOP Conference Series: Materials Science and Engineering, vol. 1203, p. 032096 (2021)
4. Arif, M.S., Ahmad, I.: Artificial intelligence based prediction of exergetic efficiency of a blast furnace. Comput. Aided Chem. Eng. **50**, 1047–1052 (2021)
5. Bai, Y., Tan, M.: Dynamic committee machine with fuzzy- C-means clustering for total organic carbon content prediction from wireline logs. Comput. Geosci. **146**, 104626 (2021)
6. Cardoso, W., di Felice, R.: Prediction of silicon content in the hot metal using Bayesian networks and probabilistic reasoning. Int. J. Adv. Intell. Inf. **07**, 268–281 (2021)
7. Blotevogel, S., et al.: Glass structure of industrial ground granulated blast furnace slags (GGBS) investigated by time-resolved Raman and NMR spectroscopies. J. Mater. Sci. **56**(31), 17490–17504 (2021). https://doi.org/10.1007/s10853-021-06446-4
8. Wang, Y.H., Zhang, H., Jiang, Z.G., Zhao, G.: Research of coke rate prediction of blast furnace based on operative characteristics of auxiliary resources. Adv. Mater. Res. **605–607**, 1792–1797 (2012)
9. Cardoso, W., di Felice, R., Baptista, R.: Artificial neural network for predicting silicon content in the hot metal produced in a blast furnace fuelled by metallurgical coke. Mater. Res. **25**, 20210439 (2022)

10. Chen, M., Wan, X., Shi, J., Taskinen, P., Jokilaakso, A.: Experimental study on the phase relations of the SiO2- MgO-TiO2 system in air at 1500°C. JOM **74**, 676–688 (2022)
11. Chizhikova, V.M.: Best available techniques in the blast- furnace production. Metallurgist **64**, 13–35 (2020)
12. Cardoso, W., di Felice R., Baptista, R.: Artificial neural networks for modelling and controlling the variables of a blast furnace. In: IEEE 6th International Forum on Research and Technology for Society and Industry (RTSI), pp. 148–152 (2021)
13. Carro, K.B., et al.: Assessing geographic and climatic variables to predict the potential distribution of the visceral leishmaniasis vector Lutzomyia longipalpis in the state of Espírito Santo Brazil. Plos One **15**(9), e0238198 (2020)
14. Fontes, D.O.L., Vasconcelos, L.G., Brito, R.P.: Blast furnace hot metal temperature and silicon content prediction using soft sensor based on fuzzy C-means and exogenous nonlinear autoregressive models. Comput. Chem. Eng. **141**, 107028 (2020)
15. Cardoso, W., di Felice, R., Baptista, R.: Mathematical modelling of a solid oxide fuel cell operating on biogas. Bull. Electr. Eng. Inf. **10**, 2929–2942 (2021)
16. Hou, Y., Wu, Y., Liu, Z., Han, H., Wang, P.: Dynamic multi-objective differential evolution algorithm based on the information of evolution progress. Sci. China Technol. Sci. **64**(8), 1676–1689 (2021). https://doi.org/10.1007/s11431-020-1789-9
17. Ibragimov, A.F., Iskhakov, I.I., Skopov, G.B., Kirichenko, A.N.: Using oxygen-enriched blast during the operation of shaft furnaces of the Mednogorsk Copper-Sulfur combine LLC. Metallurgist **63**, 62–69 (2019)
18. Cardoso, W., Di Felice, R.: A novel committee machine to predict the quantity of impurities in hot metal produced in blast furnace. Comput. Chem. Eng. **163**, 107814 (2022)
19. Jantre, S.R., Bhattacharya, S., Maiti, T.: Quantile regression neural networks: a Bayesian approach. J. Stat. Theory Pract. **15**(3), 1–34 (2021). https://doi.org/10.1007/s42519-021-001 89-w
20. He, F., Zhang, L.: Prediction model of end-point phosphorus content in BOF steelmaking process based on PCA and BP neural network. J. Process Control **66**, 51–58 (2018)
21. Cardoso, W., Di Felice, R.: Forecast of carbon consumption of a blast furnace using extreme learning machine and probabilistic reasoning. Chem. Eng. Trans. **96**, 493–498 (2022)
22. Jiang, Y., Zhou, P., Yu, G.: Multivariate molten iron quality based on improved incremental Randon vector functional-link networks. IFAC PapersOnLine, 290–294 (2018)
23. Kang, Y.-B.: Progress of thermodynamic modeling for sulfide dissolution in molten oxide slags: sulfide capacity and phase diagram. Metall. and Mater. Trans. B. **52**(5), 2859–2882 (2021). https://doi.org/10.1007/s11663-021-02224-4
24. Kurunov, I.F.: Ways of improving blast furnace smelting efficiency with injection of coal-dust fuel and natural gas. Metallurgist **61**(9–10), 736–744 (2018). https://doi.org/10.1007/s11015-018-0557-6
25. Quesada, D., Valverde, G., Larrañaga, P., Bielza, C.: Long- term forecasting of multivariate time series in industrial furnaces with dynamic Gaussian Bayesian networks. Eng. Appl. Artif. Intell. **103**, 104301 (2021)
26. Cardoso, W., Di Felice, R., Baptista, R.: A critical overview of development and innovations in biogas upgrading. In: Iano, Y., Saotome, O., Kemper Vásquez, G.L., Cotrim Pezzuto, C., Arthur, R., Gomes de Oliveira, G. (eds.) Proceedings of the 7th Brazilian Technology Symposium (BTSym'21). BTSym 2021. Smart Innovation, Systems and Technologies, vol. 295, pp. 42-50. Springer, Cham (2022). https://doi.org/10.1007/978-3-031-08545-1_4
27. Paulo, A., Krzak, M.: Evolution of technology and the market of steel raw materials in the period 1915–2015. Technology Press, Kraków, Poland (2018)
28. Li, W., Zhuo, Y., Bao, J., Shen, Y.: A data-based soft-sensor approach to estimating raceway depth in ironmaking blast furnace. Powder Technol. **390**, 529–538 (2021)

29. Pavlov, A.V., Polinov, A.A., Spirin, N.A., Onorin, O.P., Lavrov, V.V., Gurin, I.A.: Decision-making support in blast-furnace operation. Steel in Translation **49**(3), 185–193 (2019). https://doi.org/10.3103/S0967091219030082

30. Rasul, M.G., Tanty, B.S., Mohanty, B.: Modelling and analysis of blast furnace performance for efficient utilization of energy. Appl. Therm. Eng. **27**(01), 78–88 (2007)

31. Cardoso, W., Di Felice, R., Baptista, R.: Artificial neural network-based committee machine for predicting the slag quality of a blast furnace fed with metallurgical coke. In: Iano, Y., Saotome, O., Kemper Vásquez, G.L., Cotrim Pezzuto, C., Arthur, R., Gomes de Oliveira, G. (eds.) Proceedings of the 7th Brazilian Technology Symposium (BTSym'21). BTSym 2021. Smart Innovation, Systems and Technologies, vol. 295, pp. 66-73. Springer, Cham (2022). https://doi.org/10.1007/978-3-031-08545-1_6

32. Reynolds, Q.G., Rhamdhani, M.A.: Computational modeling in Pyrometallurgy: part I. JOM **73**(9), 2658–2659 (2021). https://doi.org/10.1007/s11837-021-04794-9

33. Cardoso, W., Di Felice, R., Baptista, R.: Mathematical modelling to predict fuel consumption in a blast furnace using artificial neural networks. In: García Márquez, F.P. (eds.) International Conference on Intelligent Emerging Methods of Artificial Intelligence & Cloud Computing. IEMAICLOUD 2021. Smart Innovation, Systems and Technologies, vol. 273, pp. 01-10. Springer, Cham (2022). https://doi.org/10.1007/978-3-030-92905-3_1

34. Kina, C., Turk, K., Atalay, E., Donmez, I., Tanyildizi, H.: Comparison of extreme learning machine and deep learning model in the estimation of the fresh properties of hybrid fiber-reinforced SCC. Neural Comput. Appl. **33**(18), 11641–11659 (2021). https://doi.org/10.1007/s00521-021-05836-8

35. Kong, W., Liu, J., Yu, Y., Hou, X., He, Z.: Effect of w(MgO)/w(Al2O3) ratio and basicity on microstructure and metallurgical properties of blast furnace slag. J. Iron. Steel Res. Int. **28**(10), 1223–1232 (2021)

36. Cardoso, W., Di Felice, R., Baptista, R., Machado, T., Galdino, A.: Evaluation of the use of blast furnace slag as an additive in mortars. REM – Int. Eng. J. **75**, 215–224 (2022)

37. Muchnik, D.A., Trikilo, A.I., Lyalyuk, V.P., Kassim, D.A.: Coke quality and blast-furnace performance. Coke Chem. **61**(1), 12–18 (2018). https://doi.org/10.3103/S1068364X18010040

38. Muraveva, I.G., Togobitskaya, D.N., Ivancha, N.G., Bel'kova, A.I., Nesterov, A.S.: Concept development of an expert system for selecting the optimal composition of a multicomponent blast-furnace charge and functional and algorithmic structure. Steel Transl. **51**, 33–38 (2021)

39. Cardoso, W., et al.: Modeling of artificial neural networks for silicon prediction in the cast iron production process. IAES Int. J. Artif. Intell. **11**, 530–538 (2022)

40. Liu, Y., Wang, Y., Chen, L., Zhao, J., Wang, W., Liu, Q.: Incremental Bayesian broad learning system and its industrial application. Artif. Intell. Rev. **54**(05) (2021)

41. Matino, I., Dettori, S., Colla, V., Weber, V., Salame, S.: Two innovative modelling approaches in order to forecast consumption of blast furnace gas by hot blast stoves. Energy Procedia **158**, 4043–4048 (2019)

42. Cardoso, W., Machado, T., Baptista, R., Galdino, A., Pinto, F., Luz, T.: Industrial technological process for welding AISI 301 stainless steel: focus on microstructural control. In: Iano, Y., Saotome, O., Kemper Vásquez, G.L., Cotrim Pezzuto, C., Arthur, R., Gomes de Oliveira, G. (eds.) Proceedings of the 7th Brazilian Technology Symposium (BTSym'21). BTSym 2021. Smart Innovation, Systems and Technologies, vol. 295, pp. 34-41. Springer, Cham (2022). https://doi.org/10.1007/978-3-031-08545-1_3

43. Liang, W., et al.: Application of BP neural network to the prediction of coal ash melting characteristic temperature. Fuel **260**, 116324 (2020)

44. Matino, I., Dettori, S., Colla, V., Weber, V., Salame, S.: Application of echo state neural networks to forecast blast furnace gas production: pave the way to off-gas optimized management. Energy Procedia **158**, 037–4042 (2019)

45. Itman, A., Silva, R., Cardoso, W., Casteletti, L.: Effect of niobium in the phase transformation and corrosion resistance of one austenitic-ferritic stainless steel. Mater. Res. **17**, 801–806 (2014)

46. Li, J., Hua, C., Qian, J., Guan, X.: Low-rank based Multi- Input Multi-Output Takagi-Sugeno fuzzy modeling for prediction of molten iron quality in blast furnace. Fuzzy Sets Syst. **421**, 178–192 (2021)

47. Matino, I., Dettori, S., Colla, V., Weber, V., Salame, S.: Forecasting blast furnace gas production and demand through echo state neural network-based models: Pave the way to off-gas optimized management. Appl. Energy **253**, 113578 (2019)

48. Itman, A., Cardoso, W., Gontijo, L., Silva, R., Casteletti, L.C.: Austenitic-ferritic stainless-steel containing niobium. Revista da Escola de Minas: REM **66**, 467–471 (2013)

49. Cardoso, W., Baptista, R.: Laves phase precipitation and sigma phase transformation in a duplex stainless steel microalloyed with niobium. revista materia **27**, e13200 (2022)

50. North, L., Blackmore, K., Nesbitt, K., Mahoney, M.R.: Methods of coke quality prediction: a review. Fuel **219**, 426–445 (2018)

51. Pandey, T.N., Jagadev, A.K., Dehuri, S., Cho, S.B.: A novel committee machine and reviews of neural network and statistical models for currency exchange rate prediction: an experimental analysis. J. King Saud Univ. – Comput. Inf. Sci. **32**(9), 987–999 (2020)

52. Radhakrishnan, V.R., Mohamed, A.R.: Neural networks for the identification and control of blast furnace hot metal quality. J. Process Control **10**(6), 509–524 (2000)

53. Rhamdhani, M.A., Reynolds, Q.G.: Computational modeling in Pyrometallurgy: Part II. JOM **73**(9), 2885–2887 (2021)

54. Saxén, H., Pettersson, F.: Nonlinear prediction of the hot metal silicon content in the blast furnace. ISIJ Int. **47**(12), 1732–1737 (2007)

55. Semenov, Y.S., et al.: Experience of using manganese- containing materials in blast-furnace charge. Metallurgist **63**(9), 1013–1023 (2020)

56. Sohn, S.K.I.: Application of complex systems topologies in artificial neural networks optimization: an overview. Expert Syst. Appl. **180**, 115073 (2021)

57. Cardoso, W., Di Felice, R., Baptista, R.: Perspectives on the sustainable steel production process: a critical review of the carbon dioxide (CO2) to methane (CH4) conversion process. In: García Márquez, F.P., Lev, B. (eds.) Sustainability. International Series in Operations Research & Management Science, vol. 333. Springer, Cham (2023). https://doi.org/10.1007/978-3-031-16620-4_17

Automatic Instructional Feedback, and a Lecture Hub System: A Strategy Towards Nurturing the Acquisition of a Structured Engagement Behavior

Victor Obionwu[1]($\boxtimes$), Vincent Toulouse[1], David Broneske[2], and Gunter Saake[1]

[1] University of Magdeburg, Magdeburg, Germany
obionwu@ovgu.de
[2] German Centre for Higher Education Research and Science Studies, Hannover, Germany

Abstract. Several intervention strategies, and systems have been proposed and developed to facilitate the understanding of the SQL language, and it's skill acquisition. However, most of these interventions are mainly structured around a battery of assessments and mostly overlooking the participants' engagement patterns. Ergo, large amounts of easily avoidable errors, most of which are syntactic, are generated in the course of a student's exercise task engagements. However, as evident in the body of literature, structured learning engagements potentially increases an individuals' awareness of the medium of instruction and the instruction. Thus, In this contribution, we provide a strategy to automatically derive and improve instructional feedback, our agency for structuring students learning engagement via a mapping between SQL exercises, lecture slides, and respective cosine similarity which reaches a precision value of 0.767 and an $F_{\beta=0.5}$ value of 0.505. We also describe the SQLValidaor lecture hub, an environment that facilitates our understanding of students engagement process.

Keywords: Text mining · Filtering · Instructional feedback · learning analytic · Natural language processing · Activity mining

1 Introduction

Learning a new programming language, particularly when it is the first one, is relatively difficult for most students, and introductory programming courses are considered challenging by students required to take it as a part of their degree courses [19, 21]. However, It has been shown that instructional feedback conveniently nudges students towards a structured learning interaction trajectory, while mitigating the frustration that comes with learning, and acquiring cognitive skills [15]. However, the on-hand availability of instructors during lecture, and exercise sessions in traditional educational settings, a characteristic feature that brings instructional feedback into direct play, has proved

This work was supported by the German Federal Ministry of Education and Research [**grant number 16DHB 3008**].

difficult to replicate in flipped and full online scenarios. Thus, online tools and platforms such as Moodle [5], LearnDash [8], Blackboard [12], SQLValidator [16] etc., have employed chat system as a means for integrating the instructor's presence. However, interaction with chat systems are restricted to availability. Ergo, students engaged in flipped, and full online learning scenarios while having the lecture videos, and other support tools mostly rely on their personal ability during exercise task engagements sessions, especially when the task requires coding. A consequence of the absence of instructional feedback is the continuous repetition of easily avoidable errors, as shown in Fig. 1.

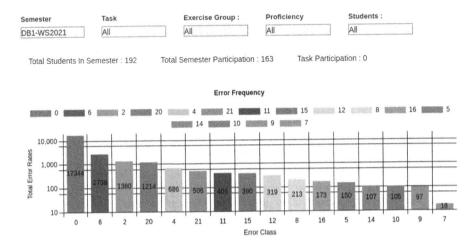

Fig. 1. Error Count.

These error classes [16] describe the possible errors that can occur in the SQLValidator exercise task administration system in the course of an exercise session. Code 0 represents the syntax error, and with respect to the database table, code 2 represents the Count error. Further under the table scope, code 3 represents order error, code 4 represents name error, code 6 represents table row count error, code 20 represents table content error, and code 21 represents table row order error. Under the foreign keys scope, code 17 represents fkname error, code 18 represents fkref table error, and code 19 represents fkref column error. Under the scope of constraints, code 7 represents constraint count error, code 8 represents primary key error, code 9 represents unique key error, code 10 represents foreign key error, and code 11 represents general keys error. For errors relating to the schema structure, code 5 represents column count ct, code 12 represents data type error, code 13 represents isnull error, code 14 represents is default error, code 15 represents is default error, and code 16 represents table name error [17].

Thus, to structure student's learning interaction behavior, as well as provide automatic instructional feedback, we have adopted two strategies, the use of a recommendation system, and a lecture hub. Our recommendation previously pointed students to lecture slides which offered no instrumentation as we could see how they interacted with the lecture material. Our system relies on content-based filtering since the pedagogical aspects of our lectures, their corresponding exercise tasks, projects, and the proficiency level of the students are already known [4]. Based on this information, feedback provided to students are enriched with recommendations that point to sections of our lecture hub. Compared to the state of the art efforts at student SQL learning engagement improvement, optimization, and skill acquisition, our strategy:

– provides meaningful automatic instructional feedback during individual online exercise sessions.
– fosters structured learning engagement, and SQL skill acquisition by linking respective SQL theory with corresponding exercise tasks.

This work is an extension of [18], and compared to the extended work, this version

– gives detailed insight on the recommendation workflow.
– introduces, and describes the lecture hub, an analytic environment that gives us insight into student's learning interaction.
– details the minimal cosine value optimization, and corresponding discussion.
– and a detailed description of the join detection process and other strategies.

Overall, this paper presents a significant extension in comparison to the conference paper [18].

In the following, we first present related work. In Sect. 3, we present the workflow of our implementation and in Sect. 4, we describe the lecture hub. We describe the SQL exercise analysis in Sect. 5, and in Sect. 6, the concept of comparing slides and exercises described. In Sect. 7, we describe an implementation, and in Sect. 8, we evaluate our detection strategies. In Sect. 9, we discuss the performance of the evaluation, after which we summarize, and indicate directions for future efforts.

2 Related Work

In a survey conducted in 2021 by Stack Overflow, SQL was selected as the third most used programming language[1]. Thus, several systems have been developed to foster SQL learning. An educational tool developed by Arizona State University enables the students to learn about relational query languages by letting the students solve their homework assignments using the tool [7]. However, the students receive their feedback directly from the interpreter, and thus we assume the feedback to be too technical to be understood by class participants with minor knowledge about SQL. In comparison, our recommendation points the students to the material of the lecture that explains the correct usage of SQL concepts, and hence the students quickly understand which command they have used incorrectly. Another tool to support students at learning SQL is the SQL-Tutor developed by the University of Canterbury [13] and used at many universities around the globe. The tool prompts students to solve SQL-related exercises and, while doing so, it provides different stages of feedback to the students. The feedback

---

[1] https://insights.stackoverflow.com/survey/2020#technology-programming-scripting-and-markup-languages-all-respondents,lastaccesson09.12.2022.

although is restricted to the task at hand and is not utilizing the learning materials of the course. Finally, there is the SQL Tester [11] that is employed at the University of Manchester. The SQL Tester is used to assess and grade the SQL knowledge of students during a 50-minute test that consists of ten SQL exercises. However, the students only received the regular error messages from the RDBMS as feedback. We are not aware of any research that is trying to improve the SQL learning experience by automatically connecting exercises to the material of the lecture.

3   Recommendation Workflow

In Sect. 1, we gave a motivated on the importance of instructional feedback. The recommendation of a lecture slide which requires the execution of several processes, and decisions, is our main strategy for integrating instructional feedback in the SQLValidator [16]. In this section, we give detailed description on how it works. The workflow is shown in Fig. 2. Each process contains an index number, employed in describing the respective action in the description.

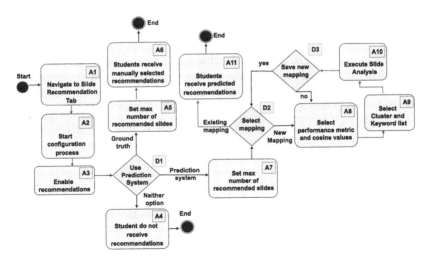

Fig. 2. Recommendation Workflow.

The recommendation process in the frontend starts once the student submits a solution, and an error condition occurs. Depending on the respective task, a recommendation will be generated. In the backend, recommendation is generated by performing content analysis of the exercises, and slides by recognizing the features of SQL keywords. Using the keywords, a mapping between the lectures and slides will be established. Due to this mapping, the feedback presented to students can be enriched with recommendation as to which section of the slide is most similar to a particular exercise. To carry out this process, the administrator will first navigate to the slide recommendation tab, A1, and initiate the process, A2. In A3, one of three different recommendation states, ground truth, prediction system, and no recommendation must be selected. if the choice of no recommendation is selected, A4, the student will not get any recommendation. This serves as a way of loosely coupling the recommendation system with the SQLValidator task management system should there be a decision not to use the recommendation. We further use this option for A/b testing so that a particular group of students does not receive recommendations while another group receives recommendations and in the end, we compare the performance of both groups to ascertain if the recommendation was helpful for the students.

The next option is to choose whether to use the ground truth or predicted recommendation. Once the ground truth is selected, we indicate the maximum number of recommended slides, A5. This number is stored in the database so that for future attempts of a question, the DB will be queried to set the number of recommendation sent to students. In A6, the student will receive an optimal recommendation chosen by an expert. The path to manual recommendation has high effort as lots of time needs to be spent in choosing which slide is suitable for which exercise, and in cases where the order of slides changes, the processes will need to be repeated. A more attractive option will be to use the prediction system, A7. On selecting this option, we also specify the number of recommendation that will be given to the student. For optimum recommendation, we select slides with high cosine similarity.

in the next option, a mapping is chosen. A mapping comprises the recommendations for each exercise and meta information as performance values and the specific semester it was created. In A8, the Administrator can choose to use an existing mapping or create a new one. For a new mapping, a set of configuration as minimum cosine value, cosine cutoff, join detection, etc., has to be specified to prevent incorrect recommendations. The minimum cosine value ensures that recommended slides achieves at least a similarity minimum value of 0.5. In A9, the cluster and keyword list is selected. These lists are created from a pool of SQL keywords. This pool exceeds that current number of keywords currently used in the slide so that future slide modifications will not lead to the modification of the list. However, if there is an unknown keyword, the list has to manually updated. The next action is the execution of the slide analysis, A10. Once the process of computing the similarity between lecture slides, and exercises is done, a visualization is generated for each recommendation. After checking the recommendations, the evaluation settings which consists of the performance settings as accuracy, precision, recall, specificity, f-measure, and f-beta are also checked. At this point, the administrator can choose to make the mapping persistent, in which case, it is stored in the database. However, if the mapping does not achieve appropriate performance, it will not be stored in the database. Once a mapping is active, recommendation is generated for each exercise, and thus a slide location feedback. In A11, students that encounter errors in the course of their exercise engagements will receive a recommendation that directs the student to the lecture hub. In the next section, describes the SQL exercise analysis.

4   The Lecture Hub

The instructional feedback system is insufficient as recommendations that point to a lecture slide is an end on its self as indicated by the activity analysis we derived from

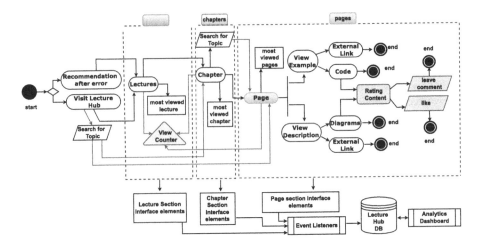

Fig. 3. Lecture Hub.

Moodle. It is important to know how student interact with lecture materials, and the recommendation they received. To this end, we developed the lecture hub, shown in Fig. 3. The lecture hub allows us the ability to track student activity in real time. It has a lecture page, and each lecture has several chapters, and each chapter has multiple pages. The click, hover, scroll etc., and other Event listeners employed to track student activity in this platform. Thus say a student encounters an error, and receives a recommendation and clicks the link that takes them to the lecture hub, at time t1, we will be able to track their interaction until they return for a retrial at time tn. Thus, we now have the capacity of tracking the provenance of a student's learning interaction. The lecture hub also has a rating system that allows us to receive feedback from student on their experiences, and all the lecture hub activities are displayed in the SQLValidator dashboard.

5   SQL Exercise Analysis

In order to support the students in solving their exercises, it is necessary to know which SQL topics are featured in the exercises. Our strategy for topic extraction is similar to the topic extraction for the lecture slides. Thus, we essentially analyze the appearances of SQL keywords in the exercise solutions, and by computing tf, idf, and tf*idf values, we estimate which keywords describe the exercise best. We note here that our used exercise task administration environment has an inbuilt set of solutions for each exercise task. The SQL exercise analysis workflow is shown in Fig. 4. The respective activities are briefly described in the following sections.

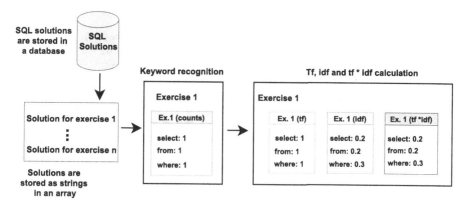

Fig. 4. Concept of SQL exercise analysis.

Querying Stored Solutions. The solution to each SQL exercise is stored in a database along with other information about the exercises such as an ID, and locale preferences. Our objective only requires the exercise solutions and their IDs, which are obtained by querying the database. The result is stored as an associative array with the key being the ID of an exercise, and the index value containing the solution in string format. Compared to the lecture slides, preprocessing is not required as the solutions are already formatted. Next, we recognize the keyword. This operation is similar to the one done for the lecture slides. The keyword recognition activity block in Fig. 4 shows a sample list of recognized keywords.

Keyword Analysis. In the next step, we calculate the tf, idf, and tf*idf values for each keyword of a page. Considering the exercise displayed in Fig. 4, the keyword that has the highest idf weight is the WHERE keyword with the SELECT and FROM keywords having a lower idf value. The tf*idf computation shows that the topic of the page is about the usage of the WHERE keyword.

6 Concept of Comparing Slides and Exercises

In the previous Sects. 5, we described the process of converting both slides and SQL exercises into a format that allows us to compare them. The comparison is done by computing the cosine similarity between the lecture slides, and SQL exercises [18]. A depiction of this process for a hypothetical Exercise 1 is shown in Fig. 5. It consists of the following steps: merging of previous analysis, computation of cosine similarity, and mapping of exercises to pages with the highest cosine similarity.

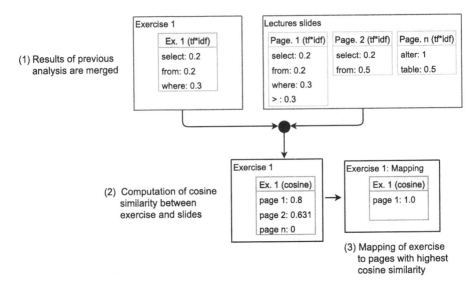

Fig. 5. Concept of combining the analysis results for the lecture slides and SQL exercises together [18].

Merging of Previous Analysis. The results of the slides and exercise analysis are merged into a list during the first step of the comparison process. For each exercise, we now have access to the tf*idf values from every page with respect to this exercise. Figure 5 shows the mapping between Exercise 1, and each page alongside the result of their keyword analysis. The three keywords SELECT, WHERE and FROM were identified in Exercise 1 with their tf*idf values of 0.2, 0.2, and 0.3. Page 1 contains the same keywords and tf*idf values as Exercise 1 plus the keyword " > " with a tf*idf value of 0.3. The second page features the SELECT and FROM keywords with tf*idf values of 0.2, and 0.5. The last page contains the ALTER and TABLE keywords with values of 1 and 0.5.

Computation of Cosine Similarity. The cosine similarity calculates the angle between two-word vectors. In our use case, the word vectors consist of keywords recognized from a query or lecture slide. The calculation of the angle is shown in Fig. 6. The dot product of two vectors a and b is divided by the lengths of both vectors. A low angle between those vectors means that the content of the vectors is similar, while a high angle expresses dissimilar content. An advantage of using the cosine angle as a similarity metric is that the length of the vectors is not relevant. In our use case, we employed this method. As a result, the cosine similarity for each page of the lecture is calculated in regard to Exercise 1. The result shows that Page 1 has the highest cosine similarity of 0.8 followed by Page 2 with 0.631, and Page n with 0. The page with the best cosine value, in this case, Page 1, is then selected to be mapped to Exercise 1, and hence recommended to students having a problem with Exercise 1. A further feature of our system is the clustering of keywords clustering which we discuss next.

$$cosine(a, b) = \frac{a \cdot b}{\|a\| \cdot \|b\|} = \frac{\sum\limits_{n=1}^{N} a_i, b_i}{\sqrt{\sum\limits_{i=1}^{N} a_i^2}\sqrt{\sum\limits_{i=1}^{N} b_i^2}}$$

Fig. 6. Formula for cosine similarity by [22].

Keyword Clustering. A cluster is a group of objects differentiated based on their similarity and dissimilarity [6, 10]. Thus, keywords are grouped such that members of a group are more similar to other keywords in the same group and dissimilar to the members in other groups. Our system has a feature that allows the creation of clusters consisting of an arbitrary number of keywords [9]. To the end that after tf*idf values for each keyword are calculated, members of the cluster are scanned for the highest tf*idf value [20, 26]. This value is applied to each member of the cluster. The reasoning for clustering keywords is the presupposition that the occurrence of specific keywords leads to a certain SQL topic. For example, clustering the keywords < and > employed as a range selection increases their tf*idf value compared to other keywords in the page that are not part of the cluster. Thus, the clustered keywords have a higher influence following the cosine calculation. Thus, it is more likely that the resulting recommendation will point to a page about range selection. We have in the past sections introduced the background and conceptual framework for our recommendation system. The next section, implementation, will show a sample process of mapping lecture slides to exercise tasks.

7   Implementation

Keywords, being a vital part of our system as they are used every time we search for the occurrence of certain SQL keywords, we implemented a tool to create a customary keyword lists that contain specific SQL keywords selected by the administrator.For example, there are SQL keywords available in our implementation, such as CONCAT, that are currently not mentioned in the lecture. Since this could also change in the future, our implementation already supports a wide variety of keywords. We now show the process of mapping slides to exercises by walking through a recommendation for Exercise *E* that is about the update operation:

Update wine set vintage = vintage +1
Where color = 'red';

The keyword analysis for Exercise *E* is displayed in Table 1 with WHERE and UPDATE recognized once and the equality sign twice. The idf values reveal that the UPDATE keyword is the rarest keyword of these three with an idf of 1.82 compared to 0.301 for the WHERE keyword and 0.519 for the equality sign. A tf*idf value of 0.91 is assigned to the UPDATE statement which means that it is the most important SQL keyword for the Exercise *E*.

Table 1. Keyword analysis for exercise E [18].

keywords	count	tf	idf	tf-idf
Where	1	0.5	0.301	0.151
Update	1	0.5	1.82	0.91
=	2	1	0.519	0.519

Table 2. Keyword analysis of the recommended page to exercise E [18].

Chp: 2, Page: 34, Cosine: 0.984

keywords	count	tf	idf	tf-idf
where	1	0.5	0.507	0.254
update	2	1	1.109	1.109
in	1	0.5	0.273	0.137
=	2	1	0.556	0.556
as	1	0.5	0.316	0.158

Our system declares the 34th page of the second chapter as the most similar slide of the lecture. The keyword analysis for this slide is shown in Table 2 with the keywords WHERE, IN, AS recognized once and UPDATE and equality sign twice. The cosine similarity between Exercise E and the recommended page with 0.984 is close to one, which resembles a high similarity.

Table 3. Keyword analysis of the recommended page to exercise E [18].

keywords	where	update	in	=	as
Count	1	1	1	1	1

7.1 Recognition Strategy for Joins

The recognition of SQL keywords is done by applying pattern matching between a list of relevant SQL keywords and the content of slides and exercises. The recognition of joins however needs a more sophisticated effort because joins in SQL can either be created with the JOIN keyword or by the usage of the WHERE keyword. In case of a join in the form of the WHERE keyword, simply counting the number of keywords would lead to an increase of recognized equality signs and WHERE keywords, but a JOIN would not be recognized. We have implemented a way to recognize those disguised joins in our implementation. An example of a join formulated by using the WHERE keyword can be observed in an excerpt from the 21st page of the sixth chapter, visualized in Fig. 7.

```
select Name, Vintage, PRODUCER.Vineyard
from WINES, PRODUCER
where WINES.Vineyard = PRODUCER.Vineyard
```

Fig. 7. Excerpt of page 21 of chapter six featuring a join formulated with the WHERE keyword [18].

The keyword analysis of Fig. 7 is displayed in Table 3. The SQL keywords SELECT, FROM, WHERE and = are recognized once. The desired behaviour would be to recognize the keywords SELECT, FROM and JOIN once each.

To recognize the join from the example shown in Fig. 7, our implementation exploits that the structure of those join statements is following a specific order, as displayed in Fig. 8. The bold marked steps 1, 3, 5 and 7 are used in our recognition method. Since each of those joins starts with the WHERE statement, our function notices the occurrence of the WHERE statement. After encountering a WHERE keyword, the function is searching for the appearance of a dot symbol followed by an equality sign, which in turn is followed by another dot symbol.

1. **Where keyword**
2. name of table A
3. **dot symbol**
4. name of a column
5. **equal sign**
6. name of table B
7. **dot symbol**
8. name of a column

Fig. 8. Order of join statements formulated with the WHERE clause [18].

Figure 4 shows the conceptual implementation of the join recognition. We are using the array $\$join\_stack$ that stores the elements 'where', '.', '=', '.' in this exact order. In Line 3, the content of a page is read in as one-liners. For each word, we test if this word is equal to the first element in the $\$join\_stack$. If the word is equal to the first element we remove it from the stack. This will be repeated until the stack is empty indicating that each keyword necessary to describe a join has been found and therefore we increment the $\$join\_counter$ variable. The $\$join\_stack$ is being filled again with keywords and we resume the join detection until every word of the page has been read in. In the end, we return the number of detected joins stored in the $\$join\_counter$ variable of Line 12.

Table 4. Method to recognize joins in the WHERE clause [18].

1	$ join_stack = [ ] ;
2	array_push ($ join_stack , ' where ' , ' ' , ' =' , ' n . ') ;
3	foreach ($uni_gram as $ index =¿ $ entry) :
4	if (preg_match ($ join_stack [0] , $ entry) != false)
5	if (sizeof ($ join_stack) ¿ 1) array_shift ($ join_stack) ;
6	else {
7	array_shift ($ joins_tack) ;
8	array_push ($ join_stack , 'where ' , ' ' , '=' , ' ')
9	$ join_counter++;
10	}
11	end foreach ;
12	return $ join_counter ;

Table 5. Keyword recognition of page 21 from chapter six after enabling join detection [18].

keywords	select	from	join
Count	1	1	1

Considering the example of Fig. 7, we are now able to correctly declare the recognized keywords in Table 5. There is one JOIN keyword detected, while the WHERE and equality sign disappeared.

8   Evaluation

Being that our objective is the integration of automatic instructional feedback into online exercise sessions, we resorted to adding the recommendation feature to our exercise administration tool, SQLValidator. This required the analysis of our lecture slides, and SQL exercise tasks. The keyword list has a significant influence on the mapping between slides and exercises. Thus, based on the performance, we collated a list of relevant keywords from a pool of SQL keywords containing 58 elements. The chosen list of keywords is displayed in Table 6.

Furthermore, to evaluate the usefulness of a mapping between slides and exercises, a ground truth is required. Thus, we manually labeled the SQL exercises so for each exercise there is a stored selection of recommendable lecture slides. The decision of which slides shall be recommended for a particular exercise might be a topic of discussion. Depending on the experts' view, the selection of suitable slides can be either flexible or strict. As a result, the evaluation is greatly influenced by the experts' labeling. We mitigate this problem by using multiple experts in the labeling process instead of a single expert.

Table 6. Selected SQL keywords for the keyword list.

Relevant SQL keywords					
select	distinct	where	and	or	not
null	update	delete	min	max	count
avg	sum	like	in	between	as
join	union	group	having	exists	any
all	case	create	<	<=	>
>=	round	=	drop	alter	constraint
unique	primary	foreign	check	default	view
concat	substring	select distinct	natural join	left join	right join
full join	primary key	foreign key	create view	create table	group by
order by	insert into	insert	order		

8.1 Performance Measures

We will evaluate the performance of our implementation by computing several performance metrics. In the following, we will shortly present each of the performance measures and explain how they help us assess the performance of our implementation.

Accuracy. The accuracy metric describes the fraction of correct predictions that the model made by dividing the number of true negative and true positive instances by the total number of instances. In our case, the accuracy resembles the fraction of slides that were correctly predicted as being recommendable plus the number of slides that were correctly not recommended to the students. An accuracy of zero means that there were no correct predictions while accuracy of 1.0 implies that there is no false prediction [3,24].

Precision. The precision metric is derived by dividing the number of true positive predictions by the number of true positives and false-positive predictions. In our context, we use precision to estimate how likely it is that a slide recommended to students is meant to be recommended [2,24].

Recall. The recall metric derives the fraction of relevant instances that were retrieved from the number of instances predicted as true. In our use case, the recall value tells us how many slides that are labeled as positive were recommended to the students [2,24].

F-measure. In the previous two paragraphs, we mentioned the precision and recall performance metrics. By using the F-measure, we combine both metrics into one formula and are thus able to find a balance between them [23]. Considering our use case, we think that the precision is more important than the recall metric. A high precision value means that almost every slide that is recommended was labeled by us as useful and thus the probability of students wasting their time, studying a slide that will not improve their understanding of the exercise, is low. The F_β enables us to put more emphasis on one of the metrics, and therefore we chose to weigh the precision value in a way that resembles its significance. A β value of 1.0 is identical to the f-measure mentioned above, while a β value of zero only considers the precision. Therefore, we chose 0.5 for our β parameter.

8.2   Baseline Evaluation

The baseline evaluation of our system derives a mapping between slides, and SQL exercises by purely computing the cosine similarity without using any additional parameters. Only the preferred way of calculating the idf values has to be selected. Using the baseline approach means that only the slide with the highest cosine similarity will be selected for recommendation. If multiple slides are sharing the best cosine value, then they are recommended. The confusion matrix of the baseline approach using the idf_{sub} computation is shown in Table 7. In our implementation, there are 180 slides, and 66 SQL exercises resulting in 11.880 entries in the confusion matrix. Out of the 70 entries predicted as positive, 38 were positive. There are 11.810 entries in the column predicted negative with 178 counted as false negative and 11632 as actually negative. The table cell of true negative entries is of interest to us since it contains a little more than 98% of all entries. This imbalance of instance distribution is expected because there are 180 possible recommendations for each exercise but usually, only a few slides for each exercise are labeled as recommendable. Suppose there is an exercise for which we selected three pages as appropriate. If our implementation recommended a random slide for this exercise, which turns out to be inappropriate for this exercise, there would still be 176 slides correctly classified as not recommendable and because of this 176 entries are added to the true negative cell. This effect is reinforced by using the baseline approach, since the recommendation is restricted to only recommend the pages with the highest cosine value, further decreasing the number of slides that are recommended. Furthermore, for the baseline evaluation, the idf value of a keyword can also be calculated by considering for all available pages, the number of occurrences of the keyword. Thus, we will refer to the sub-chapter-wise idf calculation as idf_{sub}, and the collection-wise idf values will be referred to as idf_{col}. The result for the baseline approach in combination with the idf_{col} calculation is shown in Table 8. The variation in the idf calculation is barely showing in the classification since the idf_{col} method predicts 66 instances as positive compared to 70 positive predictions in the idf_{sub} computation. The difference in negative predictions is also negligible with 11.810 negative predictions in Table 7 and 11.814 in Table 8.

Table 7. Confusion matrix of baseline approach with idf_{sub} [18].

	pred. pos	pred neg
actual pos	38 (TP)	178 (FN)
acutal neg	32 (FP)	11632 (TN)
total	70	11.810

Table 8. Confusion matrix of baseline approach with idf$_{col}$ [18].

	pred. pos	pred neg
actual pos	38 (TP)	178 (FN)
acutal neg	28 (FP)	11636 (TN)
toal	66	11.814

Table 9 shows the performance metrics with respect to the confusion matrices from Table 7 and 8. The accuracy of both idf calculations is rather high with 0.982 using idf$_{sub}$ and 0.983 using idf$_{col}$. This is mostly due to the previously described fact that most of the pages are correctly classified as true negative. The precision value of idf$_{sub}$ is slightly lower than the precision for idf$_{col}$ method with 0.576. That means slightly more than half of our baseline's recommendations are correct recommendations. Each of the remaining metrics recall, F-measure and $F_{\beta=0.5}$ are rather similar for both idf computations. The recall value for both methods is 0.176 which implies that around 17% of the slides classified as recommendable are selected by our system. The F-measure, which is influenced by the precision and recall metrics equally, reaches 0.266 with the idf$_{sub}$ and 0.27 with the idf$_{col}$. The most important metric in our use case is the $F_{\beta=0.5}$ which equates to 0.383 for the idf$_{sub}$ calculation and 0.396 for the idf$_{col}$. The performance metrics of the collection-wise idf approach are slightly better than the subchapter-wise idf. Therefore, we will focus on the collection-wise idf calculation technique in the next section because the peak performance will be achieved by using idf$_{col}$. Hence, when referring to the baseline approach, we mean the baseline approach using the collection-wise idf from now on. In the following sections, we will try to improve the recommendation performance by utilizing our already introduced optimizations of join detection, clustering of keywords and minimal cosine values.

Table 9. Performance metrics for baseline approach [18].

Metric	value$_{sub}$	value$_{col}$
Accuracy	0.982	0.983
Precision	0.543	0.576
Recall	0.176	0.176
F-Measure	0.266	0.27
$F_{\beta=0.5}$	0.383	0.396

8.3 Detecting Joins

Using pattern matching in combination with a list of relevant SQL keywords is insufficient for the detection of joins that are formulated with the WHERE keyword. Hence, we used a different method for join detection described in Sect. 8.3. Figure 10 shows the confusion matrix of our join detection alongside the rate of change compared to the baseline approach using collection-wise idf values. Applying the join detection yields a positive effect on the classification results. The number of true positive predictions increased by 15.8% while the number of false-positive predictions decreased by 21.4%. The join detection also has a beneficial effect on the false negative and true negative predictions, although they profited percentage-wise significantly less compared to the positive predictions. This is because the number of instances in the column of negative predictions is higher than the number of instances in the second column, and thus the false negative and true negative table cells are less affected percentage-wise. The performance metrics of the baseline approach with and without the join detection are shown in Fig. 11. Each of the performance metrics increased with the activated join detection. The accuracy value increased almost negligible from 0.983 to 0.984. The recall and F-measure improved more with 0.176 to 0.204 and 0.27 to 0.312 respectively. Especially noteworthy is the increase in the precision value from 0.576 to 0.667 through enabling the join detection. In the next section, we show the effect of keyword clustering.

Table 10. Results of activated join detection compared with baseline approach [18].

Idf_{col}	pred. pos	pred neg
actual pos	44 ↑ 15.8%	172 ↓ 3.4%
acutal neg	22 ↓ 21.4%	11642 ↑ 0.052%
total	66 ±0	11.814 ±0

Table 11. Performance comparison with and without join detection [18].

Metric	¬(join detection)	join detection
Accuracy	0.983	0.984
Precision	0.576	0.667
Recall	0.176	0.204
F-Measure	0.27	0.312
$F_{\beta=0.5}$	0.396	0.459

8.4   Clustering Keywords

In Sect. 6, we introduced keyword clustering. In this section, we show how keyword clustering improves our slide recommendation. One strategy to find viable cluster candidates is to take a look at exercises for which there is no correct recommendation. These exercises are then analyzed based on the respective keywords they have in common with their desired recommendations. These keywords that are featured in both the exercise and its desired recommendations are then selected to be part of the cluster. This approach could not be successfully applied in our use case since clustering these shared keywords had a negative effect on other recommendations and thus decreased the performance. In our strategy, we analyzed our data set and identified specific keywords that need to be clustered. This cluster consists of the keywords <,>=, and SELECT. This process of choosing suitable keywords is manual. Table 12 depicts the confusion matrix for this clustering approach. The clustering leads to 4.6% more true positive predictions, while the false positive recommendations were lowered by 9.1%. The performance metrics are displayed in Table 13 alongside the comparison to the former best approach without cluster usage, but with join detection. The application of the cluster causes the accuracy to increase from 0.983 to 0.984. More notably, the precision rises from 0.667 to 0.697. The recall value increases slightly from 0.204 to 0.213. The improvement of both the recall and precision values causes the F_β value to increase from 0.459 to 0.479. Especially, the improved precision and F_β metrics imply that the clustering of keywords enables our system to recommend useful slides to the students.

Table 12. Confusion matrix of cluster application [18].

	pred. pos	pred neg
actual pos	46 ↑ 4.6%	170 ↓ 1.2%
acutal neg	20 ↓ 9.1%	11644 ↑ 0.02%
total	66 ±0	11.814 ±0

Table 13. Performance comparison with and without clustering [18].

Metric	¬cluster	cluster
Accuracy	0.984	0.984
Precision	0.667	0.697
Recall	0.204	0.213
F-Measure	0.312	0.326
$F_{\beta=0.5}$	0.459	0.479

The improved performance due to the clustering is attributable to two more mappings between exercises and slides that are now done correctly. One of the exercises for which the prototype found the correct recommendation will be referred to as task E and is shown below:

> **SELECT** job, MIN (ALL salary) AS min_salary
> **FROM** employee
> **GROUP BY** job;

The keyword analysis for task E yields the results shown in Table 14 with the recognized keywords SELECT, GROUP BY, GROUP, AS, MIN, and ALL. The MIN and ALL keywords have the highest tf*idf value with 1.217 assigned to it and therefore they are the most important keywords for this exercise.

Table 14. Keyword analysis for task E from the SQLValidator.

task G				
keywords	count	tf	idf	tf*idf
select	1	1	0.087	0.087
group by	1	1	1.121	1.121
group	1	1	1.121	1.121
as	1	1	0.405	0.405
min	1	1	1.217	1.217
all	1	1	1.217	1.217

The recommendation before clustering is incorrect since the recommended page is not helpful to the students. The chosen page is the twenty-fourth page of the ninth chapter "Views and Access Control". Page 24 contains information about the problems with aggregation views although task E does not feature any information about views. Hence, the recommendation of page 24 is not useful for students that are challenged by exercise E. Table 15 displays the keyword analysis for page 24. The keywords WHERE and HAVING were recognized once, and the keywords SELECT, GROUP BY, <, MIN, GROUP twice. The highest tf*idf values are reached by the keywords MIN at 1.556 and < with 1.352 (Fig. 9).

The recommendation to task E should contain information as to how the GROUP BY keyword can be used to aggregate data. Instead of recommending page 24 of the ninth chapter, the independent labelers chose page 61 of the sixth chapter, displayed in Fig. 10 as a good fit for task E since it visualizes the process of using the GROUP BY clause.

The keyword analysis for our desired recommendation is shown in Table 16. Page 61 contains the three SQL keywords AND, GROUP BY and GROUP once with the GROUP BY keyword reaching a tf*idf of 1.109 and the GROUP clause following at

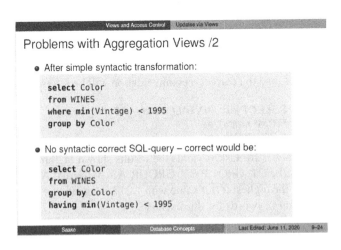

Fig. 9. Incorrect recommendation of page 24 from chapter nine to task E before clustering [18].

Table 15. Keyword analysis of the incorrectly referred page 24 from chapter nine.

keywords	count	tf	idf	tf*idf
Chapter: 9, Page: 24, Cosine: 0.682				
select	2	1	0.347	0.347
where	1	0.5	0.484	0.242
group by	2	1	1.109	1.109
group	2	1	1.051	1.051
having	1	0.5	1.301	0.651
<	2	1	1.352	1.352
min	2	1	1.556	1.556

1.051. The comparison between Table 15 and Table 16 shows that the cosine similarity of page 61 with 0.625 is lower than the cosine value of 0.682 from the current recommendation. In order to change the recommendation from page 24 to page 61, we need to influence the cosine similarity between task E and the slides by creating a suitable cluster. At first, we tried to create clusters of keywords that are both contained in task E and our desired recommendation of page 61. Unfortunately, every cluster that used this approach lead to a performance decrease and therefore a different strategy was necessary in order to establish a correct mapping for exercise E. Instead of increasing the cosine similarity of our desired recommendation, we can also decrease the cosine similarity of the current recommendation by utilizing a cluster. Page 24 contains the < and SELECT keywords with the SELECT clause being also shared with task E. We have a cluster in use that contains the SELECT and < statements and thus changes the tf*idf values of page 24. The performance evaluation of page 24 is shown in Table 17 with the SELECT keyword having a tf*idf value at 1.352 instead of 0.347. The increased tf*idf value causes the similarity between task E and page 24 to shrink and thus the new cosine value equals 0.625. The cosine similarity of page 61 does not change in respect to exercise E because our desired recommendation does not share any keywords with the cluster. The unchanged similarity of 0.64 is sufficient in order to be chosen for recommendation in task E, since the former cosine value of page 24 decreased. Our cluster contains three keywords in total, with the >= clause not being mentioned yet.

In our research, we observed a performance decrease when using a cluster that only contains the SELECT and < keywords. We believe that using the cluster without the >=yields a side effect to the other exercises, which is why we chose to include >= in our cluster.

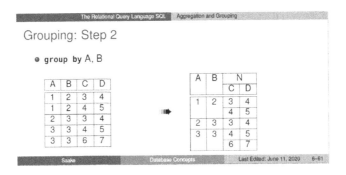

Fig. 10. Page 61 of the sixth chapter which should be chosen for recommendation [18].

Table 16. Keyword analysis for page 61 from chapter six.

Chapter: 6, Page: 61, Cosine: 0.64				
keywords	count	tf	idf	tf*idf
GROUP BY	1	1	1.109	1.109
GROUP	1	1	1.051	1.051
AND	2	1	0.499	0.499

Table 17. Keyword analysis for page 24 from chapter nine after clustering.

Chapter: 9, Page: 24, Cosine: 0.625				
keywords	count	tf	idf	tf*idf
select	2	1	0.347	1.352
where	1	0.5	0.484	0.242
group by	2	1	1.109	1.109
group	2	1	1.051	1.051
having	1	0.5	1.301	0.651
<	2	1	1.352	1.352
min	2	1	1.556	1.556

8.5   Minimal Cosine Value

In the course of optimizing our recommendation, we have observed that there are some exercises for which the best slide recommendation has a rather low cosine similarity. These cosine values range from $[0 - 1]$ with zero meaning no similarity and 1.0 being almost identical. Thus, a recommendation with a cosine value of 0.1 is most likely not very helpful to the students. In this type of scenario where the best recommendation has a low cosine value, we resolved not to make any recommendation as it will not be helpful to students. To enforce this rule, we included an option to set a minimal cosine similarity that has to be reached for any page in order to be recommended [1,14,25].

Table 18 shows results of a further extension of the baseline approach with a minimal cosine value at 0.2, 0.4, 0.6. The second column of the table contains the performance for the baseline approach using idf_{col} with the extensions introduced in Sects. 8.3 and 8.4. The baseline approach uses a minimal cosine value of zero because there is no threshold implemented that restricts pages with low cosine values from being recommended. The third column displays the performance values for a minimal cosine value of 0.2. A comparison between the baseline approach and a minimal cosine value of 0.2 shows that the minimal cosine value has a small positive effect on the performance. The precision, F-measure and $F_{\beta=0.5}$ slightly increase while the recall value remains unchanged. This implies that the minimal cosine value filtered out slides that were incorrectly recommended. Using a minimal cosine value of 0.4 increases the performance further with a precision value of 0.767 and an $F_{\beta=0.5}$ of 0.505. The recall value is still unchanged, which means that by setting the minimal cosine value to 0.4, there are just incorrect recommendations being filtered out. The fifth column displays the performance of setting the cosine value to 0.6. There is a slight decrease in all metrics compared to the previous column. This is because increasing the cosine value eventually leads to correct recommendations being filtered out. Since our focus is on maximizing the F_β and precision values, we set the minimal cosine value to 0.4.

Table 18. Performance metrics for evaluated minimal cosine values.

Metric	baseline	$\cos\text{-}\min_{0.2}$	$\cos\text{-}\min_{0.4}$	$\cos\text{-}\min_{0.6}$
Accuracy	0.984	0.984	0.985	0.984
Precision	0.697	0.708	0.767	0.763
Recall	0.213	0.213	0.213	0.208
F-Measure	0.326	0.327	0.333	0.327
$F_{\beta=0.5}$	0.479	0.483	0.505	0.498

9 Discussion

The performance evaluation shows that we achieved our goals at providing a method to optimize student learning engagement during online SQL exercise task engagement. However, there are still challenges with SQL keywords which are regularly used in the English language. In the following, we explain the remaining problems of our implementation when recognizing these keywords.

One problem we encountered during our research was that some SQL keywords such as AND, IN or AS are regularly used in the English language without any SQL context. Since the lecture slides are written in English, problems arise when counting the number of times these keywords are used in a SQL environment. This is challenging for our recommendation process if the encountered keyword rarely appears in the corpus as it would receive a high idf weight, leading to a great influence in deciding the topic of the page. In the case of a page populated with many SQL keywords, the negative effect of one incorrectly recognized keyword might be mitigated by the tf*idf

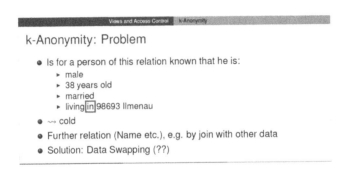

Fig. 11. Slide 40 from chapter nine that contains a SQL keyword not used in a SQL context.

values of the other keywords. If the page only has a small number of keywords, it might happen that a word like IN or AND not used in any SQL context will mislead the recommendation process for this page.

Fig. 11 displays page 40 of the ninth chapter which contains the IN keyword, although it is not used in any SQL context. Table 19 presents the keyword analysis of this page. The keywords JOIN and IN are recognized and the tf*idf value for both is shown in the fifth column with 0.699. By incorrectly recognizing the IN keyword on page 40 of the ninth chapter, it might result in linking this page to an exercise that requires the students to understand the correct usage of the IN keyword, although the page does not hold any information about the IN keyword.

Table 19. Tf*idf analysis for page 40 from chapter nine which features a SQL keyword in a non SQL context.

Chapter: 9, Page: 40				
keywords	count	tf	idf	tf*idf
in	1	1	0.699	0.699
join	1	1	0.699	0.699

10 Summary and Future Work

This research is targeted at structuring learners' learning behavior by reducing by removing or reducing the cycle of trials and errors that continue until frustration sets in or an understanding of the task requirement is manifested. Thus, we have implemented a strategy in which suitable slides from lecture materials are mapped to respective SQL exercise tasks and recommended to students in the occasion of an error condition during online exercise engagements. We achieved a precision value of 0.767 and $F_{\beta=0.5}$ value of 0.505, and have the ability to optimize our mapping with respect to performance values, and student feedback, thus justifying our strategy. SQLValidator is an evolving playground. A future direction is the implementation of an activity workflow generation system. This will enable the elicitation of the retrospective and prospective provenance of student's learning engagement.

Acknowledgement. We thank all reviewers for their constructive feedback. This work was supported by the German Federal Ministry of Education and Research [**grant number 16DHB 3008**].

References

1. Agrawal, R., Phatak, M.: A novel algorithm for automatic document clustering. In: 2013 3rd IEEE International Advance Computing Conference (IACC), pp. 877–882. IEEE (2013)
2. Alvarez, S.A.: An exact analytical relation among recall, precision, and classification accuracy in information retrieval. Boston College, Boston, Technical report BCCS-02-01, pp. 1–22 (2002)
3. Bradley, A., Duin, R., Paclik, P., Landgrebe, T.: Precision-recall operating characteristic (P-ROC) curves in imprecise environments. In: 18th International Conference on Pattern Recognition (ICPR 2006), vol. 4, pp. 123–127. IEEE (2006)
4. Charu, C.A.: Recommender Systems: The Textbook (2016)
5. Costello, E.: Opening up to open source: looking at how Moodle was adopted in higher education. Open Learn. J. Open, Distance e-Learn. **28**(3), 187–200 (2013)
6. Diday, E., Simon, J.: Clustering analysis. In: Fu, K.S. (eds.) Digital Pattern Recognition. Communication and Cybernetics, vol. 10, pp. 47–94. Springer, Berlin (1976). https://doi.org/10.1007/978-3-642-96303-2_3
7. Dietrich, S.W.: An educational tool for formal relational database query languages. Comput. Sci. Educ. **4**(2), 157–184 (1993)
8. Friska, J.: Development of e-learning application as a learning media for production écrite débutant (2020)
9. Habibi, M., Popescu-Belis, A.: Keyword extraction and clustering for document recommendation in conversations. IEEE/ACM Trans. Audio, Speech Lang. Process. **23**(4), 746–759 (2015)
10. Jain, A.K., Murty, M.N., Flynn, P.J.: Data clustering: a review. ACM Comput. Surv. (CSUR) **31**(3), 264–323 (1999)
11. Kleerekoper, A., Schofield, A.: SQL tester: an online SQL assessment tool and its impact. In: Proceedings of the ACM Conference on Innovation and Technology in Computer Science Education, pp. 87–92. ITiCSE 2018, Association for Computing Machinery (2018)
12. Machado, M., Tao, E.: Blackboard vs. Moodle: comparing user experience of learning management systems. In: 2007 37th Annual Frontiers in Education Conference-global Engineering: Knowledge Without Borders, Opportunities Without Passports, pp. S4J–7. IEEE (2007)
13. Mitrović, A.: Experiences in implementing constraint-based modeling in SQL-Tutor. In: Goettl, B.P., Halff, H.M., Redfield, C.L., Shute, V.J. (eds.) Intelligent Tutoring Systems, pp. 414–423 (1998)
14. Muflikhah, L., Baharudin, B.: Document clustering using concept space and cosine similarity measurement. In: 2009 International Conference on Computer Technology and Development, vol. 1, pp. 58–62. IEEE (2009)
15. Obionwu, C.V., Harnisch, C., Kalu, K., Broneske, D., Saake, G.: An intervention strategy for mitigating the prevalence of syntax errors during task exercise engagements. In: 2022 International Conference on Engineering and Emerging Technologies (ICEET), pp. 1–6. IEEE (2022)

16. Obionwu, V., Broneske, D., Hawlitschek, A., Köppen, V., Saake, G.: SQLvalidator-an online student playground to learn SQL. Datenbank-Spektrum, pp. 1–9 (2021)

17. Obionwu, V., Broneske, D., Saake, G.: A collaborative learning environment using blogs in a learning management system, pp. 213–232 (2022)

18. Obionwu, V., Toulouse, V., Broneske, D., Saake, G.: Slide-recommendation system: a strategy for integrating instructional feedback into online exercise sessions, pp. 541–548 (01 2022). https://doi.org/10.5220/0011351000003269

19. Pelánek, R., Effenberger, T., Čechák, J.: Complexity and difficulty of items in learning systems. Int. J. Artif. Intell. Educ. **32**(1), 196–232 (2022)

20. Ramos, J., et al.: Using TF-IDF to determine word relevance in document queries. In: Proceedings of the First Instructional Conference on Machine Learning, vol. 242, pp. 29–48. Citeseer (2003)

21. Riese, E., Bälter, O.: A qualitative study of experienced course coordinators' perspectives on assessment in introductory programming courses for non-CS majors. ACM Trans. Comput. Educ. (TOCE) (2022)

22. Sidorov, G., Gelbukh, A., Gómez-Adorno, H., Pinto, D.: Soft similarity and soft cosine measure: similarity of features in vector space model. Computación y Sistemas **18**(3), 491–504 (2014)

23. Sokolova, M., Japkowicz, N., Szpakowicz, S.: Beyond accuracy, F-Score and ROC: a family of discriminant measures for performance evaluation. In: Sattar, A., Kang, B. (eds.) AI 2006. LNCS (LNAI), vol. 4304, pp. 1015–1021. Springer, Heidelberg (2006). https://doi.org/10.1007/11941439_114

24. Sokolova, M., Lapalme, G.: A systematic analysis of performance measures for classification tasks. Inf. Process. Manage. **45**(4), 427–437 (2009)

25. Strehl, A., Ghosh, J., Mooney, R.: Impact of similarity measures on web-page clustering. In: Workshop on Artificial Intelligence for Web Search (AAAI 2000), vol. 58, p. 64 (2000)

26. Wu, H.C., Luk, R.W.P., Wong, K.F., Kwok, K.L.: Interpreting TF-IDF term weights as making relevance decisions. ACM Trans. Inf. Syst. (TOIS) **26**(3), 1–37 (2008)

Author Index

A. Cuzzocrea et al. (Eds.): DATA 2021/2022, CCIS 1860, p. 243, 2023.
https://doi.org/10.1007/978-3-031-37890-4

Printed in the United States
by Baker & Taylor Publisher Services